Assembling Financialisation

Assembling Financialisation

Local Actors and the Making of Agricultural Investment

Zannie Langford

berghahn
NEW YORK · OXFORD
www.berghahnbooks.com

First published in 2024 by
Berghahn Books
www.berghahnbooks.com

© 2024 Zannie Langford

All rights reserved. Except for the quotation of short passages
for the purposes of criticism and review, no part of this book
may be reproduced in any form or by any means, electronic or
mechanical, including photocopying, recording, or any information
storage and retrieval system now known or to be invented,
without written permission of the publisher.

Library of Congress Cataloging-in-Publication Data

Names: Langford, Zannie, author.
Title: Assembling financialisation : local actors and the making of agricultural investment /
Zannie Langford.
Description: New York : Berghahn Books, [2024] | Includes bibliographical references and
index.
Identifiers: LCCN 2023021770 (print) | LCCN 2023021771 (ebook) | ISBN
9781805390947 (hardback) | ISBN 9781805390954 (ebook)
Subjects: LCSH: Agricultural development projects--Australia, Northern. | Financialization--
Australia, Northern. | Australia, Northern--Economic conditions.
Classification: LCC HD2155.N57 L35 2024 (print) | LCC HD2155.N57 (ebook) |
DDC 338.106/09429--dc23/eng/20230801
LC record available at https://lccn.loc.gov/2023021770
LC ebook record available at https://lccn.loc.gov/2023021771

British Library Cataloguing in Publication Data
A catalogue record for this book is available from the British Library

ISBN 978-1-80539-094-7 hardback
ISBN 978-1-80539-382-5 epub
ISBN 978-1-80539-095-4 web pdf

https://doi.org/10.3167/9781805390947

CONTENTS

List of Illustrations	vi
Preface	vii
Acknowledgements	x
List of Abbreviations	xi
Introduction	1
Chapter 1. Assembling Financialisation	10
Chapter 2. A Brief History of Northern Development	38
Chapter 3. The Investment Proposition	54
Chapter 4. Making Land Valuable	74
Chapter 5. The Moral Economies of Debt	91
Chapter 6. How to Get an Investor	107
Chapter 7. 'Unlocking' the Indigenous Estate	121
Chapter 8. COVID-19 and Seven Years of 'Developing Northern Australia'	142
Conclusion. Messy Assemblages	158
References	182
Index	214

ILLUSTRATIONS

Figures

2.1. The region of Northern Australia	39
4.1. Land value of Australian pastoral zone beef farms by ownership type	77
4.2. Capital value of beef farms in Australia's pastoral zones	78
4.3. Return on investment from income of Australian pastoral zone beef farms	83
4.4. Return on investment from capital appreciation of Australian pastoral zone beef farms	84
5.1. Land value of Australian pastoral zone beef farms with corporate ownership	94
7.1. Assetisation as a continuum	125
8.1. NAIF loan value by industry	146
8.2. Farmland value annual growth rates	148
8.3. Foreign ownership of Australian agricultural land	149
8.4. Foreign ownership of Australian agricultural water	153

Tables

3.1. FIRB reports on foreign ownership of agricultural land	59
3.2. FIRB reports on foreign ownership of water entitlements	60
8.1. Australia's largest foreign landowners	150

PREFACE

In 2016, when I began the research for this book, foreign investment in Australian agricultural land was widely covered in the national news. The main issue at hand was the sale of an iconic Australian cattle business, S. Kidman & Co., to foreign investors. The 117-year-old family-owned company was the largest private holder of Australian land, with properties spanning four states with a total area of 101,000 km² – a land area larger than that of Iceland and representing about 1.3% of the total area of Australia. It had been valued at $390 million dollars, an asking price putting it out of reach of most Australian companies and investors. Over a period of eighteen months, a series of foreign-led bids from mostly Chinese companies were made, and these were rejected by the Australian Treasury due to concerns over the 'national interest' (S. Morrison 2016a, n.p.). Ultimately, Australian mining magnate Gina Rhinehart tendered a bid for 67% ownership, with 33% ownership by Chinese property developer Shanghai CRED, which was approved, and the sale was completed. In the process of these political negotiations over the desirability of foreign investment in land, it was resolved that the government should compile, and publish, a register of foreign land ownership in Australia, after which the issue of foreign investment in agricultural lands largely disappeared from public attention. However, the debate was ultimately unresolved: was it good, in the end, that the Kidman properties were bought by a Chinese-Australian consortium rather than a Chinese company? What difference does the structure of investment ownership and management make to local places, apart from issues of national interest? Who decides the structure of the investment, and why? And how are such investments ultimately assembled?

Obscured in a general discussion of ownership, and simplistic takes on what might be good and bad for Australia, is the vast number of people involved in setting up an investment deal. Take the Kidman sale, for example: the properties were independently valued at $390 million when the company was first listed for sale. But the Kidman company is unique, posing challenges for even the most experienced independent land valuers. What are the effects of the valuer's decisions and on what features is it based? What formula is used to reach the valuation? And what about the valuer – what do they think about foreign investment and does it affect the way in which they value land? And what about the Kidmans themselves and entrepreneurial family farmers like them – what role do they have in negotiating the structure of ownership of land? What is the role of banks, which fund the majority of farmers? And what is the role of local government officials, who work to promote the region to foreign investors? What part is played by Indigenous Australians, who increasingly have legally recognised rights to land and seek to capitalise on them? These local people all work to influence the structure of a deal, and yet they do not feature in most of the debates around financial investment in land in the Australian media, except perhaps as caricatures constructed to represent political positions.

This book takes a closer look at local people, most of whom live and work in Northern Australia. It asks the following questions: what is their role in making agricultural investment in Northern Australia and how does the diverse range of work that they do change the face of Australian agribusiness? Through interviews with professionals such as land valuers, bankers, farmers, government officials and Indigenous organisations, who work at the interface of foreign investment and local rural development, this book examines the assumptions, preferences, moralities, geographies and decisions of these individuals. Through this process, it aims to contribute to a grounded understanding of financialisation as assembled by a diverse range of work, beyond the simplistic polarised accounts that dominate public debate.

This work began in 2016, with the majority of research undertaken between 2017 and 2019. At the time I began my fieldwork, there was a lot of contention around foreign land ownership, but also a strong government push to attract foreign finance, particularly for the purpose of rural development in Northern Australia. The Northern Territory government was supporting a range of large-scale development schemes, such as Quintis sandalwood and the Seafarms $1.5 billion proposed prawn farm, both of which have since collapsed under financial and economic pressures. At the same time, Indigenous corporations and their hired intermediaries were seeking to attract finance and were drawing up prospectuses to promote their lands as investment opportunities. Cattle station values were high, banks were lending money on generous terms, and foreign investors were looking to partner with local farm managers to oversee their land-based investments. I sensed an almost manic energy from some and also, by those who had seen it all before, a quiet cynicism about the hype. The history of failed Northern development schemes was well known, but promoters of new schemes said that this time would be different – this time, this model, this source of finance, this technology. And the question that lingered through many of my interviews was: would it?

The reality of farmland investment is that it takes a range of concerted work to make investment happen in remote, 'underdeveloped' landscapes, and that any number of things can go wrong. Entrepreneurship is uncertain and what makes businesses work is harder to pin down than the reasons why they can fail. This book provides insights into the people who try to make it happen, who undertake ongoing work towards the construction of farmland investments in remote, 'underdeveloped' areas of Australia. Some of this work can be considered done, for now – having resulted in the construction of an investible asset. Some of it is ongoing, and whether (and for how long) it will form a sustainable asset remains to be seen. Studies of agrifood financialisation have often embraced normative ideas of what financialisation is, does and means for the rural people who are affected by it. This is understandable since in many cases the impacts of financialised processes have been severe and negative. But it is important to avoid generalisations, and in a place like Northern Australia, with a large, remote Indigenous population, where social needs are high and government development programmes have frequently been insufficient or ineffective, it is important to ask again what financialisation is and does, and how local people participate in it. This book takes up this task.

ACKNOWLEDGEMENTS

I would like to thank all the people who generously gave their time to this project for kindly sharing their professional insights with me. Without their generous contributions, this work would not have been possible. Thank you also to my Ph.D. supervisors Geoffrey Lawrence and Kiah Smith for their support during my candidature, and to Lyn, for being my home away from home while on fieldwork. I also thank the reviewers of my published work, who have greatly supported the development of my ideas. Special thanks to the reviewers of the proposal and manuscript of this book for their very helpful comments and suggestions. Further thanks to the funders of this research, the Australian Research Council (Discovery Project 160101318) and the Australian Government Research Training Program.

ABBREVIATIONS

ABARES	Australian Bureau of Agricultural and Resource Economics
ABC	Australian Broadcasting Corporation
ABS	Australian Bureau of Statistics
ALEDA	Aboriginal Land Economic Development Agency
BAV	Beast Area Value
CDNA	Communicable Diseases Network Australia
CEO	Chief Executive Officer
CFO	Chief Financial Officer
CLC	Central Land Council (Northern Territory)
COO	Chief Operating Officer
CSIRO	Commonwealth Scientific and Industrial Research Organisation
EBITDA	Earnings Before Interest, Tax, Depreciation and Amortisation
FIRB	Foreign Investment Review Board
GL	Gigalitres (1 GL = 1,000 megalitres)
ha	Hectares
ILSC	Indigenous Land and Sea Corporation
KAI	Kimberley Agricultural Investment company
km	Kilometres
MLA	Meat and Livestock Australia
NAILSMA	North Australian Indigenous Land and Sea Management Alliance
NLC	Northern Land Council (Northern Territory)
NT	Northern Territory
NTRB-SPs	Native Title Representative Bodies and Service Providers
QLD	Queensland
ROI	Return on Investment
SA	South Australia
VIC	Victoria
WA	Western Australia

Introduction

Agrifood Financialisation

Over the last twenty years, substantial investments have been made in agricultural land and agribusinesses globally (Deinger and Byerlee 2011; Bjørkhaug, McMichael and Muirhead 2020; Smith, Lawrence and Langford 2023), leading to concerns about the implications of a global 'land rush' (Arezki, Deinger and Selod 2015; Cotula 2012; Ouma 2014, 2020; Fairbairn 2020). These financial investments play a role in restructuring agrifood industries in ways that may see a reorientation of national food systems towards the needs of financial investors (Lawrence, Richards and Lyons 2013; Sippel 2015). They can also create a neorentier landholder base (Gunnoe 2014), compromise the viability of family farms (Alston 2004; Weller, Smith and Pritchard 2013; Smith 2015) and concentrate monopoly power in food distribution systems (Lawrence 2005; Burch and Lawrence 2009; Carolan 2012; Isakson 2014; Clapp 2017; Magnan, Davidson and Desmarais 2022). Some have framed these issues as the 'financialisation' of food systems – a perspective that raises concerns about the increase in profit-making from financial rather than productive activities (Krippner 2011). Concern extends to the management of companies according to the needs of distant shareholders rather than local communities, consumers and producers (Lazonick and O'Sullivan 2000; Crotty 2003; Milberg 2008; Baud and Durand 2012; Li 2015; Gunnoe 2016; Li and Semedi 2021), and the potential increase in food price volatility and food insecurity that may accompany these shifts (Isakson 2014; Clapp 2017; Kinda et al. 2022).

However, despite widespread disquiet about the issues associated with financial investment in agriculture, little is known about how this investment occurs in practice. Financial investors are often positioned as sites of power, leading to assumptions that the investments they make occur continuously, inevitably and homogeneously. However, investments in land and agribusinesses do not simply 'appear' when regulation is relaxed (Ouma 2015a). 'Successful' and 'failed' attempts at asset creation are co-constitutive (Borras et al. 2022). They are negotiated, contested and facilitated by a diverse range of actors, both distant and local, who assemble land-based investments across diverse geographies. These actors use a range of calculative tools and devices to structure investments and perform their agency in diverse ways. Financial agrifood investments are the result of ongoing work, and this work is difficult, messy and often unsuccessful. As Williams writes, 'instead of financialization at work . . . we need to think about financialization *as* work and thus the forms of labour that have enabled the financialization of food' (2014, 410, emphasis in original). This focus on work allows us to overcome the 'black-boxing' of the actual processes through which financialisation occurs (Poovey 2015; Ouma 2016) and explore how they work in practice – and how they might be altered. As Ouma (2015b, 124) observes, there is an urgent need to 'relocate[e] [markets] in the realm of politics and sociotechnical practice at a time these have gained a sheer metaphysical quality'. Rather than allowing finance to remain an abstract concept, '[r]eckoning finance into a practical activity discloses capital's own methods such that they might be both reappropriated and redeployed' (Martin et al. 2008, 128). Revealing how technical processes proceed, and the moral and practical choices that shape their operation, makes them available for renegotiation (Callon, Lascoumes and Barthe 2009). This book examines some of these processes and reveals some of the key decisions and value judgements that underpin them.

Assemblage Approaches

A poststructural assemblage ontology informs this approach. While recognising the importance of structural analysis of global changes such as financialisation, it is also useful to locate power in micro-negotiations that are 'global in scope but microsocial in character' (Knorr Cetina and Bruegger 2002, 907). This privileges the work of local actors who mediate financial investments into land and agribusiness as sites of study, recognising, for example, how small things can become powerful scripting devices for subsequent work (Latour 1992). Examples here are how a tool for assessing the value of pastoral land in remote parts of the Northern Territory (NT) could come to be a powerful driver of speculative behaviour across the region, or how planning tools being developed by one Indigenous group for their land today might become important organising principles across wide areas in the future.

The contribution of this book lies in its focus on local people and places. Emerging literature on financialisation as work has revealed how land and agribusinesses are approached by financial actors and reconfigured to form income-yielding assets (Visser 2017; Ducastel and Anseeuw 2017, 2018). In such studies, financial actors are positioned as the site of power and the decisions that they make are uncovered to understand how these actors generate certain patterns of global investment. However, less attention has been paid to local actors 'inside' a place, who champion certain sites of investment and work to assemble them in particular ways and for diverse reasons. As Henry and Prince observe:

> grasping the incorporation of agriculture into finance means getting beyond the office towers of international finance centres and into the places where the necessary connections with agriculture can be made . . . Smaller places many of us have never heard of . . . are a part of this space, and they play vital roles. (2018, 991)

In local spaces, farmers seek equity partnerships to expand their own businesses; Indigenous organisations seek investors for community development; local governments seek finance capital to fund rural development; and private sector mediators such as land valuation specialists work to moderate markets. These local mediators pursue their own projects, which may not be connected by a desire to engage in financialisation in any political way, but nevertheless 'modify a state of affairs by making a difference' (Latour 2005, 71). These actors are often viewed within the wider literature on financialisation as powerless against global finance. Yet as this book demonstrates, in Northern Australia they are central to the process of negotiating financial investments and can exert agency in powerful ways. This recognition requires that scholars 'expand the cast of actors, human and nonhuman, that participate, or are made to participate in the drawing together of generally fragile assemblages' (Henry 2017, 102). This book contributes to this task through a case study of local actors operating in remote Northern Australia.

Northern Australia is a particularly important case study for understanding the work of financialisation by local intermediaries. It differs from more intensively farmed and heavily populated areas of southeastern Australia, in which financial investors target established and operating farms. In contrast, investments in Northern Australia are occurring largely in 'greenfield' projects. A greenfield site is an undeveloped parcel of land earmarked for commercial development, one in which new agricultural crops or methods are being introduced to increase output from farming or to allow for pastoral intensification. The risky and experimental nature of these investments introduces a speculative aspect that makes Northern Australia, from an investment perspective, more similar to an emerging farmland market than the established markets in the Global North. This feature is alluded to in the Commonwealth Government's 'Developing Northern Australia' White Paper, which introduces a 'value proposition' for the region: 'Northern Australia: Emerging opportunities in an advanced economy' (Australian Government 2015a, 7). In this context, financial investments are particularly risky and vulnerable to failure, and specialist knowledge of the environment is needed. These characteristics makes local people particularly important to financial investors, as they provide unique skills and expertise, and therefore become powerful brokers of local knowledge. In such contexts, local firms and people may valorise their local knowledge to 'affirm their essential role as gateway to the country and its agricultural value chains' (Ducastel and Anseeuw 2017, 201). Furthermore, local farmers and Indigenous organisations may be particularly willing to engage with financial investors because they often lack finance for development. Some seek to engage with finance, but on their own terms and in ways that will benefit local regions and populations. Local actors are often essential intermediaries to negotiating land-based investments, and these investments are difficult to assemble, requiring innovation and experimentation. These features empower local people and make Northern Australia an important site in which to study the ways that local mediators contribute to the assemblage of financialisation.

The work of investment negotiation occurs at the interface of global and local; a site of 'friction' in which 'heterogeneous and unequal encounters can lead to new arrangements of culture and power' (Tsing 2004, 5). Taking this interface as a site of study sees larger global patterns as assembled by these moments of negotiation, innovation and contestation. It remakes local mediators as important actors in the financialisation of land and agribusiness, asking how they perform their work and what implications these negotiations might have for investment policy. Attention to this work reveals unexpected ways in which diverse people, acting with tools developed in specific places at specific times, and moving across diverse geographies that constrain and alter the way in which negotiations occur, assemble new connections between Northern Australian land and global finance. This focus requires attention to the everyday practices of a range of local actors involved in mediating and negotiating investments. This book examines key processes occurring at this interface: where local government officials seek to both attract and control financial investment into rural spaces; where professional land valuers seek to control the value of the land; where rural bankers exert moral judgements about how much money should be lent to whom; where family farmers negotiate equity partnerships with global investors; and where Indigenous organisations seek to attract investment into their lands through processes of assetisation. Their labour is spatially situated; it occurs at particular sites that themselves are complex sociotechnical assemblages in which people work to remake relationships between finance and agriculture (Henry and Prince 2018). Three broad themes have shaped the direction of this enquiry: human agencies, tools and geographies.

First, individual human actors are embedded in professional networks with rules, conventions and cultures that engender particular processes of decision making (Ho 2009) and may live or work in communities and workplace cultures with particular spatial and historical features, which in turn shape individual values and pursuits (Muniesa et al. 2017). Yet individual people negotiating and mediating financial investments also have their own preferences, values and agendas that shape the way in which they undertake this work. A focus on these individual human agencies encourages exploration of the ways that these individual and cultural factors shape their work.

Second, financial tools (such as reports and templates) and calculative devices (such as valuation formulae) shape the way in which investments are organised and enacted. For example, a land valuation formula requires certain variables to be entered and prevents the user from entering others. Such devices shape the way that humans interact with them, constraining the possibilities available to them. This power can be understood as agency of a nonhuman actor (Latour 1992, 1996). What histories and geographies do these tools emerge from, and how are they used by different actors in pursuit of divergent goals? Tools and calculative devices are not neutral (Lagoarde-Segot 2015; 2017; Lagoarde-Segot and Paranque 2017), but contain histories of decisions that have moral and ethical dimensions, and that create a range of results that may be far removed from their original intention. They 'script' (Latour 1992) investment negotiations in important ways. Tsing (2004, 6) observes that: 'Roads create pathways that make motion easier and more efficient, but in doing so they limit where we go. The ease of travel they facilitate is also a structure of confinement.' Similarly, tools that guide the investment negotiation process facilitate the process, but also shape the results it creates (Mackenzie 2006; Henry 2017). A focus on these tools and calculative devices and how they are replicated, adapted and reproduced in the process of investment mediation and negotiation reveals their influence on investment patterns.

Third, in the literature on farming and financialisation, authors are increasingly calling for attention to be paid to the geographically and temporally situated manifestations of finance. This is to understand financialisation not as an inevitable and homogeneous process of expansion, but as difficult work that moves across geographies in different ways (see Higgins and Larner 2017a; Forney, Rosin and Campbell 2018b; Ouma 2015b, 2020). In Northern Australia, geography has critically shaped development trajectories and the environment has been a constantly present nonhuman actor in financial negotiations. This context underpins the agencies and tools used in this work, as we see not only the financialisation of agriculture, but also the 'agriculturalization of finance' (Henry and Prince 2018). Rather than focusing on how 'universalizing, totalizing, and disembodied processes . . . manifest themselves in similar ways in different places' (Larner, Le Heron and Lewis 2007, 223), increased attention to spatially and temporally situated negotiations reveals how spaces shape investment negotiations and change the appearance of financialisation. Explicit attention to the geographies in which negotiations occur reveals how local places shape investment structures.

This book explores the work of local actors working at the interface of global investment and local spaces, examining how these human actors negotiate their work using particular tools in particular places. The information drawn upon in this book was collected as part of a larger project examining agrifood transformations in Northern Australia from 2016 to 2020, for which more than 100 semi-structured interviews were undertaken. This research draws on a subset of forty of these interviews focusing specifically on intermediaries to land and agribusiness in Northern Australia. Participants were purposively sampled according to their professional involvement in forging connections between local agrifood production and finance, and comprise a range of professionals, including land valuers, bankers, consultants, lawyers and government officials. The insights gained from these professionals generate a highly spatial understanding of financial investment, located in a specific cultural and geographical landscape at a particular time. They highlight power dynamics between actors and spaces of unequal negotiation where some groups are able to exert influence over others. They describe places where finance flows easily and spaces where the work is contested, difficult and forms unstable links. They reveal hidden tools that are shaping flows of investment in Northern Australia and show how these tools are contested and exploited by different actors. Taken together, this reveals a picture of the difficult, unstable and disordered work involved in financialisation, and highlights the importance of microlevel processes in effecting large-scale patterns.

Assemblage approaches are sometimes criticised for providing a depoliticised account of global processes isolated from an imperative to act. This book seeks to demonstrate that, on the contrary, the suspension of normative judgements of actors, tools and processes can reveal important insights into how these diverse actors interact to create a range of unexpected local impacts, and that these insights are often key to the design of more effective policy responses. Each chapter of the book examines in detail the work of a different group of actors and offers recommendations for policy based on the particular dynamics identified within. The result - if not explicitly political – is not disengaged: the recommendations generated target specific rural policies and aim to support a more sustainable agrifood system.

The Structure of the Book

Chapter 1, 'Assembling Financialisation', introduces the literature on financialisation that frames the inquiry of this book. It outlines relevant contributions to understanding financialisation as a global, sectoral and asset-level process, highlighting the range of ways in which it has been conceptualised. It also details the utility of the assemblage approach used in this book and discusses issues of power and ethics in research with professionals. This chapter frames the key question driving this book: how does financialisation occur in practice and in what ways do local actors and spaces shape its form?

Chapter 2, 'A Brief History of Northern Development', provides an overview of historical financial investments in Northern Australian land and agribusinesses, highlighting the long history of these investments and the role of the state in moderating them. This information highlights the need to study financialisation in differentiated spatial and historical contexts, nuanced by local policies, environments, communities, values and histories. It demonstrates the importance of Northern Australia as a case study: in such a remote region, where agricultural production expertise is rare and hard-earned, local actors are key intermediaries to financial investments.

Chapter 3, 'The Investment Proposition', introduces the contemporary work being done to market Northern Australia as an investment destination. It introduces the programme on 'Developing Northern Australia' and how it envisions the future of the region and its form of development. Drawing on interviews with local government officials, it explores how they seek to attract investors to Northern Australia, as well as how they work to control investor activities in order to create local benefit. It suggests that the Northern development programme can be considered a financialising form of governance, and also examines the contradictions inherent in the ongoing work of government officials to re-establish influence in these development pathways.

Chapter 4, 'Making Land Valuable', explores how the value of Northern Australian land is made, and unmade, by interactions between human actors such as valuation specialists, bankers, investors and farmers with calculative tools for valuing land. It describes two tools used for pastoral land valuations in the region – the Beast Area Value and the Return on Investment – and explores how these tools are used by a range of actors in strategic and sometimes competing ways. It describes the moral reasoning of valuation specialists as they seek to control markets, as well as efforts by investors and others to adapt and exploit valuation devices. It considers the importance of environmental and geographical particularities in shaping the use of valuation devices, and explores how these environments are made commensurable to facilitate investment across diverse geographies. The understanding of how land is made valuable by the work of specific local professionals provided in this chapter offers important context to the following chapters, which discuss other ways in which people seek to create and communicate investment value.

Chapter 5, 'The Moral Economies of Debt', explores the traditional financiers of the region: banks. It examines the work of rural agricultural finance specialists who are the most common connection between local farmers and global finance. It also explores the challenges faced by these specialists in their work and how banker–client relationships both shape and are shaped by understandings of morality in lending in the region. It provides insights into the traditional debt financing of agriculture in the region and the ways in which it is changing with growing financial investment in Northern Australian pastoralism.

Chapter 6, 'How to Get an Investor', explores a source of finance rapidly growing in appeal to local farmers: equity investors. It provides a case study of one farming family that formed a joint venture with a large foreign institutional investor and describes the vast amount of time and resources expended by this exceptional family in this pursuit. It highlights the role of external accountancy firms as consultants to this process in creating legal structures for joint ventures, and explores how farmers work across financial and farming spaces to negotiate farming–finance links, valorising their specialist environmental knowledge and management expertise as they do so. The exceptional experience of this farming family suggests limits to the expansion of this form of investment for a wider cohort of farmers, which has implications for policy on approaches to development financing in the region.

Chapter 7, '"Unlocking" the Indigenous Estate', explores the work of Indigenous corporations, showing how they mobilise a range of tools in their pursuit of finance for development across diverse environments and geographies. It outlines a series of initiatives by Indigenous organisations in Northern Australia as they seek access to global capital pools and describes the experiences of a range of professionals as they work to transform Indigenous land into an asset for investment.

Chapter 8, 'COVID-19 and Seven Years of "Developing Northern Australia"', examines what has changed since the White Paper on Developing Northern Australia was first introduced in 2015. It revisits major themes in Northern development introduced in Chapter 4 and considers progress towards some of the goals that were outlined for the programme, including in large-scale greenfield agricultural investment, private financing of infrastructure, patterns of land and water ownership, Indigenous agricultural development and pastoral development. It considers the impact of COVID-19 on farmland investment and highlights the intensification of investment in established industries such as pastoralism, as well as the limited progress made in other areas.

The concluding chapter, 'Messy Assemblages', argues that financialisation is usefully conceptualised as an assemblage of irreducibly complex processes that develop differently in different locations, and that policy initiatives could effectively target these microlevel processes to shape the role that finance plays in rural industries.

Through this approach, this book demonstrates the value of social science studies of economic systems and practices to provide insights into the actual processes through which the financialisation of agrifood industries proceeds. The research is grounded in Northern Australia and provides practical evidence that contributes to understanding and improving investment outcomes there. It recognises that 'finance is . . . not only a technical activity, but has social, moral, and . . . political aspects' (Lagoarde-Segot and Paranque 2017, 659), and aims to explore and reveal the assumptions and value judgements that underpin these aspects. The goal is that they can be made available for public debate in order to support a more informed and nuanced approach to the challenges of governing investment.

Chapter 1

ASSEMBLING FINANCIALISATION

The concept of 'financialisation' has been increasingly used since the early 2000s to describe a range of structural economic changes associated with significant growth in financial markets. Studies of financialisation seek to understand how the role of finance in economies, industries and lives is changing through contemporary financialised globalisation. However, the term has been used in a wide variety of ways to refer to vastly different processes, occurring at different scales. This diversity of approaches has led to criticism that financialisation is 'a highly malleable concept, made up of a plethora of contested narratives' (French, Leyshon and Wainwright 2011, 800) posing the danger that it 'will become a chaotic concept, a blanket term which is stretched too far to cover a range of related, but fundamentally different projects' (French, Leyshon and Wainwright 2011, 801). Indeed, it has recently been criticised as signifying little more than 'a vague notion of "the (increased) contemporary importance of finance"' (Christophers 2015, 184), a concept that is used post hoc to imply coherence among a range of fundamentally different processes. However, others have argued that 'financialization is an emerging concept which – when grounded in particular settings – is capable of providing important insights into the ways the finance sector is altering the nature of economic and social life' (Lawrence 2015, 204), and that increased scholarly attention to developing its meaning and applications are central to its explanatory usefulness.

At the global level, financialisation describes broad changes in the influence of finance capital in the global economy. At this scale, financialisation encompasses a shift from industrial to finance capitalism, an increasing circulation of capital globally that displaces industrial production in the 'real' economy and has far-reaching influences over global economic and social networks. At the industry level, surplus global capital enters different industries and locations to varying extents, leading to the financialisation of industries and places – for example, the financialisation of American biotechnology industries, Australian pastoralism or British welfare services. The extent to which certain industries or geographical locations undergo financialisation depends on a range of factors, from global circumstances (such as global inflationary pressures) to localised government policy (such as tax incentives to invest in certain industries), to characteristics of the industry itself (such as risk-return ratios). At the local level, capital entering certain industries and locations financialises enterprises and resources to different extents, as businesses and resources are structured into financial investments across diverse geographies. At this level, histories, geographies, values, tools, beliefs, communities and people interact with finance to structure investments in geographically and spatially variegated forms. Just as global processes influence local uses of finance, these micro-processes assemble larger systems. Studies of the financialisation of land and agribusiness typically privilege a particular scale as the site of study (be it the nation of Australia or a rural bank lender), but must be cognisant of processes occurring at other scales. The next three sections of this chapter review literature on financialisation as a global, industry-level and local process respectively.

Global Financialisation

The study of financialisation as a global process typically draws on structuralist political economy to identify major global and historical trends. Conceptualised in this way, financialisation is the 'increasing importance of financial markets, financial motives, financial institutions, and financial elites in the operation of the economy and its governing institutions' (Epstein 2002, 3) and a 'tendency for profit making in the economy to occur increasingly through financial channels rather than through productive activities' (Krippner 2012, 4). Global studies of financialisation describe a shift from industrial to finance capitalism, and although they vary in their interpretations of the shifts occurring, generally they see it as a feature of neoliberal capitalism (Clapp 2017; Schmidt 2016; Clapp and Isakson 2018a). Van der Zwan's (2014) review of financialisation literature identified three approaches to financialisation studies: those who see financialisation as a regime of accumulation; those who see it as associated with the growing dominance of shareholder value as a measure of value; and those who study the financialisation of everyday life. The first two are of particular interest to studies of agrifood transformations and will be reviewed here, although the financialisation of everyday life is also relevant, particularly as it relates to changing farmer subjectivities (see Chapter 6).

Financialisation as a Regime of Accumulation

Global studies of financialisation see the rise of finance as closely related to neoliberal capitalism. Empirical studies have shown instances in which profits have increasingly accrued to financial rather than productive business endeavours since the 1970s (Epstein 2005; Krippner 2005; Orhangazi 2008). These studies suggest both that financial companies are increasingly profitable through payments from productive industries (Crotty 2003), and that productive companies are also profiting from financial activities (Krippner 2005). Arrighi (2010, 371) sees these shifts as a feature of late-stage capitalism, in which an overstretched economy is no longer able to generate profits from material growth, and accumulation switches to the financial sector to delay a crisis of capital accumulation. In this explanation, the limits to productive growth in the economy are reached, and profit-making switches to the financial sector (thus temporarily overcoming limits to 'real' growth). As Russi (2013, 16) observes, the financial sector is increasingly disconnected from productive growth, frequently projecting much higher growth rates than the 3–5% GDP growth in the productive economy. Viewed in this light, financial expansions are not only cyclical phenomena linked to business cycles, but also represent a 'fundamental reorganization of the regime of accumulation' (Arrighi 2010, 371). This switch from productive to financial profit making creates the 'illusion' of growth (Sokol 2017, 679) based on a 'parasitic' finance that extracts profits at the expense of investment in the real economy (Sokol 2017, 681). In a financialising economy, firms compete not in the product market, but in financial markets (Boyer 2000, 118), leading to a slowing accumulation as the economy is increasingly organised around financial engineering rather than productive considerations (van der Zwan 2014, 104). This has been termed the 'neoliberal paradox' (Crotty 2003), in which an increasingly competitive financial market demands higher and higher returns on investment, while intense competition in global production markets makes it impossible to achieve these returns.

Financialisation at this scale is conceptualised as a global process arising from long-term historical processes. It points to financialisation as a type of 'finance-led capitalism' that serves the capitalist class and has 'empowered those individuals and institutions that derive their incomes from financial assets and transactions . . . at the expense of wage-earners and households' (van der Zwan 2014, 104–5). In this way, financialisation is implicated in income inequality (Stockhammer 2015), declines in labour protection (Hein 2015), unemployment (Husson 2015) and rising levels of indebtedness (Lapavitsas 2009), creating an unstable economy vulnerable to crisis and collapse (Stockhammer 2013). It is argued that the global financial crisis was an inevitable collapse of an inherently unstable system (Blackburn 2006; Michailidou 2016). Many of these global studies point to financialisation as both the result of neoliberal political projects that deregulated financial industries (Kotz 2010) and as a driver of neoliberal policies (Duménil and Lévy 2004). According to this view, financialisation is a 'logic of capitalism' (van der Zwan 2014, 106) in which investors seek profit without productive investment (Cordonnier and van de Velde 2015), and states can work to financialise or definancialise industries through regulations that exert control over investment activities. If financialisation is a reversible process linked to government approach to business and finance, the government becomes a key actor in financialisation (O'Neill 2019). This approach emphasises the importance of national regulation to moderate global influences of financial flows on national economies, as well as within national economies.

Financialisation as an Organising Principle

The structural changes in business management associated with financialisation have led to an increasing number of corporations being run according to principles of shareholder value in 'a shifting metric of success in corporate management' (Gunnoe 2016, 1096). A related stream of literature focuses on these management practices as a key aspect of financialisation. The rise of shareholder value, as both a tool for decision-making and measure of business success, has ideological as well as practical implications. The idea that finance should serve the needs of shareholders over all other stakeholders leads firms to increasingly measure their performance based on their return on equity, to seek short-term returns and to interpret their results according to international investment standards (van der Zwan 2015). Under the logic of shareholder value, firms may distribute profits to shareholders rather than reinvesting them in the business (Lazonick and O'Sullivan 2000; Crotty 2003; Milberg 2008; Baud and Durand 2012). This approach is argued to shift the balance of power from workers to capital holders (Froud 2006; Erturk 2008; Benedikter 2011) and has knock-on effects, including increased lending to households and indebtedness of workers (Lapavitsas 2009; Stockhammer 2013).

As well as a business management tool, shareholder value is also increasingly a discursive construct (Ho 2009, 150–56; van der Zwan 2014). The rise of shareholder value and financial metrics as dominant measures of value has been described as a 'progressive obliteration of alternative ways of assembling and "'processing" the world' (Russi 2013, 7), with some going as far as to call it a 'collective addiction' (Teubner 2011, 3). The restructuring of business to primarily serve the needs of capital holders (rather than workers, environments, communities and consumers) is presented as a neutral framework for efficiently organising society, when in fact it contains important value judgements about the role of businesses in society (Lagoarde-Segot 2015; 2017; Lagoarde-Segot and Paranque 2017). Business no longer exists to serve (local) customers and provide (local) employment, but to generate profits for (distant) shareholders. This discourse is pervasive and is increasingly used to justify the management of financial corporations with limited regard to their many nonshareholder stakeholders (see Ho 2009; Ascher 2016). By presenting a shareholder value orientation as efficient and ideologically neutral, it legitimises 'the social violence of financial booms and busts' (Ho 2009, 4). This can be seen as a 'roll-out' neoliberalising process (Peck and Tickell 2002) in which legitimising shareholder value as the dominant business management tool has required 'the political work of stabilising acceptable truth' (Lewis, Le Heron and Campbell 2017, 165). Academic work on this topic has argued that the ideal of shareholder value and the value judgements it implies need to be critically examined and overturned, arguing that 'economy and finance have to be embedded in environmental and social welfare . . . rather than the opposite' (Lagoarde-Segot 2017, 122). This raises questions about the role of finance capital in social enterprises (Artis 2017; Mawdsley 2018a; Langley 2020), an idea that will be explored in Chapter 7. Financialisation conceived of as the rise of shareholder value thus extends definitions of financialisation to include ideological implications of the increasing importance of financial measures of value in shaping societies, as well as the practical implications of this.

Global studies of finance such as those discussed here have usefully shed light on global dynamics. However, it is necessary to also pay attention to the spatially and temporally variegated forms of financialisation in order to understand how it is facilitated and resisted at different scales in different places. Global studies sometimes risk overlooking practical aspects of finance (MacKenzie and Millo 2003; MacKenzie et al. 2007), such that '[f]inancialisation is rendered abstract, anonymous and teleological: "finance" becomes the driving force behind its own expansion' (van der Zwan 2014, 106). Such an approach is vulnerable to presupposing coherent political projects (Campbell and Rosin, 2011) assuming 'both intent and efficacy on the part of the capitalist class' (van der Zwan 2014, 106), without giving sufficient consideration to the contested historical processes embedded in places and enacted by a range of actors, and the unexpected arrangements through which they proceed (see, for example, Newman 2017). To go beyond these understandings of financialisation, it is necessary to pay closer attention to the historical and political contestations through which financialisation has been negotiated at the national and industry levels. The next section reviews literature at this scale with a focus on agrifood industries.

Agrifood Financialisation

Industry-level studies of financialisation explore how changes in global patterns of accumulation affect different industries and locations to different extents. The increased power of capital globally increases the supply of capital potentially available to agriculture, particularly as investors increasingly look to hedge risk through portfolio diversification (InvestAg-Savills 2011; Anseeuw et al. 2012; Cotula 2012). However, capital does not flow into all sectors and locations equally: the path of financial investment does 'not necessarily follow a linear, homogenous, and automatic path. It encounters difficulties and resistance. It meets favourable and unfavourable contexts and developments' (Muniesa et al. 2017, 55). Financialisation plays out differently between locations and industries. Geographically, areas of the United States, Canada and the European Union have undergone extensive financialisation facilitated by neoliberal policy choices (see Epstein 2005; Orhangazi 2008; Krippner 2012), while certain countries, such as France, have national policies that constrain financialising processes in a range of industries (see Muniesa et al. 2017, 53–65). In addition, certain industries such as biotechnology (Mirowski 2012) and mining exploration (Le Billon and Sommerville 2017) have been particularly attractive to financial investors due to the promise of potentially massive returns. In contrast, agricultural production has traditionally been considered an unattractive asset class for investment (Martin and Clapp 2015), although this does not generally extend up the supply chain (Burch and Lawrence 2013). Looking more closely at how these different locations and industries have been affected by financialisation reveals more complicated and contested paths of finance.

There are a range of factors contributing to the historical undesirability of agricultural assets. Returns to agriculture are often lower than other asset classes, partially because family farmers are often willing to supply goods more cheaply than a commercial venture would allow (Mann and Dickinson 1978) and to exploit their own labour (Smith 2015). Primary production markets are often undifferentiated, making it unlikely that profit through monopoly control of a product will be possible. Agricultural production often operates over long timeframes that are unsuitable or undesirable to many investors. There are a range of environmental, social and market risks associated with primary production. Specialist skill is required to manage agricultural properties, such that management skill is a strong determinant of profitability. As a result, investors have traditionally been less interested in these assets due to their high risk and limited rates of return, and have instead tended to invest in agriculture indirectly through social relationships such as debt and contract production (Mooney 1982) in a process termed subsumption (Goodman and Redclift 1985). Increasingly, though, investors are looking to invest directly in agricultural production. This trend has been linked to restructuring of the agricultural sector with a shift towards neoliberal government policy in the 1970s (Larder, Sippel and Argent 2018) and increasing power of financial actors (Lawrence 2017), as well as to the effects of the Global Financial Crisis on investment priorities (Fairbairn 2014).

Interpreting the Financialisation of Farmland

Academic research has sought to understand what financial investment in land and agribusiness means for food systems and rural communities. Studies of changes in food systems warn against the volatility of finance and the risks of introducing this to primary production, in which there are a range of stakeholders such as producers, consumers, rural communities and environments. They highlight concerns about food systems reorienting their activities towards the generation of financial profits for external shareholders (Williams 2000; Burch and Lawrence 2013; Isakson 2014; Kuns et al. 2016). In particular, changes in the ownership and control of farmland operations are said to risk rising farmland prices and a neorentier landholder base (Gunnoe 2014; Magnan and Sunley 2017), volatile and increasing food prices (Ghosh et al. 2012; Clapp 2014), decreasing national sovereignty over food supply (Lawrence et al. 2013; Sippel 2015) and the declining viability of family farms (Alston 2004; Weller et al. 2013). Private equity-based investments are often geared towards speculation, may lack transparency and may pursue a process of 'creative destruction' in which the search for efficiency leads to ruthless streamlining of businesses (Ho 2009; Daniel 2012). In addition, large financial entities may actively reshape the agricultural landscape in the regions in which they operate (Salerno 2014). Rather than being highly efficient, many financialised investments are based on low land prices and a regime of low wages (Cochet 2018), which compromises the ability of land to support livelihoods and operate sustainably (Clapp and Isakson 2018b). New financial tools facilitating investments in land and managing uncertainty open farmers up to new risks and opportunities (Isakson 2015), and there is a need to understand to what extent the use of these tools is 'simply about the management of risk, and to what extent they are about generating profit at the expense of others' (Visser, Clapp and Isakson 2015, 547). Financial products are often volatile, risky and unstable, and these features can be projected onto food systems.

Several studies have explored how financialisation is reshaping agriculture according to the logics of finance. Kuns, Visser and Wästfelt (2016) showed how short-term, speculative shareholder-orientated management strategies compromised the long-term viability of large farming investments in Russia and Ukraine. Similarly, in the US forestry sector, adoption of shareholder value compromised long-term viability and led to industry decline, but was considered successful by the shareholders who profited from it (Gunnoe 2016). This highlights the disjuncture between land conceived of as a financial and productive asset and the different measures of success used by different stakeholders. As Li (2014, 590) notes, there are a range of perspectives on 'what land is (its ontology), what it can or should do (its affordances) and how humans should interact with it'. As such, the movement of finance into agriculture has raised substantial concerns, more so than in industries in which nonfinancial stakeholders can be harder to identify or may be in more powerful positions (such as the aforementioned areas of biotechnology).

These studies of the financialisation of agriculture usefully explore agri-food transformations, their structural drivers, and their impacts for nations and communities. They describe major transitions in the organisation of capital and the impacts on food and land. However, an emerging literature argues that while these studies describe *what* is happening, they say less about *how* it is happening, and highlight the need for attention to the way in which calculative devices, geographies and human agencies enable the movement of finance into different industries. As Williams notes:

> [Weight] must be placed on the question of *how* these developments have unfolded in practice – that is, the specific practices, devices, technologies and operating assumptions through which agriculture has been reconfigured as a type of investment and thus made amenable to the epistemic demands of finance. (2014, 409, emphasis in original)

The emerging literature on this topic addresses a key gap in studies of financialisation by exploring the ways in which connections between finance and agriculture are being formed in practice by a range of actors in local places at the level of individual land-based assets.

Asset-Level Financialisation

Structural and sectoral studies of financial networks have alerted us to a range of processes that are changing agricultural landscapes. These processes are not 'homogenous and inevitable', but uncertain, reversible, contested and 'driven by specific entrepreneurs . . . [who] play an active role in structuring and mediating demand and supply' (Ducastel and Anseeuw 2017, 200). They are temporally and geographically variegated, creating unexpected outcomes in different contexts. In order to understand these outcomes, there is a need to study financialisation 'from below' (Ouma 2014, 162) and to examine the specific financial processes and actors that make decisions rather than leaving intact this 'black box' package of assumptions, ideas, values and tools. The people of interest range from those directly involved in structuring investment opportunities, such as investors and entrepreneurs, to people and organisations that take a seemingly peripheral role in the investment process. These are 'market mediators' (Bessy and Chauvin 2013) such as agents, consultants, evaluators, marketers, debt financiers, insurances agencies and government personnel, who introduce professional norms, calculative constraints and creative opportunities to the investment process.

By studying these actors and understanding their 'drivers, strategies and legitimating discourses' (Visser, Clapp and Isakson 2015, 547), grounded information can be elicited to both improve policy responses and to open up financial activities to public debate in a project of 'technical democracy' (Callon, Lascoumes and Barthe 2009). Tsing's 'Ethnography of Global Connections' (2004) powerfully nuances structuralist approaches to global movements such as financialisation by seeing 'generalization to the universal as an aspiration, an always unfinished achievement, rather than the confirmation of a pre-formed law' (Tsing 2004, 7). She argues that 'universal aspirations must travel across distances and differences, and we can take this travel as an ethnographic object' (Tsing 2004, 7). Her work focuses on spaces of 'awkward engagement' (Tsing 2004, xi), the 'sticky materiality of practical encounters' (Tsing 2004, 1) where people come together from different backgrounds to negotiate new ways of doing things. Because creating connections involves *work*, these configurations are not fixed and inevitable, but an uncertain space in which global futures are contested (Tsing 2004, 2). These studies emphasise a need for detailed understanding of these processes in order to understand the reality they create. They do not emphasise a binary of 'real' and 'nonreal' financial processes, but consider financial calculations to be real because they are real in their effects (Muniesa 2014, 19–20). Three approaches have been particularly instructive in studying 'work': exploring the *agencies* that direct this work; the *tools* that guide it; and the *geographies* that shape it, as introduced in the Introduction. These will each be explored in turn below.

Human Agency

Studies of the effect of human agency on micro-processes of financialisation recognise structural constraints, but privilege – as a site of study – the human actors who assemble financialisation. These people are embedded in a place, and have lives and assumptions and values developed through social contracts with those around them. They are situated in a particular place and time, in a network of friends and colleagues with interconnecting social relations. Yet they are also embedded in global networks, often trained in professions with their own values and professional socialisation processes. They engage, virtually, with a range of professionals and people who, in turn, are enmeshed in their own virtual and real networks. These people 'work to stitch together aligned interests across significant messiness, deep tensions and conflicting interests' (Lewis, Le Heron and Campbell 2017, 166). From this perspective, financialisation is 'the resultant of a background of management cultures and practices' (Russi 2013, 29). It is embedded in everyday practices, 'organized social assemblages . . . [of] employees following routines, people with shifting professional identities enmeshed in global political configurations and working with complex technocratic apparatuses' (Muniesa et al. 2017, 58). This book takes up the need for studies of finance as constituted and reproduced through social interaction, pursuing 'a deeper understanding of agency, especially by probing the psychological and cognitive origins of the ideas, orientations and motives that guide actors' (Bell 2017, 724).

Professional communities are increasingly important social networks, and workplace cultures strongly influence behaviour. People value social affiliation (Baumeister and Leary 1995) and – through education (Szelényi 2013) and work experience – are socialised into professional networks that often have their own ways of speaking, thinking and moralising (Higgs 2013). Since the 1970s, 'academic finance has . . . shaped the perceptions, attitudes, beliefs, and behaviour of finance graduates – a societal impact . . . magnified by . . . concomitant global deregulation and expansion of financial markets' (Lagoarde-Segot and Paranque 2017, 658). In situations where people feel particularly uncertain, group identification becomes even more important to finding ways of working and providing the justifications for that work (Hogg 2009). Cultures are evolving and self-sustaining systems (Geertz 1973; 1983), and professional cultures are practised and sustained in situated office spaces, in virtual networks and discursive framings. Economic systems are imperfectly reproduced by these people, and it is in these processes of reproduction that change is possible (Abolafia 1998). This centres interactions between people as a key site for the study of the economy.

In the field of financial mediation, Karen Ho's *Liquidated: An Ethnography of Wall Street* (2009) offers important insights. Ho applied Bourdieu's notions of disposition and habitus to investment bankers, describing a localised office culture that values hard work, intelligence and risk taking, and moralised investment banking activities as an essential part of economic operation by ensuring that '[t]he best operation should survive' (Ho 2009, 157). She shows how investment bankers projected their own values about risk-taking, short-terminism and competitiveness onto workers. She also chronicled how Wall Street has a view of its own 'cultural superiority . . . which in turn serve[s] as a catalyst and justification for spreading its culture and dominance' (Ho 2009, 71). In contrast, Hertz's ethnography of Shanghai traders described more uncertain and contested moralities (Hertz 1998, 139) and a greater influence of the state. Studies into these microcultures of finance are invaluable in terms of understanding the pervasiveness of social networks and personal values in financial decision making. Studies of these sites of power show how cultural norms of isolated powerful groups can assemble broad global changes. As Ho noted:

> Locating the supposedly abstract market in sites with particular institutional cultures localizes the market, demonstrating its embodiment, and shows how it is infused with the organizational strategies of [financial organisations]. (2009, 6)

However, it is not always possible to locate the market in geographical space, and virtual interaction increased dramatically during the COVID-19 pandemic (see, for example, Kilcullen et al. 2022). Financial communities increasingly interact in virtual space in networks dispersed across the globe (Gusterson 1997). Locating these dispersed networks may involve multiple spaces or no space at all, and requires the development of novel approaches to 'follow . . . subjects' into these virtual places of interaction (Gusterson 1997, 116)

Muniesa (2014) and colleagues (Muniesa et al. 2017) have studied a number of important financial processes in detail to analyse how this work is done by people who come to a particular place, with a particular set of professional tools, as well as with their own self and preferences. For example, Muniesa examines aspects of professional socialisation, showing that:

> becoming a businessperson . . . requires . . . changing the way one thinks and the way one behaves; also the way one values things . . . above all, you become someone else − a leader, hopefully − and this becoming is only marginally about knowing things. It is, above all, about reaching a felicitous mentality, about acquiring a disposition. (2014, 96)

This 'disposition' affects the approach people take to their work. Finance is a social interaction, and social interactions are underpinned and justified by moralities (Fourcade and Healy 2007; see also Li 2007b). Viewed in this way, all economies are moral economies (Sayer 2015; Palomera and Vetta 2016), and understanding moral reasoning, and the ways in which professional communities re-create it, is of primary importance. As Sippel points out:

People do not 'strip off' their social and cultural baggage when they engage in economic activities. They fluidly move within different spheres of value and make use of various and potentially diverging or incompatible justificatory principles for determining worth. (2018, 554)

The presence of culturally constructed moralities in driving financial activities demonstrates that finance is 'both empowered and limited by its cultural specificity' (Tsing 2004, 57) – empowered to expand its reach on subjective moral grounds, and yet limited by narrow conceptions of value which constrain its activities. These anthropological perspectives provide important insights into the movement of finance, both in terms of an ontological focus on interpersonal negotiations and in providing methodological contributions to the study of professionals.

Tools

As well as moralities, professionals inherit certain tools and calculative norms. From this perspective, financialisation is 'not a deterministic process . . . [but rather] a sharing of calculative practices and informational devices' (Russi 2005, 29). These pre-established technical and discursive norms simplify financial work, but they also naturalise judgements about value and remove them from a sphere where they can be examined and contested. Objects, tools and calculative devices have agency, since they 'script' user behaviour (Latour 1992), and digital agricultural technologies have further facilitated assetisation processes (Higgins and Bryant 2020; Duncan et al. 2022). As Tsing (2004, 6) describes: 'Roads create pathways that make motion easier and more efficient, but in doing so they limit where we go. The ease of travel they facilitate is also a structure of confinement.' According to Ouma (2016), it is important to re-examine the value judgements hidden within these calculative frameworks that are often taken for granted. Of particular note in this project is the work of Muniesa and colleagues, who have written on a number of important financial practices. For example, investors may see a company's value not as the sum of its parts (warehouses or stockpiles), but as its earning potential (and potential for growth) in the future (Muniesa et al. 2017, 62). From this perspective, the imagined future of the business is the source of its value rather than its current (objective) existence, as Chapter 4 will explore. Similarly, Discount Cash Flow (DCF) models, widely used to assess returns on investment, weigh the value of future societal wellbeing against that of today through the use of the 'discount rate' variable – what Muniesa et al. (2017) argue is a radical proposition normalised by repetition (see also Fairbairn 2020). Similarly, the use of shareholder value as a dominant measure of value has been normalised as a neutral judgement, when in fact the exclusion of other stakeholders (workers, communities, environments and future generations) has serious practical and ideological implications (Lagoarde-Segot 2015; 2017; Lagoarde-Segot and Paranque 2017).

Mackenzie's book *An Engine, Not a Camera* (2006) explores the operation of economic theories of finance and shows, for example, how new mathematical models for portfolio selection are required to be simple enough to use but also complex enough to avoid being seen by peers as trivial (Mackenzie 2006, 245). Understanding the technical norms of finance professionals, their equations and what their variable inputs represent is an important part of questioning financial reasoning and reproduction. As Henry and Scott (2017, 110) observe, 'decisions about how and what to count are political decisions about what counts, and what socio-material worlds should look like'. The tools that are used, for example, to measure value are so influential that there is a shift in some sectors from competing in productive spheres to competing in valuation spheres, in which different actors may exert strategic agency to improve their performance by exploiting different aspects of valuation processes rather than optimising the process itself (Kornberger 2017). Chapter 4 will explore this by investigating the way in which companies respond strategically to different valuation norms and formulae.

The practical implications of these tools are demonstrated by their application to the assetisation of agrifood industries. Ducastel and Anseeuw (2017) showed how investors made decisions about what to invest in according to their ease of incorporation into existing financial models and spreadsheets, selling off some productive enterprises because they could not fit neatly into their existing measurement systems. In the case they describe, a failure to establish calculative norms for managing cattle made it unviable for investment. Visser (2017) showed the assetisation of land to be a contested and reversible process, requiring substantial work for a land-based investment to be rendered profitable, manageable and legitimate, and, once done so, to be maintained as such. He showed how in Russia, this process required work to structure investment products and, where it was unsuccessful, led to the withdrawal of finance from certain regions. Ouma (2015b) showed how technical measurements were used as instruments of control over Ghanaian farmers, when a firm that experienced fluctuations in demand from buyers would pass this risk on to farmers by rejecting their fruit. The firm would claim the fruit to be of low quality, as measured by their own instruments for measuring sugar content (an instrument that the farmers did not possess) (Ouma 2015b, 157). Henry (2017) explored how prices for red meat in New Zealand are assembled by materialities, infrastructures and artefacts, denaturalising these prices to highlight their spatial and historical specificity. Magnan and Sunley (2017) showed that investors typically paid higher prices, bought more quickly and were interested in particular regional areas, although it is important to be sensitive to the differences between different types of investors (Celik and Isaksson 2013; Sippel 2018). In the field of social impact investment, Dempsey and Bigger (2019, 517) show how creating environmentally friendly asset classes 'does not always hinge on extinguishing other-than-capitalist-social relations but rather attempts to mobilise and harness such differences, including non-profit-seeking values, logics and relations'. In their example, innovation in the management of a range of different types of value proves a core part of creating assets based on environmental benefit. These studies indicate the importance of organising devices, which allow land – and its diverse range of affordances – to be standardised, organised and traded as a financial investment (Ouma 2018b).

Geography

Financialisation scholars are increasingly attentive to the 'geographies of financialisation' (Hall 2011, 80; see also Leyshon and Thrift 2005 [1997]; French and Kneale 2009; Hall 2010; 2012; French et al. 2011; Mawdsley 2017). This focus is particularly important in the study of agrifood systems (Williams 2014; Ouma 2015a; 2016; Henry and Prince 2018), yet studies of the financialisation of farmland often focus on powerful international financial centres and 'virtual space largely removed from the physical act of . . . agricultural production' (Clapp 2012, 156). Relatively less attention has been paid to the (often) remote spaces in which financial connections are made (Ouma 2016). Rather than viewing the connection between agriculture and finance as an 'unnatural coupling' (Ghosh 2010), it is necessary to view global and local processes as mutually co-constructed (Çalışkan and Callon 2009), and to see finance as connected to, and forged in, rural spaces (Williams 2014). As Henry and Prince (2018, 989) argue, finance and agriculture are mutually constitutive, such that alongside the financialisation of agriculture, we also see the 'agriculturalization of finance' in which 'finance has been transformed by its relationships to agricultural logics, subjectivities, and practices' (Henry and Prince 2018, 1004). It is important to study 'the makeshift links across distance and difference that shape global futures – and ensure their uncertain status' (Tsing 2004, 2) in order to see how financialisation plays out differently in different places as a result of geographically and historically affected work.

Several works have been important in this regard. Ouma's book *Assembling Export Markets* (2015a) explores how connections between global markets and local places are forged through contested local processes, with markets being 'shaped by a 'plurality of aspirations' (Ouma 2015a, 127) associated with local projects. His more recent work similarly sought to ground global transitions in local places (Ouma 2020). With studies from New Zealand and Tanzania, he revealed how, despite public discourse contrasting 'good' local farmers with 'bad' foreign investors, these investors often had greater capacity for environmental stewardship and participation in organic or environmentally sustainable practices, though they do so to capitalise on price premiums and maintain investment values (Ouma 2020, 143, 153). Visser's study of assetisation of farmland in Ukraine and Russia highlighted the way in which a failure of an investment firm to account for the materialities of farming resulted in failed and reversible attempts at asset-making, showing how 'global, macro trends that supposedly lead to land shortages . . . do not automatically translate into rapid commoditization and asset making around the globe' such that 'land that promises to become a profitable asset may become less valuable and less asset-like overtime' (2017, 196). Similarly, Ouma (2018) discussed the challenges faced by those who seek to legitimise agriculture as an asset class, in which the social affordances of land are reasserted by those who resist its conversion to a pure financial asset. Henry and Prince observe the 'performance of rurality' by financial actors who '[i]n finding ways to insert themselves into agricultural relationships have to build new infrastructures, create new ways of knowing the uncertain, variable materialities of agricultural production, and . . . perform particular versions of rurality in order to be trusted' (2018, 1003). Li's (2007c; 2014) work emphasises the embeddedness of land in social, cultural and environmental relations, showing that:

> To turn it to productive use requires regimes of exclusion that distinguish legitimate from illegitimate uses and users, and the inscribing of boundaries through devices such as fences, title deeds, laws, zones, regulations, landmarks and story-lines. It's very 'resourceness' is not an intrinsic or natural quality. It is an assemblage of materialities, relations, technologies and discourses that have to be pulled together and made to align. To render it investible, more work is needed. (Li 2014, 589a)

This work is deeply embedded in place, such that 'economic relations are never narrowly economic, or reducible to simple market exchanges . . . such exchanges are always simultaneously political, socio-cultural, socio-ecological and dependent on human-non-human relations and environmental valuation' (Lewis 2018, 98). These studies highlight the significance of the particular spatial situations in which financial connections are made, and the importance of grounded studies that are capable of understanding the mutually constitutive relationship of agriculture and finance.

Together, the emergent work on agencies, tools and geographies of asset-level financialisation demonstrates a shift in recent literature on the financialisation of agriculture towards seeing financialisation as a global microstructure constituted through contested negotiations that assemble and are constrained by broader influences. However, the connections between these local negotiations and descriptions of global changes are not uncontested; some authors have argued that financialisation is an 'unhelpful signifier' (Christophers 2015, 187) for describing the diverse projects through which financialisation is assembled. Jacobs and Manzi (2019, 1) suggest that 'the concept [of financialisation] has most utility for researchers when applied historically, to make explicit how the variegated, situational and adaptive practices that are now in place have their origins in earlier stages of capitalist development'. In this sense, the concept of financialisation provides little to support the project of understanding short-term, unique projects. However, connecting diverse, situated projects to larger patterns of change allows their significance to be grasped; the connection between local developments and wider structural factors that constrain them is central to understanding them as a whole. As Brenner et al. write of neoliberalism:

> empirical evidence underscoring the stalled, incomplete, discontinuous or differentiated character of projects to impose markets or their coexistence alongside potentially antagonistic projects . . . does not provide a sufficient basis for questioning their neoliberalised, neoliberalising dimensions. (2010, 332)

From this perspective, it is important to recognise the financialised and financialising dimensions of micro-practices alongside their specificity. Schmidt (2016, 143) suggested that '[i]f capitalism is the commodification of all things, financialization is the capitalization of all things', and this makes it available for study at a range of scales. This book takes as its focus the spaces of remote Northern Australia and offers a series of case studies of locally situated processes of negotiation that shape the form of financial investment. This evidence highlights how investment patterns are co-constructed by local and financial actors in ways that are often not clearly identifiable as intentionally financialising or definancialising in nature.

Assemblage Approaches

While structural political economy approaches have usefully highlighted the extent and impacts of financialisation in agrifood industries, they are less useful in explaining the diverse range of outcomes from financial investments or accounting for situations in which results are not predicted by prevailing power dynamics. Nonrepresentational, relational ontologies, such as Actor-Network Theory and assemblage approaches, offer ways to untangle the micro-processes that lead to macrolevel changes in agricultural industries. In agrifood studies, assemblage approaches are increasingly being used to examine these micro-processes (e.g. Ouma 2015a; Lewis et al. 2016; Henry 2017; Le Billon and Sommerville 2017; Forney, Rosin and Campbell 2018b). Assemblage thinking is not strictly a theory, since theories seek to explain patterns; rather, it is an ontology (Bennett 2010) that has important implications for how we think about individual responsibility, government regulation and structural changes in financial markets. An assemblage approach 'shifts the emphasis from studying [global change] as a relatively unified and ascendant formation to interrogating the relationship between heterogeneous elements that do not have a logically necessary . . . coherence' (Higgins and Larner 2017a, 6). An assemblage approach highlights the power of these day-to-day negotiations and opens up the field of study not only to financial institutions and their employees, but also to unexpected actors who – as a side effect of their own projects – contribute to and alter broader global changes (see Higgins and Larner, 2017a). Such a focus 'inquires into the makeshift links across distance and difference that shape global futures – and ensure their uncertain status' (Tsing 2004, 2). An assemblage approach suggests that individuals can play a part in reconstituting economic relations. This requires a rethinking of agency in the study of financialisation, since it implies that financial intermediaries do not passively reproduce economic systems, but often actively 'work to stitch together aligned interests across significant messiness, deep tensions and conflicting interests' (Lewis et al. 2016, 166). Exploring how diverse types of 'work' create financialising effects is important for understanding broader global changes. Mirroring patterns in studies of neoliberalism – where the emphasis has shifted away from studying neoliberal governance as a homogeneous entity towards a study of the diverse processes associated with 'neoliberalisation' (Peck and Tickell 2002) – studies of financialisation processes can reveal how heterogeneous actors relate to each other in ways that create effects associated with financialisation. They can also challenge notions of financialisation as a homogeneous and inevitable force of change.

The concept of assemblage is used as the ontological framework for this book. Assemblage Theory emerges from the work of Deleuze and Guttari (1987) and offers four key insights for studies of the financialisation of agrifood systems (see Anderson et al. 2012): first, it emphasises that agrifood investments are dynamic assemblages of heterogeneous component parts (elements); second, it directs attention to the independent existence of these elements (beyond their relationships with other elements); third, it views agency and power as distributed and causality as nonlinear; and, finally, it dissolves the divide between structural and micro-processes. I will now discuss each of these in turn.

The Processes of Assembling Heterogeneous Parts

Assemblage is a translation of the French word *agencement* originally used by Deleuze and Guttari (1987). The translation does not fully convey the meaning of the original, which refers to both the *result* and the *process* of assembling: assemblage as a noun and assemblage as a verb. The latter meaning is a core component of an assemblage approach, which directs attention to the movement through which relations between elements emerge and shift. Assemblage is 'an ongoing process of forming and sustaining associations between diverse constituents' (Anderson et al. 2012, 174), and assemblage approaches emphasise the *heterogeneity* of elements of an assemblage. These heterogeneous elements include human and nonhuman actors of varying complexity and scale, dissolving social divisions such as social-material, near-far and structure-agency (DeLanda 2006). For financialisation studies, it suggests that not all actors who financialise are intentionally financialising; rather, that diverse elements relate to each other in a range of ways to create a range of unexpected structures, and that unexpected tools, animals, grasses and people can form part of a financialising assemblage. An assemblage can vary in its size and behaviour, and can comprise a variety of elements and relations. This view of social structures as comprised of diverse heterogeneous elements draws attention to the *work* of assemblage through which these elements are drawn together (Williams 2014). As Li notes:

> Assemblage flags agency, the hard work required to draw heterogeneous elements together, forge connections between them and sustain these connections in the face of tension. It invites analysis of how the elements of an assemblage might – or might not – be made to cohere. (2007c, 264)

This focus on work and processes of assembly emphasises the difficulty of maintaining relations between elements. Anderson et al. (2012, 177) note that assemblages are 'both the provisional holding together of a group of entities across differences and a continuous process of movement and transformation as relations and terms change'. This provisionality flags the potential for change and for *disassembling* of structures – as Visser (2017) has shown, we can observe both processes of assetisation, in which deliberate and innovative work on the part of specific financial intermediaries saw the creation of assets from remote farmland, while we can also see, over time, *deassetisation* as the desirability of these assets is only partially maintained. For studies of financialisation, this creates space to consider *definancialisation* and what this might look like in a range of contexts. From this angle, financialisation is not viewed as a hegemonic project, but as a pattern that results from a diverse range of projects undertaken by a variety of actors. It is important to avoid assuming a coherent project of financialisation (or neoliberalism; see Higgins and Larner 2017), but instead to view financialisation as an assemblage of 'multiple, contradictory and overlapping projects and practices' (Higgins and Larner 2017b, 5) that are not readily identifiable as financialised in nature.

Assemblage thinking is therefore an 'ontological priority' (Massumi 2002) that gives rise to 'an ethos of engagement with the world that is deliberately open as to the form of the unity, the types of relations involved, and how the parts will act' (Anderson et al. 2012, 176). This approach is consistent with Williams' (2014) call to study financialisation as work, and with a 'weak theory' approach to tracing 'the multidirectional and interrelated dynamics of change in diverse economies' (Gibson-Graham 2014, 151).

The Exteriority of Relations

From this focus on heterogeneity of elements arises the emphasis on 'relations of exteriority'. Relations of exteriority occur between two elements that are not defined by their relationship; the relationship does not affect their identity. This is in contrast to 'relations of interiority', which occur where the identity of one element relies on its relation to another (for example, a mother–child relationship). As DeLanda (2016, 2) describes, 'if a relation constitutes the very identity of what it relates it cannot respect the heterogeneity of the components, but rather it tends to fuse them together into a homogeneous whole'. The focus on relations of exteriority differentiates assemblage approaches from other relational theories such as Actor Network Theory (Callon 1984; Law and Hassard 1999; Latour 2005), and Anderson et al. (2012) argue that this is the central contribution of assemblage theory over other relational theories. In a relation of exteriority, a thing is 'conditioned, but not determined, by its relations' (Anderson et al. 2012, 177) and is therefore autonomous from surrounding elements. While heterogeneous parts may come together through relations within an assemblage, these relations do not fuse the elements, but remain open to change and renegotiation. This view emphasises the distinction between an element's capacities (which are independent of the assemblage) and its properties (which are the actualisation of certain capacities that occur as a result of the element's relations in the assemblage). As Anderson et al. (2012, 179) note, 'all of an entity's capacities cannot be definitively named and known in advance. All that can be known is how specific capacities play out in relation to, or with, the properties and capacities of other entities'. A thing's position within an assemblage can enable or constrain its capacities for action, such that 'entities are never fully actualized within any of the relations that constitute an assemblage' (Anderson et al. 2012, 179); they retain independent existence. The unity of an assemblage is provisional, and the properties of the components of an assemblage cannot explain the behaviour of the whole. As such, while Actor Network Theory suggests that relations 'format' the world (Latour 2005), assemblage theory emphasises the temporary nature of such relations and their opportunity for renegotiation.

As such, an assemblage is 'a multiplicity which is made up of many heterogeneous terms and which establishes liaisons, relations between them ... the assemblage's only unity is that of co-functioning: it is a symbiosis, a "sympathy"' (Deleuze and Parnet 1977, 52). The relationship between parts is temporary and provisional. This approach removes the assumption that combinations and relations, once made, will endure and merge into an organic whole, but asks us to question how certain forms endure across differences and distances. For example, in an assemblage approach, a financial investment in a farm would not come to be seen as a fixed and unified whole, but would remain a series of alliances between diverse and heterogeneous entities such as the farmer, the land and each of its elements, the investor, the reporting devices through which the farm is managed, the wider regulatory structure and so on. These entities are themselves assemblages that are constantly in flux. As such, viewing investments in this way highlights how change in any of the parts can shift the assemblage and lead to dissolutions and new alignments. The assumption becomes one of movement rather than of stability, creating a view of investments and finance that is less structured and predictable in nature.

This also prevents us from understanding the effects of an investment based purely on an analysis of its component parts; rather, the interaction of a diverse range of elements creates an assemblage that functions in unique ways. This approach highlights the need to avoid assuming that investments occur and interact with land and communities in any predefined way, but to remain open to exploring the diverse range of relations that may arise. Actors do not require an intention to engage with financialisation in any political way. This approach removes the need to identify any component parts as 'financialising' or 'financialised' in nature; rather, all parts of an assemblage retain their independent features, but may *behave* in financialising ways as a result of their position in the assemblage. This approach is able 'to expand the cast of actors, human and nonhuman, that participate, or are made to participate in the drawing together of generally fragile assemblages' (Henry 2017, 102). It is not only financial actors who financialise; it may also be local people, farmers, community members, environments, valuation devices, rural bank lenders and so on. There is no broader financialised unity, but rather 'a multiplicity of political forces always in competition with one another, producing unintended outcomes and unexpected alignments' (Larner, Le Heron, and Lewis 2007, 243). These actors actualise in unique ways in particular assemblages but, if removed from the assemblage and entered into a new assemblage, may behave in new ways and generate different results. Actors whose interests facilitate one farmland investment may behave differently in another context as a result of a new expression of their capacities and interests; this implies a distinct approach to thinking about the agency of elements of an assemblage.

Distributed Agency and Nonlinear Causation

Assemblages include both human and nonhuman actors. Human actors work to assemble broader patterns, but do so in pursuit of a range of collective and individual goals. Nonhuman actors are not mere objects upon which action is taken, but have agency that critically shapes the assemblage (Lewis et al. 2013; Rosin et al. 2017). In an assemblage:

> the individual, purposeful human actor is not only displaced as the sole possessor of agency, but no action is possible without the coming together of a diverse arrangement of people, things, texts, technologies and so on. The agency of people and things, in other words, is necessarily relational. (Fredriksen 2014, 3)

This requires a 'rethinking of agency in distributed terms and causality in non-linear, immanent, terms' (Anderson et al. 2012, 186). Agency is viewed as distributed across a range of possible actors who relate to each other and perform their work in different ways. This is not to imply that distributed agency equates to equally distributed power (Fredriksen 2014). Individual people can influence the assemblage and its parts to different extents, and it is critical 'to attend to the forms of power through which particular relations are held stable, fall apart, are contested and are reassembled' (Anderson et al. 2012, 180). It also lends itself to a rethinking of causality. Both the assemblage as a whole and its parts have agency and can transform the parts and the whole of the assemblage (Anderson et al. 2012, 186). Causality is viewed as a nonlinear process (Anderson et al. 2012, 180) and, as such, it is not possible to reduce the causality of an assemblage to either a direct cause and effect or to complete randomness; rather, causality emerges through a range of different practices that are linked in a provisionally ordered social field (Li 2007c, 285; Anderson et al. 2012). Connolly (2005) suggests thinking about 'immanent causality', in which, where assemblages meet novel circumstances, randomness may be introduced, leading to unpredictable results. It highlights the way in which assemblages may behave in different ways in different contexts due to small differences in the situation – for example, a farmland investment may fail in a particular context due to a new element such as a clash of personalities between a parent company executive and a farm manager that prevents effective communication; or due to the presence of a particular organism in the soil, or community dissatisfaction, or a document produced by a short-seller. These factors can create random and unpredictable effects in an investment strategy that has had relatively consistent results elsewhere. As Anderson et al. note:

> In a non-linear system, small disturbances can have massive effects, meaning that the agency of small components is often only revealed retrospectively in specific traces or as the assemblage is later stabilized, and may remain hidden altogether . . . [such that the] creative reworking of relations in motion may render causality multiple and indeterminate, meaning that the identification of mechanical causality results from 'cuts' to the assemblage that reveal only specific interactions: causality become visible in shifts between moments of unchartered turbulence and the congealment of agencies that appear as traces. (2012, 182–83)

As such, taking an assemblage approach requires a focus on moments of interaction, and attention to the ways that particular actors engage with other assemblages and particular moments at particular times. This underlies the continual emphasis on provisionality and local context. However, an awareness of the contextual specificity of particular engagements does not prevent their relevance to wider studies on financialisation, but emphasises the need to bear in mind complexity and context when doing so, and the range of cultural and physical geographies that investment spaces work across and assemble within. This leads to a consideration of the relationship between individual elements and stability of larger assemblages as a whole.

Structure and Dynamism

A final important contribution of assemblage thinking is that it 'invites us to think outside a distinction between the structured and the unstructured' (Anderson et al. 2012, 175), resisting both microreductionism and macroreductionism. Assemblages are not fixed, but are always in a process of becoming (Deleuze and Guttari 1987; Bennett 2010), yet some forms may become durable through repetition or habit (Anderson et al. 2012, 180). As such, although assemblage thinking emphasises relationality, specific situated and relational practices can stabilise and become repetitive such that they begin to appear to possess wider structural unity and power. As implied above, these stabilities 'are themselves achievements which require all manner of human and nonhuman actions' (Hinchliffe et al. 2007, 260–61), and different parts of an assemblage can simultaneously work to stabilise and destabilise the assemblage; indeed, one part of an assemblage may participate in both of these processes through enacting different capacities (DeLanda 2006, 12). Deleuze and Guttari (1987) describe these as: (a) lines of articulation, in which heterogeneous things come together; and (b) lines of flight, in which things disperse. As DeLanda (2006, 38) notes, 'social assemblages larger than individual persons have an objective existence because they can causally affect the people that are their component parts, limiting and enabling them'.

This approach has implications for studies of financialisation by recognising the importance of linking back to wider, durable and stable assemblages, particularly those associated with neoliberalising and financialising rationalities. Certain decision-making processes, the use of particular tools for particular jobs, and types of relations between actors can stabilise and become persistent patterns that shape landscapes in important ways. For example, a technique for mapping Indigenous land and developing an 'investment prospectus' based on it might be picked up by a range of other groups working to attract investment in Indigenous land. The processes followed by the first group might then be repeated, become stabilised and come to form a durable assemblage through which very large areas of land, and very large numbers of people, come to be framed in particular ways that shape investment geographies. It is therefore important to be attentive to the stabilisation of assemblages and the range of scales at which different assemblages and their parts interact.

Methodological Implications

The above four aspects of an assemblage ontology open up new avenues for the study of financialisation. Financialisation is often viewed as a hegemonic project undertaken by actors who undertake intentional and efficient reorganisation of economic life (Ouma 2016). In contrast, an assemblage approach asks us to assume a more disordered reality, requiring a closer look at the variety of human and nonhuman actors involved in negotiating assemblages of financial investment, to see financialisation as a result of ongoing effort. Creating connections between land and global finance requires constant work to structure and maintain assemblages of financial investment. As Ouma notes:

> there is neither something natural, nor something evolutionary or inevitable, about global market connections. Markets do not simply fall out of thin air . . . nor do they befall and subjugate local actors as inexorable global forces . . . Humans . . . have to solve a range of sociotechnical puzzles in order to access, maintain, and/or expand markets. (2015b, 5)

An assemblage approach denaturalises economic rationalities such that the specific moral and practical judgements that underpin individual decisions may be explored as choices. Assemblage theory reminds us: that social and economic relations occur between heterogeneous parts that are constantly in flux; that these parts actualise different capacities as a result of their relation to other parts; that agency is distributed and causality is nonlinear and potentially unpredictable; and that structures stabilise and destabilise over time, affecting component parts and the assemblage as a whole. It becomes necessary to take cross-sectional 'cuts' of an assemblage (Anderson et al. 2012) to examine the interactions between a few key elements in order to understand the agencies involved and the causalities that result; reflecting on what these practices contribute to larger global processes while holding in mind the contextually, provisionally, historically and spatially situated nature of this moment of interaction. It requires rethinking assumptions that all actions of finance are financialising and, similarly, that all local actions constitute resistance. Rather than focusing on how 'universalizing, totalizing, and disembodied processes . . . manifest themselves in similar ways in different places' (Larner, Le Heron and Lewis 2007, 223), the approach sees these processes as assembled by the places and the people who engage with them.

Combined with awareness of broader discourses and patterns, an assemblage approach offers the possibility for more a detailed and critical view of financialisation in its spatially and temporally differentiated forms. While it problematises studies of financialisation that emphasise its structural coherence (see Christophers 2015), it is complementary to studies that identify global discourses and pressures (for example, Burch and Lawrence 2009; 2013) since 'social assemblages larger than individual persons have an objective existence because they can causally affect the people that are their component parts, limiting and enabling them' (DeLanda 2006, 38). From this perspective, an 'assemblage is held together and takes actualized spatio-temporal form, but in uncertain and open relations and configurations of sometimes multiple actors, measures and practices' (Lewis et al. 2016, 165), in a 'micro-construction of the practices' of broader global changes (Lewis, Le Heron and Campbell 2017, 164). While the approach in this book is to pay particular attention to these moments of individual and interpersonal negotiation in order to further explore their role in forming and contesting financialised futures, this must be undertaken with reference to widespread structural patterns that influence these micro-processes. The use of assemblage theory here reflects the importance of these micro-processes and the performativity of their actions.

An assemblage ontology asks us to examine the range of relations and interactions that contribute to emergent assemblages. However, in viewing financial work as deeply relational, provisional and unpredictable, 'we must also beware of the danger of aimlessly following the threads, lacking a defined endpoint and further losing ourselves in the deep entanglements of the relational processes that create our world' (Forney, Rosin and Campbell 2018, 3). It is important to identify how changes in agrifood systems are brought about by particular alignments of human and nonhuman actors; for example, how particular tools and calculative devices lead to certain patterns of investment in Northern Australian land.

Such an approach asks us to identify critical moments in the negotiation of links between global finance and local actors for examination. Tsing's (2004, 5) approach was to focus on moments of 'friction' in which 'heterogenous and unequal encounters can lead to new arrangements of culture and power'. By exploring important interactions between actors, she was able to show 'the importance of contingent and botched encounters in shaping both business-as-usual and its radical refusals' (Tsing 2004, 272). The approach in this book is to focus on the work of individuals who are involved in negotiating connections between global finance and local industry and who are able to 'modify a state of affairs by making a difference' (Latour 2005, 71). These intermediaries often play crucial roles in guiding finance and assembling the patterns through which it relates to agriculture. They include people directly involved in negotiating investments (such as farmers, Indigenous intermediaries and fund managers) as well as mediating professionals (such as lawyers, consultants, bankers, valuation professionals and government officials). These people are professionals who hold varying degrees of power, raising particular concerns around power, ethics and access. As the study of professionals poses particular challenges and is undertaken from a range of different approaches, it is worth discussing the approach taken in this book in some detail.

Power, Ethics and Access in Studies with Professionals

Ideally, finance professionals would be studied using long-term ethnographic methods that allow for direct observation of their everyday decision-making processes rather than relying on their own accounts of these processes. This could include observations and discussion with these professionals, perhaps setting up residence inside their offices. While some researchers have successfully gained access for these types of studies (see Ho 2009; Ducastel and Anseeuw 2017), in general such observation is complicated by a range of ethical, access and power considerations (Ostrander 1995; Thomas 1995). Reports commonly contain commercial information and have restricted access, access for observation is rarely granted, professionals have limited time available for participation, and a desire to look at the patterns of many actors across an industry imposes resource constraints. This raises some important concerns around data collection and use that are directly relevant to this book.

In studies of marginalised groups, social scientists have come under scrutiny in relation to the ethical implications of their work (Rylko-Bauer, Singer and Willigen 2006). In these contexts, researchers may seek to address the power imbalance between themselves and their participants by letting them 'speak for themselves', through a variety of mechanisms, including letting people read back over transcripts and make corrections. The normative bias this introduces is not widely problematised and indeed is often seen as a right of the participant in the research project, and increasingly represents the view that participants may be better placed to interpret their own society rather than the researcher. In the study of power, some have argued that there is a need to correct power imbalances in the opposite direction, perhaps through journalistic strategies (Pierce 1995). Indeed, in studies of financial mediation there is often an explicit normative agenda (Ouma 2014, 164) against the actions of the participant. However, this raises questions about whether differential treatment of participants is ethical and, if so, who decides which participants deserve protection. I prefer to take an objective stance and believe that participants – who give freely of their time to participate in a study that they believe has value – would *want* to participate in the study. This is both an ethical and a methodological choice: studies of finance rely on the cooperation of finance professionals (Ouma 2014) who are unlikely to willingly participate in a hostile study. These professionals hold power, and so are in a position to enforce their own code of ethics. They 'are out of reach on a number of different planes: they don't want to be studied; it is dangerous to study the powerful; they are busy people; they are not all in one place, and so on' (Nader 1972, 302). They may agree to participate in interviews, but may be skilled in selecting information to withhold, and in 'shield[ing] themselves from exposure or criticism' (Ostrander 1995, 139). They may declare certain parts of the conversation to be 'off the record', may require oversight of transcripts so they approve what information can be used and may exert influence that restricts publication (see Ostrander 1995, 139). In short, they can limit the information they provide to their own narrative, such that the interviewee becomes both the subject and the tool of their own self-enquiry and constructs a normative narrative of their work. What sort of information can be gleaned from these types of data?

Some argue that the information people give about their own work is of little use in critically analysing the work they do, but rather leads to 'sociologists repeating and recapitulating economists' own stories and never challenging their accounts ... never compar[ing] what they say they do with what they actually do' (Undurraga 2013, n.p.). The knowledge we can gain through interviews is by its nature partial, positioned and constructed

(Warren 2001). Mirowski (2012; 2014) argues that economic actors are unable to usefully comment on their own work because they are biased, they do not self-reflect and they do not critically analyse their own work. This has not been my experience, although different people naturally do this to different extents. Partial and positioned does not mean invalid or empty, and recognising the sorts of information we can gain and cannot gain from interviews is an important methodological challenge in the studies of elites, in which access to information is greatly constrained. Although accounts are constructed by the individuals who give them, and so are necessarily positioned and partial, they can be usefully used with critical awareness of their limitations, and the development of strategies to appropriately ground the research. Understanding how people see their own work is, in itself, a critical part of understanding processes of construction (Riemer 2011). However, it can also be used to develop understandings of what people 'actually do' (Undurraga 2013), and this research did not lead to simple repetition of a dominant narrative. There were three key reasons for this.

First, the people I spoke to were often in positions of less power than those often discussed in the literature. I noticed that among the interviewees, some were more willing to share personal stories, while others (often those in senior management or working for highly visible institutions) shared only general information consistent with published company reports. These interviewees were highly conscious of what they could and could not say, and so provided limited additional information on their own activities in interviews, although they often provided valuable information on others. However, the majority of interviewees felt that their work was difficult, and misunderstood, and that if more were known about the challenges they face, they would enjoy greater resourcing. These interviewees spoke at length about their work and the challenges they faced, as well as about others in the field.

Second, professionals do not have a unified, coherent agenda, but a diversity of opinions on the way in which work should be done, as an assemblage approach highlights. Speaking with a range of people who do similar work does not result in a series of repetitions of the same account, but rather a range of different perspectives, justifications and criticisms of other ways of doing things. We can learn from comparing these different accounts, while recognising that each is constructed by an individual in a place. For example, one interviewee described at length what they saw as the immoral behaviour of another intermediary. I then requested an interview with that intermediary to gain a different perspective on the morality of their work. By combining different accounts and opinions, I gained a variety of descriptions on financial work and how it 'should' be done.

Third, professionals are often in a much better position than the researcher to reflect on their own work and are not necessarily protective of it. These people are individuals, with their own beliefs and practices that align or conflict with industry rules and standards in various ways. An experienced professional is likely to have beliefs about their profession and how it could be improved, and is likely to be willing to pinpoint issues in professional customs or calculations, or wider political systems, that they see as negatively impacting their work. They are almost certainly much more informed about the process than the researcher, and so their own interpretation is of great value and should be seen for its merits as well as its limitations. This filtered and socially constructed knowledge provides extremely rich, valuable data, representing insights that could not be gained without the willing participation of interviewees. However, it must be used with the recognition of its partiality and positionality, and combined with accounts from other professionals to assemble an understanding of how different people undertake work. In this book I combine accounts from a range of professionals to develop an understanding of how they interact with each other and each other's work.

We can see interviews as a series of advocacies, and from these contrasting advocacies we can assemble information on the different ways of moralising a range of financing work. In this way, professionals themselves challenge each other's accounts, and the researcher becomes a facilitator for this process. From this angle, interviewing elites is a chance to present a person's own personal views and a commitment to represent all angles that were expressed in the research. In this approach, the *intersection* between information sources is critical: the combination of accounts from different people and triangulation with other sources of information to ground findings (Flick 2018). Reports, newspaper articles, textbooks on professional standards, studies of businesses, sales data and public debates can all be triangulated with interviews to build an understanding of practices as they are performed and as they are viewed by individuals. An interdisciplinary approach is needed in this analysis in order to critically analyse work in a range of fields.

This book aims to demonstrate the utility of this approach for understanding the assemblage of financialisation in Northern Australia. The next chapter introduces the historical context of Northern Australia that has shaped contemporary engagements with foreign finance.

Chapter 2

A Brief History of Northern Development

Background

Northern Australia is defined as the Northern Territory (NT) plus the parts of Queensland (QLD) and Western Australia (WA) above or intersecting with the Tropic of Capricorn (see Figure 2.1). It spans a diversity of environments, land tenures and histories. Large parts of this region have remained relatively underdeveloped in comparison to southern agricultural regions. This underdevelopment, as well as the region's unique environmental features, proximity to Asia and perceived importance to national security during the early twentieth century, are key reasons why it is viewed as a composite region of Australia – that is, 'Australia's North' (Holmes 1963; Kelly 1966; Davidson 1972). Northern Australia has a long history of seeking financial investment for development with a range of successful and unsuccessful outcomes. Investment policy in the region has evolved beyond simply attracting investment to encompass a concern with keeping benefits locally and reducing speculative financial behaviour. This history makes the region a unique place to study the ways in which investment is negotiated, the role of government in mediating these investments, and how people have sought to control finance for social benefit to local communities.

Northern Australia is an immense area of land spanning a diversity of environments, water and soil resources, communities, cultures, land tenures, histories and infrastructure developments. Environmentally, it receives similar levels of rainfall to other areas of Australia, but with more extreme seasonality

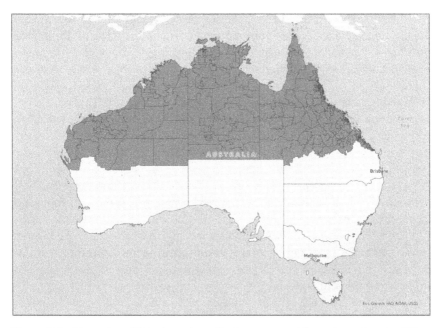

Figure 2.1. The region of Northern Australia. Image created by author using ArcGIS Pro. © Zannie Langford. Area boundaries as shown on Australian Government (2022), https://www.infrastructure.gov.au/territories-regions-cities/regional-australia/off ice-northern-australia

(Bureau of Meteorology 2016), leading to pronounced wet and dry seasons in many parts of the region. As a result, animal grazing is the main land use in the region, with the exception of the eastern coastal areas. Many areas of the region are subject to extended periods of drought, and rainfall strongly influences the productivity of pastoral enterprises. Efforts pursuing agricultural development in the region tend to focus on either intensifying the pastoral industry (such as by installing increased water bores and fencing) or on irrigated agricultural development. Both are capital-intensive activities and are considered emerging opportunities that continue to be associated with uncertain outcomes and risk.

Irrigated cropping development plans rely on either groundwater or surface water resources. Groundwater resources are limited and poorly understood in many areas, particularly the NT, though in some areas there is a concerted effort to measure and analyse existing resources to increase their sustainable usage, and at the federal government level, there are discussions to develop large dams to capture surface water for irrigation programs (Australian Government 2015a). There is also the potential for smaller-scale dams using on-farm water storage, a strategy that has been successfully undertaken by a number of growers in the NT. Groundwater resources and soil quality are the limiting factors for cropping development in much of the region (Ash 2014; Australian Government 2015a). Water is also used to intensify pastoral activities as water supplies can open up larger areas of cattle stations to grazing.

Pastoral leaseholds are common throughout the region. These are long-term ownership rights that are often sold for many millions of dollars on private land markets. These leaseholds coexist with native title rights in many areas and, as Indigenous rights to land have increased since the 1970s, the move to Indigenous land ownership has become one of the most significant changes to occur in the region. In particular, the NT has large areas of Aboriginal freehold land, which are entirely owned by Indigenous people and are generally administered through a group decision-making process overseen by Native Title Representative Bodies and Service Providers (NTRB-SPs). Their substantial landholdings make Indigenous people increasingly influential actors in Northern Development initiatives. Indigenous people also hold partial rights to land through Native Title agreements, which may give them access to land for certain activities and to have input into proposed developments, including negotiating benefits. Despite these rights, many Indigenous people in the region live in poorly serviced areas with limited economic opportunities, where health indicators and access to public services are far below levels considered acceptable in other areas of Australia (Dale 2014, 11; Australian Institute of Health and Welfare 2022). The provision of services and the development of local economies in these regions is one of the major goals of development efforts (Australian Government 2015a; Commonwealth of Australia 2021).

These diverse landscapes and features have been the target of numerous agribusiness development initiatives. From the late 1800s to the present day, the most intensive government-driven development efforts have focused on the NT, which was administered externally by South Australia from 1863 to 1911 and by the federal government from 1911 to 1978. There have also been numerous private sector initiatives in agriculture. The eastern coast has also had some agribusiness developments, but has a different relationship with external capital due to its larger resident population. The next section will consider historical capital development in Northern Australia with a focus on pastoral zones outside the eastern coastal areas.

Early Occupation

Indigenous Australians are thought to have lived in Northern Australia for at least 65,000 years by the time Europeans first attempted settlement

A Brief History of Northern Development • 41

(Clarkson et al. 2017), and at this time were organised into hundreds of Indigenous groups. They practised a range of food provisioning activities on the land, including hunting, fishing and the collection of native foods, and in some places these activities significantly transformed the landscape (Gammage 2011; Pascoe 2014; Sutton 2021). These activities were substantially interrupted by colonisation, during which time foreign species (such as sheep, cattle, pigs and buffalo) upset the fragile ecosystems upon which many of these activities were based (Wright 1997). Although Indigenous people continued to practise some food-harvesting activities, agricultural development in settler-colonial Australia largely sought to replace these through the cultivation of introduced species mostly in isolation from Indigenous practices and with little input from Indigenous people other than to provide labour. Beginning in the 1970s, legislation was introduced that allowed Indigenous people to claim formal land rights, and the resulting laws have seen Indigenous people recentred as important players in Northern Development (Australian Government 2015a). In addition, native plant and animal species are gaining increasing attention for wildlife-based enterprise development (Zander, Austin and Garnett 2014), as they are environmentally sustainable, may command niche markets and are a preferred form of employment by some Indigenous people (Austin and Garnett 2018, 184). The Indigenous business sector in Australia is growing rapidly, although much of this growth is the result of government and corporate procurement policies, and targets a narrow range of industries (Langford 2023). However, for much of Australia's colonial history, Indigenous people were largely excluded from agricultural development initiatives that sought to replace existing practices, often through violent mechanisms.

Early attempts to establish settlements in Northern Australia occurred in the NT, with several failed colonial settlements in Northern Australia from 1825 to 1849. In 1863 South Australia took over administrating the NT and established the first permanent colony of the NT just south of Darwin in 1864, at great public expense. The South Australian leaders believed that the NT could be quickly developed along a similar trajectory as South Australia, and would form a hub for tropical agriculture, support a transcontinental stock trade route and provide a gateway to Asian markets (Powell 2009 [1982]). By that time, Eastern Australia had decades of history over which a capitalist development philosophy had emerged (McMichael 1984), and this philosophy drove NT development efforts. The South Australian government was largely composed of business owners who, having seen South Australia's quick development through investment by speculators from abroad, sought the same for the NT. In the view of South Australian leaders: 'Speculation and settlement . . . were not incompatible; they had gone hand and hand in the building of South Australia' (Powell 2000, 77). These politicians were described as 'self-made men' with interests in 'business, land, mining and speculation' who hoped to profit from an NT that would be run in the same way as the economy of South Australia (Powell 2009 [1982], 77–78).

The South Australian government set about developing a plan for 'systematic colonization' (see Kittrell 1973) of the NT, a task that has been described as 'the most laborious and least successful task in [South Australian] history' (Bauer 1964, 48). They divided the NT into parcels for sale to private interests, which they believed would quickly develop the region for profit. In 1869, the Adelaide *Register* reflected the government's faith in private enterprise for development in its comment that 'the South Australian government can now freely transfer the responsibility of the NT from its own shoulders to that of the land speculators' (quoted in Donovan 1981, 164). However, delays in surveying the land and the continuing lack of economic development in the North undermined these ambitions. Many speculators lost substantial investments, and some sued the South Australian government for the return of their investment (Powell 2009 [1982], 62–64).

Despite these losses, several agricultural experiments persisted in the region, notably those by Maurice Holtze at the Darwin Botanical Gardens, who managed to grow tropical crops such as coffee, sugarcane, tobacco, arrowroot, rice, peanuts, tea and cotton (Powell 2009 [1982], 105). However, these experiments were labour-intensive and could not be replicated on a large scale. This limitation notwithstanding, the trials encouraged confidence in the agricultural potential of the region and spurred the belief that the region could be profitably developed by investors. In 1882, the journalist Sir Edward Sowden visited the NT and, after seeing these early agricultural experiments, wrote that:

> success will be general as experiments multiply. If our own capitalists do not accept to their own advantage the commercial suggestiveness of that conclusion, they will find in distant places other men who will; they will discover that foreign money will do what they might much more easily have done. The NT will not for long be the *terra incognita* it has been. The newspapers are spreading its fame throughout the world, and consular authorities and Government officials at Palmerston are frequently addressed from America, China, Mauritius, and other distant parts by men of capital and practical experience in plantation work, and asked for precise information about a place they have seen referred to in papers in the various countries where they live. (Sowden 1882, 95)

Like the South Australian government, Sowden saw a key role for urban Australian and foreign capitalists to invest in the development of Northern Australia. However, he felt that this investment must have a productive aspect and more soberly addressed the issue of speculation by people who would buy the land without developing it. He lamented the 'curses of absenteeism' (Sowden 1882, 131) that he saw on his trip and wondered 'how much longer are the lessees of the big unstocked runs going to leave their lands idol?' (Sowden 1882, 153), also observing that it was 'practically impossible to buy land in the township, for these absentees have a huge monopoly' (Sowden 1882, 130). He saw one of the greatest challenges of development of the region to be 'the really grievous hardship . . . [of t]he withering blight of grasping absentee owners' (Sowden 1882, 159), voicing an opinion that remains a major concern in Northern Development to this day – the need to distinguish between those investors who would develop the region and those who sought simply to speculate on the land.

This concern emerged in a context of very substantial speculation in NT land at the time. Following a boom in pastoral real estate in Queensland from 1881 to 1883, NT land had been divided into leaseholds and almost completely allocated. However, as Bauer observed, 'a glance at the maps is convincing proof that many of the applications were purely speculative; large areas which were unexplored and entirely unsuitable for pastoral purposes were applied for from Adelaide without the applicants ever seeing a yard of the country they claimed' (1964, 112). In 1881 most of the NT had been allocated, but within fifteen years most of the area had been abandoned and 'many bona fide graziers lost heavily on their investments' (Kelly 1966, 21).

There was a persistent gap between large corporate pastoralists and smaller family pastoralists. As Newland observed in 1887, lessees were 'either men who are prepared to spend years of their life at it until the few stock they begin with increase, men who will live hard, work hard and lie [die] hard; or capital, capital, capital' (1887, n.p., quoted in Hartwig 1965, 382). In the NT, large pastoralists have come to dominate the more productive lands in the Top End, while Central Australia has much higher family owner-ship. As Hartwig observed, in Central Australia: 'The big pastoralist financed himself for the most part; and when faith in the country deserted him he merely cut his losses and vanished from the land. His place was taken by the "small" man, who required little, if any, capital' (1965, 383). Some have suggested that companies are more resilient than family businesses because they have access to capital that allows them to overcome drought (Duncan 1967), while others argue that such companies are more likely to leave the land during periods of unprofitability (Hartwig 1965) and that the ability of family farmers to exploit their own labour is a key component of their resilience (Smith 2015). Chapter 6 will discuss changing forms of family and corporate land ownership in a contemporary context, and their approaches to environmental and financial management.

Despite these early pastoral development challenges, the pastoral indus-try in the NT and northern WA eventually grew, with pastoralists from

Queensland and South Australia spreading across the North 'by advance and retreat and then re-occupation' (Pearson and Lennon 2010, 103). They initially trialled sheep, which did poorly, before experimenting with cattle. These early explorer-settlers were driven by 'the ambition to gain a really large parcel of supposedly good country on which to establish a huge pastoral empire, well watered . . . well grassed, and close to limitless markets in Asia' (Pearson and Lennon 2010, 105). They campaigned for pastoral land rights with 'self-justification [that] arose from their *productive* occupation of imperial wastelands, [and] emphasized their economic value to colony and empire alike' (McMichael 1984, 145, emphasis in original). In this way, pastoralism spread from the more densely populated areas of South East Queensland and South Australia across Northern Australia (Holmes 1963, 149).

The expansion of pastoralism across Northern Australia vastly increased the contact that Aboriginal people had with settlers, which inevitably led to conflicts (Elder 1979). Many Aboriginal groups found their land destroyed by grazing animals that compromised their food supply. Violent conflicts were common (McMichael 1984; Powell 2009 [1982]). Aboriginal resistance was often met by 'punitive' expeditions, leading to numerous indiscriminate massacres of Aboriginal people living in the region. Many had little choice but to move from armed resistance to acquiescence, living near pastoral homesteads, trading labour and goods intermittently (Powell 2009 [1982], 99), though not always voluntarily. Their labour became essential to the pastoral industry's growth, until the introduction of equal wages in 1968 saw many dismissed and helicopter mustering taking over as the dominant approach (Pearson 2010). Until very recently, Aboriginal people have rarely been recognised as significant stakeholders in Northern Development, despite their essential role in supporting the establishment of the pastoral industry. Today, they have regained rights to substantial areas of land in Northern Australia and are increasingly involved in development efforts on these lands.

Pastoral Development

The pastoral industry performed relatively poorly until the early twentieth century due to the realities of northern weather, the high costs of sale and the outbreak of tick fever (*babesiosis*) (Powell 2009 [1982]). The South Australian government invested heavily in the NT, receiving little in return, and in 1911, after several decades of deliberations, the Commonwealth assumed administration of the NT from South Australia. The early twentieth century saw a great deal of consolidation of properties and the rise of very large pastoral empires. Large corporate interests dominated the industry through the early twentieth century – in the NT by 1927, the industry was highly concentrated, with only six lessees holding nearly half the stocked land (Powell 2009 [1982], 124).

The largest of these companies was the Vesteys company, which first entered Australia in 1913 as a multinational company with capital in excess of £1,000,000 (d'Abbs 1970, 8). Vesteys quickly acquired a series of properties representing over nine million hectares (ha) of land (Kelly 1966, 2) and built a meat works through an agreement with the Commonwealth government, although this meatworks only operated for a few years before it closed down (Powell 2009 [1982], 110–11). By 1926 Vesteys were the biggest landholders in the NT (d'Abbs 1970, 15). Vesteys' impact on Northern Development has been contentious. There were certainly areas in which its activities contributed to development goals. Vesteys pioneered some strategies for the movement of cattle (Pearson and Lennon 2010, 159–60), re-established a live cattle trade in the 1920s (Pearson and Lennon 2010, 160) and made several other technical contributions to the pastoral industry. Cattleman Max Sargent, who worked for Vesteys for many years, stated that: 'Vesteys have done more for NT development than any other firm is likely to do in the next bloody hundred years' (Williams 1981, 5, cited in Powell 2009 [1982], 161). Others have noted that Vesteys famously evaded paying tax for a number of years (d'Abbs 1970, 18), negotiated very low lease terms, had a poor Aboriginal labour rights record (d'Abbs 1970, 24–29) and closed down operations (such as the Darwin meatworks) as soon as they no longer served its international interests (Powell 2009 [1982], 111–12). At the height of company's international dealings, it was thought to be worth in excess of £2 billion, with 23,000 employees and 250,000 head cattle globally. In the 1990s, debts incurred by its London holding company forced it to divest itself of a number of it operations, and by 1995 it had sold its last NT property, ending 81 years of operation there (D'Abbs 1970). D'Abbs (1970, 4) wrote that the Vesteys group was:

> one example of how a large overseas group, dedicated purely to increasing its own profits, has been able to acquire enormous power in Australia which, unlike the political power wielded by our politicians, is not subject to any control by the people of Australia.

J.H. Kelly's 1966 work on the pastoral industry positioned the NT's lack of pastoral development as a political rather than an environmental problem. Kelly (1966) argued that powerful corporate-owned cattle interests with excessively large land holdings and very low lease rents inhibited NT development by opposing closer settlement and development policies that would make it possible, such as the construction of railways. He strongly criticised the extension of cheap, long-term lease holdings, arguing that rather than giving leaseholders a permanency of tenancy that would incentivise development, they locked in large unproductive companies interested only on running properties as cheaply as possible, and not on developing the region. He noted that 'it is better from a development and settlement point of view to have a number of resident lessees on areas of reasonable and adequate size than to have very large areas leased to non-resident companies' (Kelly 1966, 11) and emphasised:

> the great importance of railway construction in the area . . . [S]tock routes, roads and aerodromes are of secondary importance to railways both from the strategic and development point of view. Without an adequate railway system, the development of Northern Australia cannot hope to succeed. (Kelly 1966, 11)

The 1960s were profitable years for the NT beef industry, yet many stations continued to run at a loss. From 1962 to 1965, 25% of cattle stations ran at a loss and the average return on capital invested in the Barkley Tableland, a highly profitable region, was only 6.6% (Bureau of Agricultural Economics 1968, 50–52). From 1961 to 1975, the Commonwealth government spent $630 million developing 2,500 km of roads. Cattle went from being primarily walked to markets to being transported by road (Powell 2009 [1982], 161). In 1959 mining overtook pastoralism as the biggest income earner in NT. Today, the pastoral industry is dominated by large corporate interests, although less so in the more marginal areas near Alice Springs.

Agricultural Development

Agricultural development efforts were expanded as a result of the Second World War. Darwin featured prominently in the Second World War effort as a defence base for the war in South Asia, with the development of a military force of 32,000 by 1942. This context created the first substantial local market for Territory beef and food crops, and led to the establishment of animal production facilities and agricultural gardens. In 1944, 1,500 tonnes of vegetables were produced on 140 ha of new farmland stretching from Darwin to 1,200 km south, as well as chickens and 42,000 dozen eggs from Katherine (Powell 2009 [1982], 149). This example has been used to demonstrate the feasibility of agricultural production in the NT – yet, like the market gardeners before them, the military gardeners relied upon cheap Aboriginal labour (Powell 2009 [1982], 149). Supporting the military also led to the establishment of sealed highways between Mount Isa, Alice Springs and Darwin, the long-distance telephone system, improved water, and power supplies in towns and along highways (Powell 2009 [1982], 155).

After the end of the war, security threats from abroad (the Korean War of 1950–53, the Vietnam War of 1962–75 and the Indonesian confrontation of 1962–66) kept successive governments concerned with Northern Development (Powell 2009 [1982], 167), although the logic of pursuing Northern Development continued to be debated. In 1963 Holmes published *Australia's Open North: A Study of Northern Australia Bearing on the Urgency of the Times*, arguing for Northern Development for homeland security reasons as well as for national pride (Holmes 1963, 459). This book was followed by Davidson's more sober 1972 work *The Northern Myth: A Study of the Physical and Economic Limits to Agricultural and Pastoral Development in Tropical Australia*. Davidson argued that, on the contrary, a developed region is more attractive to would-be invaders than a nondeveloped region, and that Northern agricultural development would be uneconomic due to the high costs of production and 'would act as a continual drain on the Australian economy and utilize resources that could profitably be used elsewhere' (Davidson 1972, 271).

The 1950s saw the first large-scale, privately financed commercial attempts at agriculture in Northern Australia, an approach that remains highly influential in Northern Development efforts today. Funded by distant capital, a series of large agricultural ventures were attempted, as Ash (2014) has usefully summarised.[1] The Ord River scheme, although a public sector initiative, is included for its current engagements with private finance. These large-scale development efforts are worth examining as they provide insights into current agricultural development efforts, particularly as they relate to the role and effects of private finance capital in development.

The Queensland-British Food Corporation (1948–52)

The Queensland-British Food Corporation's sorghum-growing scheme operated in central Queensland from 1948 to 1952. The scheme planned to grow 100,000 ha of dryland sorghum, although it only reached 25% of its planned scale (Ash 2014). An investment of $137 million was funded 75% by the British Overseas Food Corporation and 25% from the Queensland government through low-interest loans. The main driver of the development was the need to address food shortages following the Second World War, and the project was quickly developed up to 25,000 ha of sorghum with a labour force of 320. However, the yield of two t/ha of sorghum was never achieved, with only 0.6 t/ha being achieved, and the project ended in 1952. The land was redistributed by ballot to smaller operators, and the region has since established mixed grazing-cropping enterprises that continue today. The scheme benefited from a guaranteed market in which the British government had agreed to purchase all produce; however, it suffered from a range of environmental and management issues. Ash (2014) identified the critical constraints that underpinned the failure of the scheme as overly ambitious expansion plans, centralised decision-making from Brisbane with poor communication lines, a lack of experience in the tropical environment, high management costs and interest payments, and capital constraints limiting scale-up. A number of smaller growers now successfully grow sorghum in the region, suggesting that environmental issues faced by the large scheme could have been overcome if longer time periods to develop farming strategies had been available and the financial and management structure of the operation had been more flexible.

Territory Rice Ltd (1955–61)

The Territory Rice Ltd scheme operated at Humpty Doo in the NT from 1955 to 1961. The scheme planned to grow 200,000 ha of irrigated rice, although it only reached 1.1% of its planned scale. It was initially capitalised with a $5 million investment from Australian and American investors, who entered an agreement with the Commonwealth government to lease 300,000 ha of land for 30 years. This agreement was contingent on their development of 200,000 ha of this land and the introduction of farming techniques to support the establishment of a Northern Australian rice growing industry. The scheme expected yields of 2.5 t/ha of rice, but only achieved 1.3 t/ha. The scheme was abandoned after just over five years following significant losses, and the company was placed in receivership. Ash (2014) identified critical agronomic and management constraints that undermined the scheme. Agronomically, the scheme used varieties of rice that were not well suited for the climate or for mechanised farming, the soils were unsuitable to rice growing, and there was a lack of understanding of how to plant the rice seeds (if planted too deep, they would not emerge from the soil, but if planted too shallow, they would be damaged by the region's sun and heat). From a management perspective, the operation suffered from a lack of capital to properly set up the farm, a lack of irrigation water during the planting time (due to seasonal surface water salinity), poor soil levelling, inappropriate farming equipment and methods, and poor communication on management issues between offices in Brisbane, Sydney and the United States. No subsequent rice growing industry has been established, although there continue to be efforts to do so (Brann 2019).

The Ord River Irrigation Area (1963 to the Present Day)

The Ord River Irrigation Area was an initiative of the WA and Commonwealth governments in the 1950s. Stage 1 involved the construction of a Diversion Dam at Kununurra (completed in 1963) and a main dam at Lake Argyle (completed in 1972). The programme was underpinned by substantial agronomic research into crops and farming methods that would be suitable for the region. However, less research had explored the economics of production and marketing of these goods (Ash 2014). The scheme initially focused on cotton growing; however, this scheme had collapsed by the mid-1970s due to poor cotton quality, pest issues (the cotton boll worm *Helicoverpa*) and the removal of cotton subsidies by 1972. This phase of the scheme had been intended to reach 70,000 ha, but only 12,000 ha were made available and less than 5,000 ha were actually used by 1980 (Ash 2014). From the 1980s, after cotton growing had failed to be economic, growers shifted towards a range of higher-value field and horticulture crops. In the mid-1990s, sugarcane was introduced to the region and a small mill was built, and this industry grew to cover 4,000 ha and produced 55,000 t/year of sugar. The production was not economically competitive at this small scale and production ended in 2007. Despite this, there are plans for a sugarcane industry ten times this size in Stage 2 of the Ord development. Since the early 2000s, managed investment schemes have taken hold in the Ord, growing sandalwood, African mahogany and mangoes. Today, of the 14,000 ha of irrigated land in the Ord, sandalwood covers more than half. Other crops continue to be grown, such as mangoes, melons, pumpkins, chia, chickpeas, borlotti beans and sorghum, and these cover around 6,000 ha and generate $40–50 million per annum (Ash 2014, 9). More recently, plans for the Ord River expansion (with significant foreign capital investment) are emerging, but remain uncertain.

The Tipperary Land Corporation (1967–72)

The Tipperary Land Corporation operated in the Daly River Basin of the NT from 1967 to 1972. It sought to grow 79,000 ha of dryland sorghum, although it only reached 8.7% of this scale. After several decades of post Second World War efforts towards Northern agricultural development (including research farms and land surveying), Tipperary station was purchased in 1967 by a group of Texan investors who sought to develop sorghum and cattle fattening, and estimated that a US$20 million investment would be required (Ash 2014). An initial investment of US$7 million had been raised by 1967. However, the corporation overestimated the yields that could be achieved (ignoring available evidence from field trials) and only operated for three years before experiencing financial difficulties, after which the property was sold. Ash (2014) identified critical constraints facing the scheme as a lack of adequate storage facilities on the farm (resulting in a decline in grain quality and a failure to meet export contracts), inexperienced management and labour, the use of inappropriate methods for seedbed preparation, soil cultivation and application of fertiliser, and insufficient capital.

The Australian Land and Cattle Company (1970–74)

The Australian Land and Cattle Company operated in the Camballin Irrigation Area of WA. It sought to grow 25,000 ha of sorghum, but only reached 7.7% of this area at its peak. After some small-scale rice production in the region in the 1950s and 1960s, the WA government supported the development of the area through the construction of a small dam, in return for the company that was operating at the time (Northern Developments Pty Ltd) agreeing to crop 8,000 ha of land with rice. Northern Developments had little success due to flooding, and in 1969 the Australian Land and Cattle Company took over the project. Despite substantial expansion plans, it failed to sustainably develop the area. The total investment in the project exceeded $120 million (Ash 2014). Ash (2014) identified critical constraints to the project as insufficient capital for scale-up, regulatory constraints, and problems aligning financing and farm operation schedules.

The Northern Agricultural Development Corporation (1970–74)

The Northern Agricultural Development Corporation operated at Willeroo Station in the NT from 1970 to 1974 and sought to transform the property from a low-intensity cattle grazing operation to an intensive crop production and cattle-fattening operation. Plans included the development of 80,000 ha of improved pasture, 25,000 ha of grain sorghum and the establishment of a feedlot (Fisher et al. 1977), although only about 10,000 ha of sorghum was ultimately sown. Ash (2014) identifies critical constraints facing the property as a poor fit of agronomic techniques for the environment, a failure to take account of available technical information, and poor project and financial management, including overestimation of economies of scale and overcapitalisation with very high borrowings. The Corporation was placed into receivership in 1974.

Katherine Mangoes (1982 to the Present Day)

The Katherine mango industry was initiated in the 1980s as a managed investment scheme at Manbullo Station (Wilson 1982), which collapsed financially after seven years after the trees failed to bear fruit in the timeframe planned in the investment documents (Ash 2014, and based on reports from my fieldwork). Two years later, the plantations produced fruit, and Manbullo Station is now one of the NT's largest mango producers. The mango industry has grown substantially over the last two decades and is now the NT's largest horticultural industry, with over 700,000 trees planted (Australian Bureau of Statistics 2022).

This historical literature demonstrates the longstanding challenges and contradictions facing capital-led development in Northern Australian agriculture, and sets the scene for this book as it focuses on contemporary financialisation trends in the region. In each of the cases where failure occurred, a combination of environmental and management factors led to their demise: unfamiliar climate and soil types, unsuitable plant varieties and a lack of technical understanding hampered operations. The failure to plan for initial difficulties led to capital constraints and to the ultimate abandonment of the projects. Christian and Stewart (1953, 138) categorised cropping failures in the Katherine-Darwin region as explainable by three factors: production problems (climate, soil, natural disasters, property management and land use); economic problems (market access, transaction costs and marketing difficulties); and social problems (living conditions and problems attracting farmers).

Sir William Archer Gunn, the pastoralist, industry leader and founder of Gunn Rural Management, saw these projects as being driven primarily by external factors rather than productive factors, arguing that their conception as financial projects laid the foundations for their demise. His analysis is worth quoting at length because it speaks directly to the issues associated with private financial sector funding of agricultural development projects:

> [At] Territory Rice . . . the agricultural methods used had the prime object of raising money, with no regard to agricultural knowledge. The people who managed the project did not know anything about agriculture, let alone rice. The same was true at Tipperary; the agricultural programme was aimed at raising money and satisfying the New York Stock Exchange, and they thought that the dollar would beat the agricultural programme. I know something about the Cape York Peninsular project, too; the same applied there. Gunn Rural Management, in fact, did the feasibility study and the feasibility study was thrown out of the window because it didn't help them raise the money. We were asked to do the North Australian Development Company one . . . and we told them if we did, they wouldn't invest the money, so we didn't get the feasibility study. (Gunn 1977, 179)

Clifford Stuart Christian, Chief of the Division of Land Research at the Commonwealth Scientific and Industrial Research Organisation (CSIRO) at that time, agreed that financial motives in agricultural projects could undermine their success:

> The true motivation of privately financed projects also bears examination. Speculation on land subdivision, share dealing, or foreign tax concessions could lead to a different approach to crop development from that of a scheme based on profits from crop production alone. (Christian 1977, 15)

He went further to associate these issues with the scale of very large investment schemes in the remote North of Australia:

> To be competitive, crop production in isolated areas must reduce its costs of production, yet its very isolation tends to increase them through transport and supply costs. A large scheme is therefore attractive in the belief that the size of operations means cost savings. Experience does not appear to support this contention in northern Australia. A large project has a degree of inflexibility, especially where centralized management is practised and particularly so if managed by remote control. Some northern schemes have suffered from this. A large project uses large machinery, involving high capital and maintenance costs. Unless it is suited in kind and size to the tasks required, wastage results. With large-scale operations it is difficult to apply the necessary precision of ecological management to different portions of a property in accordance with variations in land type, rainfall incidence and soil conditions . . . It is understandable that large schemes involving substantial private investment should seek returns on capital as soon as possible . . . Yet, in the absence of prior experience, haste in expanding operations only magnifies any mistakes that are made. (Christian 1977, 24)

Noting in particular a lack of financial resilience involved with large absentee ownership of agricultural schemes, Christian noted:

> A large scheme also involves financial management as well as property management. It cannot take in its belt and subsist off the land in the same way that a pioneer farmer had to do. Once in difficulties, it may fail quickly and completely. (1977, 25)

As Gunn notes, 'in the great majority of these large schemes the original policy behind the project laid down the foundations for the failure' (Gunn 1977, 179), advocating for what he describes as 'the "owner-driver" type of operation, where the man [*sic*] who operates the farm has a financial interest in the results' (Gunn 1977, 180). A CSIRO report in 2014 mirrored these sentiments, warning against a 'get big quickly' (Ash 2014, 28) approach in favour of a more gradual approach that could have 'provided an opportunity to solve problems as the industry grew' (Ash 2014, 28). Yet today, large-scale, foreign-financed agricultural development proposals continue to attract political favour, with a range of government programmes aimed at marketing Northern Australia's 'investment proposition'.

The Legacies of Development Programmes

These histories of agricultural development programmes in Northern Australia have led to some cynicism about current large-scale development efforts. Many local professionals are working in roles that require them to promote similar development initiatives, which they do with varying levels of enthusiasm. These attitudes seem to engender caution to different extents and lead to a greater concern with sustainability by those cognisant of past histories. In some cases, a level of defensiveness could be detected, which led many to define current efforts in terms of what previous efforts had been lacking. The next chapter examines contemporary Northern Development efforts and recent investment programmes in order to explore this approach and its impacts on Northern Development pathways.

Note

1. Values given in the next section are as reported in Ash (2014) and are in 2012 Australian dollars.

Chapter 3

THE INVESTMENT PROPOSITION

Developing Northern Australia

In 2015, the Commonwealth government released the first White Paper on Developing Northern Australia. The White Paper recognised the history of failed development efforts in Northern Australia, yet claimed that with the right approach, these challenges could be overcome:

> Many previous efforts to develop the north have floundered through a lack of foresight and the absence of markets in our region for high value goods and services. Through this, the first ever White Paper on Developing Northern Australia (the White Paper), the Commonwealth Government is putting in place the right policies, at the right time, to unlock the north's vast potential. This White Paper has been developed to stand the test of time – it should be the first, and last, White Paper for the north. (Australian Government 2015a, 1)

This language was typical of the White Paper, which was ambitious in its scope and sought to frame decisive action to support the Northern Development agenda. The guiding logic of the White Paper was a particular governance rationality that makes explicit an investor-led development philosophy:

> It is not the Commonwealth Government's role to direct, or be the principal financier of, development. Developing the north is a partnership between *investors* (local and international investors who provide capital and know-how)

and *governments* (that create the right investment conditions). (Australian Government 2015a, 2, emphasis in original)

The White Paper developed a 'value proposition' for these investors, forecasting potentially significant returns on investment parallel to those found in land investments in developing economies (Australian Government 2015a, 7). In it, Northern Australia is positioned as a newly discovered region that finance is yet to discover, described as an area of 'untapped potential', 'underutilized assets' and 'immense opportunities' (Australian Government 2015a, 60, 85, 55). There are numerous references in the White Paper to the need to 'unlock' this potential (Australian Government 2015a, 1, 5, 21, 35, 61, 84, 164). It is proposed to be done through large-scale, privately financed, interventions. The White Paper asserts that Northern Development 'cannot be done with incremental approaches. It will need private sector capital – and lots of it' (Australian Government 2015a, 4). It details a range of programs aimed at Northern Development, including the following:

- *Indigenous land administration*
  An announcement that $440 million would be available to support the finalisation of Indigenous land claims. A further $20.4 million was allocated to support native title holders to engage with potential investors and an additional $17 million was allocated to support leasing of Indigenous land.
- *Water infrastructure*
  Some $200 million would be allocated for water infrastructure, including an initial $25 million on feasibility studies at five locations.
- *Trade and investment*
  A range of programmes would be initiated to connect international investors and businesses with local businesses, including running a major investment forum, establishing offices to facilitate investment and reforming the regulation of fisheries and exports.
- *Research and Development*
  Some $75 million would be invested in a new Cooperative Research Centre on Developing Northern Australia to focus on agriculture, food and tropical health, as well as an additional $17.3 million for a Tropical Health Strategy and research collaboration.
- *Infrastructure*
  A range of infrastructure investments would be funded, including $600 for priority roads, $100 million for beef roads, $5 million for railroad feasibility studies, $39.6 million for air services and, most notably, a $5 billion concessional loan facility, known as the Northern Australia

Infrastructure Facility (NAIF), to distribute long-term, low-cost loans to businesses seeking to develop infrastructure.

- *Labour*
  Increased labour supply for Northern Australian businesses would be facilitated by reforming labour programmes, including for local Indigenous workers, seasonal workers (largely from the Pacific island states and East Timor) and working holiday-makers.
- *Governance*
  There would be a collection of initiatives designed to increase the visibility of Northern development agendas, including moving the Office of Northern Australia to Northern Australia, and increasing the presence of the defence force in Northern Australia.

These initiatives can be considered varieties of 'roll-out' and 'roll-back' neoliberalism (Peck and Tickell 2002), including efforts to reduce regulation and 'red tape' (Australian Government 2015a, 12) as well as substantial investments in creating conditions to favour private sector investment.

Themes in Northern Development

Several contemporary trends in Northern development have emerged in the years prior to and since the White Paper. These themes are key to understanding the core issues that respondents outlined in their interviews, which in turn indicated where appropriate 'cuts' to the assemblage could be made to reveal influential global–local relations (see Anderson et al. 2012, 182–83, and Chapter 1 in this volume). As users of assemblage approaches have noted, it is important to 'beware of the danger of aimlessly following the threads, lacking a defined endpoint and further losing ourselves in the deep entanglements of the relational processes that create our world' (Forney, Rosin and Campbell 2018a, 3). The following analysis of important themes in Northern Australian development structure the selection of points at which appropriate 'cuts' to the assemblage can be made and closer investigation pursued. The themes identified are approaches to Indigenous development, foreign ownership of land and water, infrastructure development, pastoral intensification and greenfield agriculture.

Indigenous Development

The greatest social benefits expected to be made from Northern development are in remote Indigenous communities, as these communities comprise people who live in the region permanently as a result of their connections to particular areas of land (Gerritson, Whitehead and Stoeckl 2018). In the NT, for example, outside the Darwin census area the population is 51% Indigenous, increasing to 75% for very remote regions (an area representing the vast majority of the NT's landmass) (Australian Bureau of Statistics (ABS) 2018[1]). With the increase in Native Title recognition across Northern Australia, Indigenous people are being treated more seriously as stakeholders in development. According to health and welfare experts, the social needs from remote development in Indigenous Australia are not being met, with remote Indigenous people having poorer health outcomes, fewer employment opportunities, and more limited access to goods and services than other Australians (Australian Institute of Health and Welfare 2015). The White Paper recognises that 'land is of fundamental importance to Indigenous Australians for cultural, social and economic purposes' and announces its commitment to enable them 'to leverage their land assets to generate wealth' (Australian Government 2015a, 15). This effort is supported by plans to facilitate leasing of Indigenous land and to support landholders to negotiate with investors. However, others have argued that this 'development from above' is unlikely to create substantial localised economic benefits for remote Indigenous communities as it tends to favour capital-intensive industries with small employment multipliers (Gerritson, Whitehead and Stoeckl 2018). Stoeckl (2010) describes an 'asymmetric divide' between Indigenous and non-Indigenous economies in Northern Australia, arguing that structural factors prevent economic and other gains in the non-Indigenous economy from benefiting Indigenous Australians. Rather, direct investment into Indigenous economies is often said to be required (Gerritson, Whitehead and Stoeckl 2018).

Indeed, studies of successful remote Indigenous businesses have indicated that a range of non-economic factors are indicative of success. For example, Austin and Garnett (2018, 184), in a survey of three remote Indigenous enterprises, found that success was defined in a range of ways. Measures of success included individual income from employment and royalty payments to Traditional Owners (TOs), growth in the local economy, employment, pride and purpose, removal of people from stressful and potentially harmful situations, pleasure and enjoyment, improved diet, exercise, knowledge and skill development, the ability to reside 'on country'[2] for longer, increased opportunities to participate in cultural and ceremonial activities, and increased ability to engage in land management activities. This pursuit of a diverse range of benefits is in contrast with the approach of the White Paper, which focuses primarily on benefits that might accrue to Indigenous Australians as rentiers. Indeed, studies of remote businesses in Northeast Arnhem Land have shown that the ability of businesses to provide royalties sometimes conflicts with other benefits such as employment, training and other social benefits (Corey et al. 2018). Successful businesses on remote Indigenous land often offer unique employment structures and benefits to their employees (see, for example, Brueckner et al. 2014). This contrast suggests that caution should be taken when considering Indigenous development outcomes through a narrow lens of royalty payments. As Corey et al. note:

> If participation in the broader mainstream economy is a major government priority for remote communities, then less emphasis needs to be placed on royalties, and more on ensuring Indigenous employment, training and capacity building within the industry. (2018, 706)

In the NT, a series of efforts have been made to support Indigenous 'development from below' (Gerritson, Whitehead and Stoeckl 2018; see also, for example, Fleming 2015a; 2015b; Fleming, Petheram and Stacey 2015) using government funding. These efforts target areas that are unlikely to quickly earn a financial return, but are key to developing industries that could underpin future businesses. These have emphasised the importance of governance structures and labour arrangements for creating businesses that provide benefits to Indigenous people. Chapter 7 will explore these issues in considering the work that Indigenous intermediaries are doing to attract finance for development on Indigenous land.

Land and Water Ownership

The past five years have seen substantial concerns raised about foreign ownership of Australian farmland. In Northern Australia, this concern is often concentrated around pastoral properties due to the very large areas they command (Smith and Pritchard 2016). A notable example is the proposed sale of the iconic cattle company S. Kidman and Co, which controlled 1.3% of Australia's land area, to a consortium with a Chinese majority (80%) shareholder (Grattan 2016). The sale was blocked by then Treasurer Scott Morrison, who said that the sale was 'contrary to the national interest' (Grattan 2016, n.p.). The company was eventually sold to a consortium of Australian-based Hancock Prospecting (67%) and the Chinese company Shanghai CRED (33%). The protracted sale process fuelled concerns around foreign investment in land in Australia, and this concern eventually led to the production of a national 'Register of Foreign Ownership of Agricultural Land'. However, the register that was produced included only summary data, and a change in reporting metrics obscures the patterns of change over the years for which it has been presented (see Table 3.1). What is clear from the register is that land ownership can change quickly: from 2016 to 2017,

Table 3.1 FIRB reports on foreign ownership of agricultural land (data from Foreign Investment Review Board (FIRB) 2017; 2018; 2019; 2020; 2021; 2022a). Some country ownership levels for some years were not reported (n/r)

Areas in 1,000 ha	2016	2017	2017	2018	2019	2020	2021
	Total area of (partially) foreign held land	Foreign share of foreign-held land					
China	1,463	14,422	9,112	9,169	9,153	9,199	8,499
United Kingdom	27,504	16,445	9,752	10,239	9,026	8,166	8,251
United States	7,727	2,693	2,550	2,655	2,226	2,751	2,926
The Netherlands	2,976	4,708	2,509	2,540	2,796	2,802	2,817
Canada	n/a	2,130	2,034	1,984	2,129	2,610	2,451
The Bahamas	n/a	n/a	n/a	2,201	≥2,201	2,201	2,201
Switzerland	1,069	2,227	1,888	1,944	2,012	2,078	2,149
Germany	n/r	n/r	n/r	n/r	≥1,933	2,134	2,144
South Africa	n/r	648	648	648	≥1,131	1,791	1,862
Hong Kong	n/r	n/a	279	1,273	≥1,181	1,462	1,779
Other	11,408	7,242	7,801	6,579	≤11,020	4,242	4,317
Total Australian agricultural land	384,558	371,079	371,079	393,797	378,082	383,801	377,002

China's land holdings increased nearly tenfold due to the joint purchase of the Kidman properties. However, as has been shown elsewhere (Smith, Langford and Lawrence 2023), most of the land that appears in the register is owned by just ten cattle companies, making it a poor indicator of foreign influence in Australian agrifood industries.

In addition to the register of land ownership, a 'Register of the Foreign Ownership of Water Entitlements' is also produced (see Table 3.2), revealing that 9.5% of all entitlements to Australian water are foreign-owned, with China owning the largest proportion. These features point to substantial influence of foreign finance capital in land and food production in Australia. Many of these result from the sale of large, aggregated farming portfolios to international investors – for example, over the last five years, Canadian Pension fund PSP Investments made a number of large purchases of aggregated farming enterprises and are now Australia's largest agricultural investor with $5 billion in assets (Wagstaff and Miles 2022). This is reflected in Canada's growing water ownership as reflected in the register of foreign ownership of water entitlements, which results from purchase of businesses with water rights attached, as well as sales of water entitlements in isolation (Jasper 2020).

Table 3.2 FIRB reports on foreign ownership of water entitlements (data from FIRB 2022b). Some country ownership levels for some years were not reported (n/r)

Entitlements (GL)	2018	2019	2020	2021
Canada	212	295	698	810
United States	720	713	660	626
China	732	756	662	604
United Kingdom	411	394	375	377
France	139	158	158	161
Hong Kong	80	118	129	134
The Netherlands	92	98	104	109
Germany	32	58	99	108
Belgium	102	102	103	103
Switzerland	136	128	103	103
Singapore	172	171	n/r	n/r
New Zealand	100	n/r	n/r	n/r
Other	444	527	610	634
Total water entitlement on issue	38,674	39,124	39,383	39,739

Privately Financed Infrastructure

Infrastructure development proposals in Northern Australia often 'struggle to satisfy conventional cost benefit analysis, particularly when assessed against projects in the major southern cities' (Australian Government 2014, xiii). This is due to low numbers of people and businesses in remote Northern Australia, which lead to a low number of potential users for infrastructure, limiting its short-term economic benefits. As such, infrastructure development is one of the major themes of the 2015 White Paper. In addition to allocating nearly $600 million for priority roads, $100 million for beef roads, $5 million for railroad feasibility studies and $39.6 million for air services, one of the most significant funding announcements of the White Paper was a $5 billion concessional loan facility known as the Northern Australia Infrastructure Fund (NAIF). As the Northern Australia Advisory group (2015) noted, the fund was designed to address calls for 'strategic "game changing" and "nation building" infrastructure investments in the north . . . funded by the public and private sector' (cited in Australian Government 2015a, 87). It advertised that it offers long-term loans of up to thirty years at 'lower' rates than those available commercially, although the actual rate and terms of these loans are determined 'on a case-by-case basis' (NAIF 2023a, n.p.). As of April 2023, the facility had committed to $4 billion worth of deals for 29 infrastructure projects. It is notable that 72% of the total value of the NAIF loan portfolio is in the energy and resources sectors, as will be discussed further in Chapter 8.

In addition to these projects, a further $980 million has been committed to developing roads to support economic development in Northern Australia (Australian Government 2022), which is an important publicly funded infrastructure project (in contrast to the NAIF project, in which privately financed infrastructure is the goal).

Pastoral Development

There is also a strong focus on intensification of the pastoral industry in Northern Australia, and this intensification requires substantial productive investments. There have been numerous examples of purchases of large pastoral properties by foreign and Australian investors over the last decade, many of which have sought to develop properties with water and fencing infrastructure to increase the property value. One notable example is Brett Blundy's purchase of the Walhallow and Creswell Downs cattle station for $100 million in 2015 and its resale, after substantial developments, for $250 million in 2022. This trend has reinvigorated longstanding concerns about differences between family and corporate ownership, along with the role of family farmers. In the Gulf country of Queensland, Martin (2019, 131) contrasts the family operator's 'commitment to the land' with 'an understanding of property as fungible, and essentially interchangeable with any other financial asset'. He quotes one long-term Gulf resident describing the station on which he grew up as 'the deepest root' (Martin 2019, 134) and emphasises the connection to the land and the region. Conversely, he notes of Macquarie Bank's Paraway Pastoral that:

> Unlike . . . family-owned properties, Paraway's properties are run by managers, who are frequently moved between stations as they progress their 'careers' in the industry. As one Paraway station manager emphasised, 'It's a business', and the company is focused on 'the bottom line'. (Martin 2019, 131–32)

Emerging changes in family and corporate ownership will be explored in Chapter 6.

In addition to these changes, there are also shifts in Indigenous ownership and use of pastoral properties, such as the expansion of the Indigenous-owned Kimberley Agriculture and Pastoral Company (KAPCO) (Collins 2019), as well as purchases, sales and development plans from companies (such as the Australian Agricultural Company (AACo), the North Australian Pastoral Company (NAPCO), the Consolidated Pastoral Company (CPC) (majority-owned by the private equity firm Terra Firma Capital Partners) and Paraway Pastoral (owned by Macquarie Group)), and by large family-owned companies such as the Heytesbury Cattle Company, the Hughes Pastoral

Company, Stanbroke Pastoral, the Hewitt Cattle Company and the Crown Point Pastoral Company. These development plans are often partially funded by private finance capital, in models that are partially development focused and partially motivated by capital gains. These models overlap, since property development often also increases the capital value of the property beyond the value of developments. This will be explored further in Chapter 4, where I look at strategic use of pastoral land valuation practices.

Greenfield Development

One of the goals of the White Paper is to 'create greenfield supply chains across agriculture, aquaculture and previously stranded energy and minerals resources' (Australian Government 2015a, 4). This is said to be enabled by both transport and water infrastructure developments, and by facilitating investments in large-scale agribusiness schemes that will overcome trans-action costs through economies of scale. Large private sector-led schemes receive special assistance because of the favourable effect they are expected to have on Northern Development, and those that occur in the NT are given 'Major Project Status', entitling them to additional government support. To this end, several large schemes are or have been in development, including, in WA, the further development of the Ord by the Kimberley Agricultural Investment company (KAI) and, in the NT, Project Sea Dragon and the expansion of Quintis sandalwood.

Quintis

Quintis is a sandalwood-growing managed investment scheme that developed plantations across WA, the NT and Queensland. It commenced planting sandalwood under the name of Tropical Forestry Services in 1999 in the Ord Irrigation Scheme in WA and quickly grew to become the world's largest producer of sandalwood. In 2012 it expanded into the NT and undertook a programme of purchasing land with water allocations attached. It became the largest agricultural water entitlement holder in the NT, with an allocation of 51 GL of water per year (Fitzgerald 2017a). This water was allocated free of charge by the NT government through its first-come-first-served policy, in order to stimulate privatisation of water resources, and was marketed as a major benefit for producers willing to develop new operations in the NT. However, Quintis' acquisition of water entitlements was contentious, as it did so by encouraging prospective sellers to acquire a water licence and would buy properties subject to these approvals. As Quintis operations investment relations manager Malcolm Baker put it, '[i]n terms of the way we value the property, properties are always valued on how much land you can use, and the amount of land used is determined by the amount of water on it' so '[w]e have to either have the ability to buy a property that has existing water licences, or it has to have the ability for us to apply and gain a water licence for it' (Fitzgerald 2016a). In one high-profile case, Tina Macfarlane, then owner of Stylo Station and candidate for the Country Liberal Party government seat of Lingiari, applied for and was granted a water licence of 5.8 GL, and then sold her land with the attached (freely acquired) water licence to Quintis (Sorensen 2017) for a reported $5.5 million (Betts 2016). She was accused of corruption, and a review into the sale concluded that she was 'inexplicably allocated more water than she would have been able to use' (Everingham 2017), raising concerns about the way in which water resources were distributed in the NT. Quintis also bought a number of irrigated farms in the NT and changed them from food production to sandalwood plantations, using their existing irrigation licences (Fitzgerald 2017b). This led to public concern over whether sandalwood was a good use of limited land and water resources in the NT, with many locals preferring to see food (rather than sandalwood trees) grown in the NT in order to develop local economies and create jobs.

Quintis received support from the NT government through its 'Major Project Status' until its financial collapse in 2017. This collapse was caused by the release of a report by activist short-seller Glaucus (2017), which compared Quintis to a Ponzi scheme. The release of the report saw shares plummet (Poljak 2018) and the company placed in receivership. In 2018 it recapitalised with $145 million from BlackRock Advisors, LLC and its affiliates (Morse 2018), releasing a statement declaring that: 'With a restructured balance sheet, Quintis is now a well-funded private company . . . The recapitalised Company will no longer focus and rely on sales of plantations to retail and high net worth investors' (Morse 2018). Today, Quintis remains in operation, but it has recently sought to sell several of its NT properties, including the aforementioned Stylo Station, which it notes 'had underperformed for a variety of reasons' (Brann 2022a). The property includes 800 ha of sandalwood trees, which it is expected that the new owner will need to clear at additional expense (Brann 2022a). Quintis now continues to manage 12,000 ha of plantations and its Ord River plantations appear to be going well, with new trees being planted in 2022 (Brann 2022a). However, the role of sandalwood – and other forestry projects like it – in the broader Northern Development context remains unclear.

Ord River Developers

The Ord Irrigation Scheme began in the 1960s with the construction of a Diversion Dam near Kununurra to be used to irrigate large areas of surrounding farmland. However, in the years that followed with limited economic production achieved, the scheme became highly controversial. In 2012, additional farmland was released for development and KAI, a subsidiary of the Chinese-based company Shanghai Zhonfu Group (which is controlled by the property developer Wu Puingai), was named as the preferred developer of the Ord River Irrigation Area (ORIA) Stage 2 expansion, an area of over 6,000 ha. In 2014 it was reported that the company was expected to spend $700 million over six years, including a $425 million investment in a sugar mill to produce 500,000 t/year of sugar and ethanol. These early plans have been discontinued, but KAI has spent $250 million on land clearing, irrigation channels, purchasing nearby land and associated assets. The company has since trailed a series of crops, including 2,500 ha of mixed grain crops (chia, sorghum and millet) (Kimberley Development Commission 2019). However, it is now focusing its efforts on cotton, although many of the uncertainties of large-scale agricultural developments remain. As Jim Engelke, the general manager of KAI, colourfully reflected: 'I spend half my life being excited and the other half shit-scared it's not going to work' (Grigg 2018, n.p.). Nonetheless, political commitment to the proposal remains high and cotton-growing efforts are underway (Grigg 2018; Kimberley Development Commission 2019), with the KAI recently part of a consortium seeking to develop a cotton ginnery in the region (Fowler 2021). In 2022, AAM Investment Group was chosen as the preferred developer of the NT Ord Stage 3, a 67,500 ha site on which it states it will grow dryland crops including cotton (Brann 2022b). The scheme remains contentious as a result of the limited financial viability of production of many crops in the region, which has seen it mostly produce sandalwood and cotton to date rather than food, as was initially promised. Its recent iterations are examples of a financier-led approach to development, in which financial entities are chosen to develop the farmland in ways that they see fit.

Project Sea Dragon

Project Sea Dragon was a proposed large-scale aquaculture project in the NT, near the Ord River irrigation area (NT Government 2019). The project, developed by the aquaculture company Seafarms, planned to eventually reach a total of US$1.5 billion and to export 150,000 tonnes of black tiger prawns per year. The project included the main operation of a grow-out facility on Legune Station, as well as a quarantine facility in Exmouth, a processing facility in Kununurra, and a breeding centre, brood stock maturation centre and commercial hatchery in Darwin. It had major project status in the NT throughout the time of the research for this book and was widely promoted, including by Austrade, as an important investment opportunity. The project attracted millions of dollars of support from the federal, WA and NT governments over the decade since it was first announced in 2012, including an NT government investment of $56 million in remote roads to the proposed prawn grow-out site.

In 2021, Seafarms appointed a new Chief Executive Officer (CEO), Mick McMahon, who oversaw the preparation of a report into the proposed project that was released in March 2022. The report described Project Sea Dragon as 'unviable in its current form', stating that it involved 'unacceptable risk' and would 'not generate acceptable financial returns' to shareholders (Seafarms 2022a). The report led to widespread dissatisfaction with McMahon's leadership and he resigned shortly afterwards. Seafarms then appointed a new CEO, who in June released an update saying that 'the company continues to believe in the future of Project Sea Dragon and will now undertake a more detailed assessment', including engagement of new consultants, visits to large-scale prawn farms in Central America where large-scale prawn farms are common, and a re-examination of cost structures for the project (Seafarms 2022b). The future of the project remains uncertain at the time of writing.

These contemporary agricultural development projects involve finance-led approaches to development, in which investors propose and drive large-scale projects and governments play a supporting role as co-investors by providing infrastructure developments and water entitlements. These three greenfield examples highlight an interesting theme in large-scale, finance-led Northern Development efforts: projects can undergo spectacular failures, yet never decisively fail and end. Although their failure to provide wider benefits for communities and regions raises concerns about the effectiveness of this approach to development, there are so many potential reasons that projects can fail to eventuate that schemes can never be proven unviable based on individual failures. However, it does suggest the need for closer examination of the work that goes into their development and, in particular, the work of government officials and agencies in promoting them.

Investment Seeking Work in Practice

The current programme for Developing Northern Australia sees the government both seeking to reduce 'red tape' with a view that this will 'enable' investments to occur, as well as directly and significantly investing in strategies to facilitate and guide private sector investment. It is not merely private sector *companies* that they wish to invest in development, but high net-worth individuals and institutional *investors* – financial actors who may have little or no knowledge of agricultural production or related business interests, but who are engaged as the financiers of Northern Development. These investors are involved in the allocation of capital to different ventures in ways that significantly shape rural landscapes. However, they do not work in isolation, but are guided and facilitated by government programmes, as Peck and Tickell (2002) described in their analysis of 'roll out' and 'roll back' neoliberal governance. This section explores how government officials in the NT operationalise programmes that seek to attract and facilitate investment proposals.

Attracting Investment

Key to the Developing the North programme is increased access to private investment capital. The White Paper, alongside an associated Austrade document promoting Northern Australia as an investment destination (Austrade 2015), offers a 'value proposition' for the region: 'Northern Australia: Emerging opportunities in an advanced economy' (Australian Government 2015a, 7). The Austrade report seeks to promote Northern Australia as an area of 'underdevelopment' in which substantial capital gains can be made through land development (Li 2014). It does so by alluding to parallels between Northern Australia and farmland in the Global South, while simultaneously highlighting Australia's governance capacity, suggesting that Northern Australia provides the benefits of each. It suggests to potential investors that:

> In an increasingly inter-connected world it is rare for investors to be presented with high-performing yet relatively untapped markets with investor-ready projects and collaborative opportunities in place. Northern Australia is one of very few such markets remaining globally: a market full of possibility yet situated firmly within the safety and security of a successful advanced economy ... [We] are here to facilitate your path to investor success. Together, we welcome you to northern Australia, a land of limitless potential and abundant opportunity. (Austrade 2015, iv–v)

The White Paper is similarly strongly oriented towards investment attraction and is itself a participant in this process. Numerous strategies for securing investment are outlined in the White Paper, including simplifying land use arrangements (Australian Government 2015a, 18), reconfiguring native title (Australian Government 2015a, 25), providing services in remote Indigenous communities (Australian Government 2015a, 32), reforming pastoral leases (Australian Government 2015a, 36), providing tradable water entitlements (Australian Government 2015a, 41) and engaging in explicit marketing strategies, in which '[t]he Government will . . . showcase business opportunities to attract more investors to the north and reach out to its neighbours' (Australian Government 2015a, 61). Part of these marketing strategies include running an investment forum 'to attract investors and expose them to opportunities in the north' (Australian Government 2015a, 11) and the development of a prospectus for marketing Northern Australia (Australian Government 2015a, 11). These descriptions suggest a focus on bringing investors to Northern Australia, and a fervent hope and expectation that investors will take up these opportunities and develop projects.

The NT embraced this approach with particular energy. At the state NT government level, the 'International Engagement, Trade and Investment Strategic Plan 2022–2026' outlined priorities for NT agribusiness development to 'attract and facilitate investor interest in new agribusiness developments in the NT' (Department of Trade, Business and Innovation (DTBI) 2018, 12) and 'develop and deliver a pipeline of NT Government facilitated projects to leverage private sector investment in economic and iconic infrastructure and major projects' (DTBI 2018, 12). It emphasised that 'all investors are welcomed and encouraged to explore investment opportunities' (DTBI 2018, 13) and highlights Singapore, Japan, India, China and the Middle East as future sources of agribusiness investment (DTBI 2018, 16–17). The 2022–2026 International Engagement Strategy shifted the focus somewhat, listing towards high priority markets as Singapore, Japan, South Korea, Vietnam, Indonesia and North America.

Evidence from the NT government officials tasked with implementing investment attraction programmes suggest this to be difficult and uncertain work. The officials need to promote the region to investors. Remote NT agribusinesses currently face very high transaction costs due to limited infrastructure and low economies of scale. The NT government therefore seeks to attract investors to develop businesses because, as one NT government official put it, 'every product that comes along and needs to use the supply chain helps us build a supply chain that's more attractive for investors'. In this sense, financial investors are sought as a way to contribute to infrastructure development and economies of scale. However, actually bringing investment to the NT is difficult and involves substantial promotion work, which is the focus of the government departments of Austrade and InvestNT. As one official tasked with attracting investment stated:

> we have a lot of problems with financing here. We see nobody from Melbourne and Sydney coming up here . . . we issue invitations and half the time we don't get a reply. At the end of the day . . . that's what I do, attracting [overseas] investment.

The official noted that while investors were increasingly familiar with Australia as an agricultural investment location, there was frustration that private sector intermediaries such as Australia's 'big four' banks[3] operating overseas 'aren't directing many people from Shanghai to us. They're sending them all to Melbourne and Sydney'. One government official lamented that 'I'll go to . . . Shanghai and they'll [say], we don't even really know where Darwin *is*'. This official saw their role as marketing the NT to foreign investors and financial intermediaries – 'taking my big presentation and this and that and going and visiting'.

In much of Southern Australia there is considerable resistance to foreign investment, particularly from China. This appears to be far less common in the NT. One government representative said Territorians are 'pretty agnostic' as to where the capital comes from, 'as long as it works for the Territory'. Another suggested that 'compared to other States in Australia, the NT is much more open to foreign investment, full stop, and it's absolutely ambivalent about where it comes from . . . there's an open-mindedness here that you don't see elsewhere'. Indeed, there is a strong focus on foreign rather than domestic investment. This reflects perceptions of a lack of capital in Australia, as well as of investment preferences. One government official lamented that 'no one in Australia wants to put decent money into this joint', while another said that 'if it's not going to come from Melbourne and Sydney, well then bugger them. We'll get it from Tokyo, and we'll get it from Beijing'. The officials did not have strong preferences about what product should be produced with foreign capital, because 'every product helps us build scale'.

By contrast, the government officials were clear about the type of investment they sought in terms of scale and farm maturity, stating that investments in real estate or established businesses are 'not the sort of activities in which we engage'. According to one official:

> We want someone who wants to pretty much do a greenfield investment because there's not a lot of established investments. So you have to have lots of courage, you have to have pretty deep pockets, and you have to have a real vision for what you want to do and an eye to the market. So they're the kind of investors that we would spend time, effort, and energy on. The other ones, we facilitate, we're nice to them, we encourage them. Sometimes they surprise us but the ones that are the heavy hitters, they're the ones that we want.

This theme was mirrored in the emphasis many government officials put on attracting 'patient capital' – investors with long investment horizons of several decades rather than just a few years. Several noted that China was a favourable source of investment in this respect as they perceived that Chinese investors had longer timeframes than investors from other countries. Despite the limited success of large investments historically, there is a continued focus by NT government actors on attracting large investors with long timeframes and greenfield agricultural development plans. There is again a strong focus on scale as key to overcoming the challenges of Northern Australian production, consistent with shifts in agrifood industries associated with neoliberal globalisation, such as consolidation of landholdings in pursuit of 'market efficiency'.

Facilitating Investment

The White Paper on Developing Northern Australia does not go far beyond outlining proposals for investment procurement, but documents produced at the NT government level introduce more detailed planning of the ways in which private finance is expected to contribute to development outcomes. The 'International Engagement, Trade and Investment Strategic Plan 2018–2021' emphasised the need to 'grow business development capabilities to enable proactive researching, prospecting and qualifying of investment prospects' (DTBI 2018, 12). In addition, the NT government has a 'Territory Benefit Policy' designed 'to maximise the contribution to the NT economy by private sector projects in the NT' (DTBI 2019, 4). It 'challenges proponents to consider what strategies they may adopt to enhance the local benefits their project delivers' (DTBI 2019, 4), with a suggested focus on employment and workforce development of local people (particularly Aboriginal people), local sourcing of goods and services, and contribution to 'shared value' in the local community, which may include infrastructure investment, corporate social responsibility initiatives or the establishment of headquarters in the NT (DTBI 2019). There is therefore a focus not only on attracting investment, but also on seeking to place requirements for rural development upon it in an effort to capture benefits for NT rural development.

Government professionals work to implement this approach, to moderate expectations and to prevent future failure, particularly for greenfield investments, as one official described:

> It's the proven fields where blue-chip investors want to go. They want to know they're buying something that's working and that will continue to work. [But] greenfield [sites] are what we have an abundance of – foreigners often jump in but then just as quickly fall out.

Their approach is informed by the aforementioned history of failed agricultural investments in the NT that have left many sceptical about the ability of large financial actors to develop sustainable agribusinesses on the land. One official lamented that some investors think 'here's a large swathe of country that I'm going to buy and turn into a gold mine', but have 'zero understanding of the steps that it will take to achieve that outcome'. As a result, government actors are strongly focused on trying to moderate investment proposals to ensure that they are successful by explaining 'the realities of investing in the North'. One government official noted that 'there [are] people that come here with the idea that they'll make a return very quickly. If they come to us first, they'll learn that it's not a quick process. It is in fact a long, steady, slow process'. To this end, one government official spoke of the importance of:

> speaking with people, presenting to people, talking them through their investment, trying to steer them in a good way so that they have a good investment experience and they're successful. That they understand the risks, they understand all the challenges, and they understand what the opportunities might be.

The officials varied in terms of the degree of support they offered. One official went as far as to say: 'I would like to say that we act more as a business investment developer . . . we are getting ourselves more and more involved to help to shape that project'. Another saw their job as being 'kind of about hand-holding as people wander their way through this kind of maze of stuff'. This provides an interesting contrast to theory on governmentality that stresses the withdrawal of the state and the subsequent devolution of responsibility for rural problems to other actors.

One important theme was not only the issue of poorly developed investment plans, but also that of local people deliberately misleading investors in an effort to sell their properties. The difficult operational environment in Northern Australia requires a high level of skill to operate farming properties, and investors rely on local expertise when constructing a deal. Some local businesspeople have taken advantage of this to negotiate investments between investors and farm sellers, as one government official noted:

> They slide themselves into the middle there and they become this go-between. And they say, 'oh yeah I've got someone in Australia who's got this, and I've got an investor here' and they try and put them together. And some of the people I've seen doing that are bloody spivs and bullshit artists . . . We've got investors getting led up the garden path and investing in things and finding that . . . the returns are not there, or the conditions are completely different to what they expected, so they get disappointed and . . . become very, very risk averse.

Officials expressed strong moral sentiments around this work, often drawing on their own long personal histories in the region and demonstrating a desire to ensure that investments lead to long-term productive outcomes and to avoid issues associated with finance-led development. This might be considered as attempts to facilitate investment and, in doing so, reduce the negative effects that financialisation of the industry might bring.

The focus on finance for development extends to Aboriginal economic development in several places – such as the Tiwi Islands (through the Land Development Corporation), East Arnhem land (through Developing East Arnhem Land), and the Northern and Central Land Council regions (through the Aboriginal Land Development Agency) – in which government agencies are supporting Aboriginal landowners to attract investments on their land. The Tiwi Islands, for example, are working with the NT government-funded Land Development Corporation to develop an investment prospectus to assist investors to make business investments in these Aboriginal lands. From such investments, the Tiwi Island people hope that infrastructure such as roads will be developed, local markets will be stimulated and employment opportunities will be created. They are strongly focused on financial investment as a pathway to economic development than as merely an opportunity for rent income. A similar approach is being undertaken in East Arnhem land, in which a government-funded body is involved in scoping the region and providing underlying environmental and cultural assessments that will assist investors to create greenfield developments in these regions, again focused on job creation and economic growth. Government officials and government-funded bodies are involved in attracting and facilitating investment proposals for Aboriginal lands. As one professional working in this space explained:

> we are an intermediary effectively between the land owners and proponents that come in . . . our role [is] to attract investment, but it's not just to attract, but also to facilitate, so there's a process we'd step through with proponents coming through, help them with the site selection process, help with further assessment of the land, the interactions with the [Aboriginal] working group and then working up a broader agreement around the leases.

These efforts in some ways mirror development efforts being undertaken on non-Indigenous land as they aim to provide baseline assessments of land planning and business proposals in 'a pseudo process of what you'd do in town'. They were similarly focused on large-scale investments as a strategy for overcoming the costs of remoteness, noting that 'with these remote locations you'll have these logistics costs and other challenges, so it means having a certain critical mass to a project that can achieve some efficiencies. That typically puts it in the scale where it needs to be a major capital type project as opposed to a smaller grassroots one'. However, this work on Aboriginal land often goes substantially further in developing business proposals, often scoping proposals that have community support and then pitching these to investors. These developments are very strongly focused on remote economic development and job creation, as one professional described:

> our objective really is to encourage economic development, so that means local employment and local businesses . . . the way we analysed it was the yield – how much land is used for the project and how many jobs come out of that.

This work broadly aligns with logics of financialised development being undertaken across the NT more generally, but has a stronger sense of involvement in seeking to direct investors in a way that ensures social outcomes from these developments. This resonates with literature that highlights social impacts and social accountability as key concerns around financialisation (Clapp 2017). According to Cotula and Blackmore (2014, 4), for example, promoting investment by and with small-scale producers, protecting legitimate land tenure rights, ensuring transparency of process and 'leveraging pressure points to influence the conduct of brokers and intermediaries' are crucial responsibilities of governments that seek to govern global investment processes effectively.

Governance under Financialisation

The White Paper on Developing Northern Australia articulates a particular rationality of governance in which the role of providing and allocating financial resources is designated to a broadly defined category of 'investors'. Beyond a neoliberal rationality of governance (Rose and Miller 1992), the current approach seems to be an emerging *financialising* approach to governance, in which it is not only local private business but also foreign investors who are envisioned as directing development (Langford, Smith and Lawrence 2020). Studies of financialisation, and the financialisation of governance, have often viewed this rationality as a withdrawal of the state, followed by the 'appearance' of investment projects once the government has stepped back. However, investments do not simply materialise when their possibility is enabled (Ouma 2015b; 2020), and recent studies of financialisation have shown that the work of assembling global investments is difficult, uncertain, multidirectional and often unsuccessful (Ducastel and Anseeuw, 2017; 2018; Henry 2017; Henry and Prince 2018; Visser 2017; Borras et al. 2022). This is particularly true for greenfield investments in developing agricultural regions, in which there is no guarantee that investment in a region can be successfully negotiated and maintained (Visser 2017). Patterns of financial investment are geographically uneven and moving finance into remote geographies requires concentrated and sustained work.

In Northern Australia, there have been sustained efforts to imagine particular development futures based on large-scale agricultural developments. These imaginaries are most recently territorialised in the 'Developing Northern Australia' programme, and government officials seek to enact and create these futures, but in doing so run up against practical realities. This chapter has explored their attempts to attract finance and to facilitate greenfield investments. There is substantial distance between the initiatives in the

White Paper on Developing Northern Australia and the on-the-ground work of officials who find it to be difficult, frustrating and time-consuming work to bring investors to Northern Australia. In facilitating these investments, these officials struggle to convey the environmental constraints of the region. Far from simply stepping back and letting investors allocate resources, these government officials – often locals from industry backgrounds – re-enter negotiations to direct and guide investors to influence the success of their operation. Driving this local focus on attracting particular types and patterns of investment is a long history of 'failed' investments in Northern Australia. Investments fail or succeed in different ways for different actors, and attempts to guide investment are premised on an idea of what failure (and success) looks like for the North. The past failures of large-scale investment schemes underpin the construction of policy documents that assemble calculative infrastructures for measuring success and what 'good' investment should look like (see Kurunmäki, Mennicken and Miller 2019). Officials seeking to implement these programmes undertake their work informed by and co-constitutive of moral ideas about the way in which development should be undertaken (see Carrier 2018). These moral ideas shape the way in which finance is mediated in NT landscapes and form part of an assemblage of financialisation in the region. This highlights the importance of the work of this group of actors in assembling assemble financial investments in rural spaces in Northern Australia.

Notes

1. More recent census data on Indigenous population by remoteness had not been released at time of writing.
2. Country is a term often used by Aboriginal people to described the lands, waterways and seas which they are connected to (Australian Institute of Aboriginal and Torres Strait Islander Studies 2023).
3. The Australia and New Zealand Banking Group (ANZ), the Commonwealth Bank, the National Australia Bank (NAB) and Westpac.

Chapter 4

MAKING LAND VALUABLE

Conceptualising Land Value

The price of land is a central driver of investment activity, yet land prices do not arise naturally, but are constructed and negotiated by a range of actors – farmers, land valuers, bankers, investors and government officials – each with different goals and levels of influence over valuation processes. This chapter focuses on the *processes* of land valuation to contribute an understanding of how land is *made* valuable (see Kornberger et al. 2015), both by financial entities creating investment products (Ducastel and Anseeuw 2017; Visser 2017) and professional intermediaries who, 'beyond their apparent specific function (providing services of buying and selling, matching, advising and evaluating), are all engaged in activities of valuation that shape the market' (Bessy and Chauvin 2013, 84). In particular, the work of professional land and agribusiness valuers is studied in Northern Australia as there are a small number of these professionals and their work strongly influences land markets in the region.

It has often been observed that land is 'like gold with yield' (Fairbairn 2014, 589), the yield being profits from agricultural production and the gold being the land itself. This framing captures two ways of valuing land: as a commodity with inherent value related to its qualities, and as an asset whose value is related to the future income it returns. These divergent ways of valuing land are based on different understandings of its value. Commodities are valued in markets through a process of 'qualification' in which they are described according to a set of characteristics and ranked relative to each other (Beckert and Musselin 2013, 1). By contrast, assets are valued through a process of capitalisation or, more narrowly defined, assetisation: a 'form of valuation that propels a consideration of return on investment' (Muniesa et al. 2017, 11). An asset is not designed to be broken up into its component parts, but to generate sustainable and ongoing income. From this perspective, assetisation is 'what you do in order to protect something from the vagaries of commodification' (Muniesa et al. 2017, 51).

Birch and Muniesa (2020) consider the shift from commodification to assetisation to be a key feature of technoscientific capitalism, and associate this with a shift from a logic of market speculation to that of capital investment. Associated with this is a shift in 'critical analytical attention away from a focus on commodification and price speculation and towards concerns with the appropriation of value and extraction of rent through capital investment' (Langley et al. 2021, 510). However, as Braun (2020) cautions, the asset-commodity dichotomy is more fluid in practice and some goods – including land – are treated as commodities and assets by different people at different times. The pragmatic approach of Muniesa (2012) offers one way to explore land value assemblages by presupposing that land has no inherent value as either a commodity or an asset, but is made valuable through varied processes of valuation undertaken by particular actors at particular times. Exploring how a diverse range of actors assemble the value of land through contingent and contested valuation processes reveals how land values – which drive investments in land and underpin the viability of cattle properties – are generated in practice.

In Northern Australia, land has typically been valued using the Beast Area Value (BAV), a 'rule of thumb' (Vail 2014, 32) for commensurating diverse land holdings based on a simplified set of characteristics. In this valuation process, a pastoral station's value is derived from the sum of the land value, the cattle value, and the value of any infrastructure developments made to it. The land is valued as a commodity in a process of *valuation-qua-marketisation* (see Muniesa et al. 2017, 130). However, financial investment in pastoralism in the region is seeing properties increasingly valued using the Return on Investment (ROI), a measure commonly used by investors to estimate the value of an investment based on its expected future income streams in a process of *valuation-qua-capitalisation* (Muniesa et al. 2017, 130).

These different valuation devices often produce divergent land prices based on different understandings of value. Examining how value is constructed by different actors using competing valuation devices reveals the 'disputability and multiplicity of value regimes' (Kjellberg et al. 2013, 19), and how the increasing presence of financial sector actors is shifting the way in which value is constructed in the Northern Australian pastoral industry.

This chapter first describes the process for valuing land using the BAV, revealing how value is negotiated by farmers and valuation professionals. It then discusses how the ROI is driving assetisation processes in which pastoral stations are increasingly organised as assets, and how this appears to reduce the capacity for speculation on land as a commodity by treating it as an asset from which durable economic rent should be derived. Finally, it shows how the ROI and the BAV are being strategically combined in ways that incentivise development activities that do not necessarily improve station profitability. Through these studies, I argue that pastoral land is being assetised and developed in ways that are more reflective of the valuation devices that are influential in the region than of the practicalities of pastoral station management.

Land as a Commodity

In Northern Australia, land has historically been valued as a commodity following a process that arose from its particular historical and geographical context. Beef pastoral land in Northern Australia is typically low rainfall, remote land, mostly held on long-term leases administered by the Commonwealth government. The leased land provides the government with rental payments and can be bought and sold on land markets. Properties tend to be very large and sold at costs that are low on an area basis, and even relatively small properties are typically several thousand square kilometres in area. This apparently low-cost land, coupled with investment reports emphasising 'market fundamentals' such as growing middle-class populations and shrinking resource bases, have bolstered expectations of future land value rises and have fuelled financial investments. Over the past twenty years, with increasing transactions in Australian beef pastoral land (Rural Bank 2022), land prices have risen considerably and become substantially more volatile (see Figure 4.1). This effect has been concentrated on the largest, corporately owned stations, although family enterprises have also experienced appreciation as a result. This has occurred without an equivalent increase in farm incomes. Indeed, the financial viability of these pastoral investments is underpinned by gains on land value rises, which historically have made up more than half of ROI (Meat and Livestock Australia (MLA) 2021).

Prior to 1970, pastoral properties in Northern Australia had relatively little market value, and governments historically struggled to encourage people to occupy and use the land (Hartwig 1965; Powell 2009 [1982]). Apart from a few major corporate holdings, properties were typically unfenced, with very little infrastructural development (Powell 2009 [1982]). Most properties were held on leasehold, and the land itself had very little capital value, due

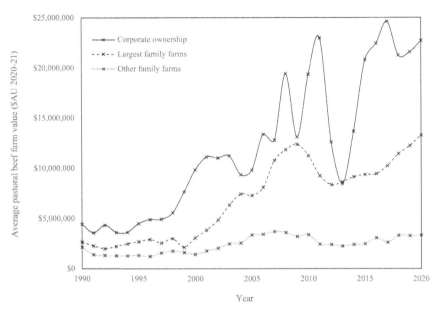

Figure 4.1. Land value of Australian pastoral zone beef farms by ownership type. Image created by the author using data from MLA (2021). © Zannie Langford. Data have since been moved and reorganised, and are now available (with different aggregation options) at https://www.agriculture.gov.au/abares/data/farm-data-portal

to the very large amounts of land available and the difficulty in profiting from it. Scarcity, a key condition for assetisation (Visser 2017) was not a key feature of the land market. Stations were typically sold on the basis of an estimate of the number of cattle that were living on them – it was the cattle, not the land, which had the most value (see Figure 4.2).

During these early years of the pastoral industry, the BAV emerged as a basic industry 'rule of thumb' (Vail 2014) to enable the buying and selling of different pastoral properties. These properties were very large and contained a variety of different land types with differing suitability for grazing. A simple tool was required to facilitate the description of these diverse landholdings according to a common metric, a process that Espeland and Stevens (1998) describe as 'commensuration' (1998, 315). The metric settled upon was the 'Beast Area' or carrying capacity of the property. Rather than selling a property based on its area, pastoralists would sell the property based on the number of cattle who could live sustainably on it. This enabled buyers and sellers in markets to quickly assess the approximate size of pastoral businesses, which varied greatly in size and land types.

Beckert and Musselin describe how goods are organised in markets through qualification, 'a collective process in which products become seen

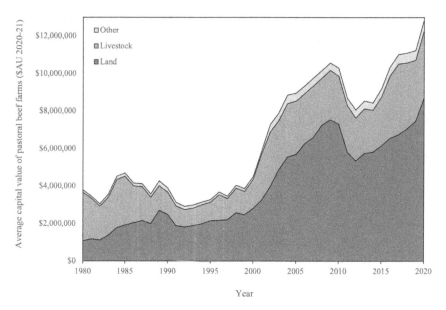

Figure 4.2. Capital value of beef farms in Australia's pastoral zones. Image created by the author using data from MLA (2021). © Zannie Langford. Data have since been moved and reorganised, and are now available (with different aggregation options) at https://www.agriculture.gov.au/abares/data/farm-data-portal

as *possessing certain traits* and *occupying a specific position* in relation to other products in the product space' (2013, 1, emphasis added). This two-step process aligns with the process for valuing pastoral land using the BAV, which involves, first, describing the property according to its physical characteristics and deriving a single figure from these for the number of cattle the property can support, and, second, ranking the property relative to other properties, which may vary by remoteness, infrastructure developments, seasonality and other relevant factors. This process is highly complex in practice, requiring specialist skillsets held primarily by professional land valuation specialists, and it is worth exploring here how these professionals undertake this valuation process.

In valuing land using the BAV, land valuers first seek to describe the land according to a limited number of its physical characteristics – a process that 'flattens' (Kornberger 2017) land's diverse 'affordances' (Li 2014, 589) into a subset of features deemed valuable. These features – such as area, rainfall, vegetation types, degradation, and availability of permanent water sources – are used to estimate the number of cattle that can sustainably live on the property in the long term. Assessing these qualities is not a trivial matter. Properties cover vast areas and often contain land that varies substantially in terms of soil types, vegetation, topography and water availability, and in many parts of Northern Australia, there is limited availability of environmental mapping data. In addition, the features of land vary substantially with weather cycles and with intensity of cattle stocking, and so vary from season to season, year to year and between decades. They are highly vulnerable to overgrazing and invasion of unwanted vegetation species, which can substantially erode the health of the land and cause permanent damage. In addition, improvements made by pastoralists (such as water developments or supplemental feeding) can be included and subtracted from valuations in different ways. As such, the number of cattle currently living on the property rarely aligns with the long-term sustainable average number of cattle that can live on the property, and it is this long-term average that forms the basis of the BAV.

As such, professional pastoral valuers need a skillset that is specialised to the cattle grazing industry and to their particular region of Northern Australia. They must combine an ability to assess environmental features of many types of pastoral land, an understanding of the behaviour of grazing cattle and an ability to assess other important features of the land that affect cattle grazing patterns. This leads to highly specialised and spatialised valuation skillsets that are not transferable across regions. As one professional valuer described:

> when we value a property we have to base a lot of it on our own experience of what we know country [land] type in that certain region can do . . . I certainly wouldn't go outside of my borders and pretend I could value [elsewhere] . . . I understand how tricky it is to understand a region up here, and there's so many nuances of our particular region that you would not know if you just flew in for a week.

The professional valuer estimates the sustainable carrying capacity through a combination of environmental observation, review of business records and interviews with local informants. They fly over and/or drive around a property to observe its environmental features and the interaction of cattle with the land. These observations last several days, depending on the size of the property, but due to the vast sizes of the properties, the observations that can be made in this time are relatively limited. As a result, the pastoralist owner or manager of a property features heavily as a key informant in the valuation process in order to point out important features of the land. As one professional valuer described:

> You always want to drive round it or be on the inspection with someone who knows the property pretty well, 'cos you obviously want them to point out [important features]. They might have been there for twenty years, so you want to pull in everything you can off them.

The pastoralist's role as informant is to indicate important features of the land to the professional valuer, as well as to provide information on the business management that helps valuers to interpret their observations. Some features are likely to increase the valuation, such as natural water sources, while others will reduce it, such as the encroachment of an undesirable weed. These features can be difficult to notice and require long-term detailed observation of the property, which are often exclusively obtained by the pastoral station owner/manager, creating a key role for them in the valuation process. One pastoralist described that in their experience, professionally determined carrying capacities were not 'instructed', but '"negotiated" . . . to a mutual agreement' (Armstrong and Armstrong 2017, 2). Indeed, one government commissioned valuation was overturned because the professional valuer had been 'insufficiently influenced by the estimates of the well-experienced owners' (*Keough and Wirth v Department of Natural Resources and Mines* 2004, 15), who had advised the professional valuer on the limitations of a property. Pastoralists thus feature as central informants in valuation processes, while simultaneously being directly affected by its outcome. This is reminiscent of a capitalisation story described by Muniesa et al., who noted that 'figures are neither blindly accepted nor completely disregarded, but are discussed, corrected and revised throughout the discussions between entrepreneurs and potential investors' (2017, 71). This occurs primarily between valuation professionals and pastoralists, but others are also involved at times. One rural agrifinance specialist described their role in property valuations in the following terms: 'we do property inspections, so we will drive around looking at a property . . . I take photos so that someone external to me can put a value on the property'. Valuation specialists emphasise their role in interpreting reports from various sources 'to make sure that the property is *correctly* described'– that is, as objectively assessed as possible, given the constraints on information.

Once the valuer has assigned the property a carrying capacity – effectively a descriptive measure of its size – the property is ranked relative to other properties for which sale prices are available. This 'requires decisions to be made about which properties are superior to others and vice versa. They effectively need to be 'ranked' in order from best to worst' (Peacocke 2017, 2). As the influential professional valuer Frank Peacocke[1] put it, 'it is the valuer's skills, I guess, to look at that one and say "It is definitely two-thirds better than that one, or 90% as good as that one"' (Economic Policy Scrutiny Committee (EPSC) 2018, 17). Assigning a BAV in this way requires robust data on recent sales and a detailed knowledge of the local market – as one professional valuer described, each valuer is 'just *constantly* monitoring the market in [their] area of expertise'. This ranking requires accounting for 'qualitative factors' (Peacocke 2017, 2) such as location, development potential and market risks. Frank Peacocke described the difficulty in obtaining these skills, stating that 'it has taken me 10 years just to get my head around the relativities. That is how long it takes' (EPSC 2018, 17).

These rankings are compared against recent sale data to estimate the value of a property. However, this task is not as simple as using market price directly, since price fluctuations in the region are often extreme and vary with weather and financial cycles. Rather, valuers attempt to differentiate between sale price and what they describe as the 'true value' (*Brewarrana Pty Ltd v Commissioner of Highways (No. 1)* 1973, 180–97) of a property. They are tasked not with assessing what purchasers *are* paying, but with predicting what they refer to as a 'rational purchaser' *would* pay for any given parcel of land. Valuations are therefore not reflective of current land markets, but of what 'rational' buyers in a hypothetical future land market could be expected to pay. As Wells J described in *Brewarrana Pty Ltd v Commissioner of Highways (No. 1)*, 'the sale price of any given piece of land is not necessarily the price at which it *ought* to have been sold, or the same thing as its *true value*' (1973, 180–97, emphasis added). In a context where land sales substantially above market prices are relatively common,[2] these sales must be excluded since they do not represent predictable behaviour of this hypothetical rational purchaser. Professional valuers therefore do not use all past sales equally as evidence of market activity, but assess the *quality* of the sale in deciding how much weight to give it in predicting future behaviour. One professional valuer highlighted the need to 'keep bringing it back to the hard evidence, culling out the bad evidence', and lamented sales that they believed to be excessively above market prices, noting that:

> when [the valuer] analyses the sale, [they] need . . . to find out who bought it, why, and how much due diligence they did, and also who else was in the running for the property, and how far behind were they, and how much do they know. If you get one where the agent will say 'These folks really did their due diligence', then you say that's good evidence from a well-informed purchaser in this market, so that's *good* evidence.

Valuers assess whether buyers did their due diligence by comparing the price paid with an estimate of the value of the land as calculated using the ROI – treating the land as an asset. This is a contemporary development that has altered the process for valuing land using the BAV and suggests that they consider the 'true value' of the land to be that produced by valuing the land as an asset and, by extension, that the true form of the land is that of an asset. This reflects the market for professional land valuations, which are used by nonspecialist investors to guide their purchasing decisions, by banks as an assessment of the value of pastoralists' assets in making decisions about how much finance to extend, and by governments as the basis of lease rates payable. These actors value the land not as a home or as something with inherent environmental, cultural or social value, but as an asset with a definable financial value.

This reveals that BAV valuations are assembled by a host of geographically situated human and nonhuman actors, from pastoralists and land valuation professionals to government lease policies and bank lending ratios. The resulting land market reflects the work of these diverse actors undertaking valuation processes, and the interactions between them. Although this historical device nominally treats land as a commodity, it is increasingly influenced by a view of land as an asset that should return a stream of future income that affects the advice that valuation professionals offer in their reports. The next section explores the process for valuing land using the ROI.

Land as an Asset

The ROI values land as an asset. It is calculated as the sum of returns from farm income and returns from capital gains, as shown below (adapted from Beattie 2021).

$$ROI = ROI_{income} + ROI_{capital\ gains}$$

where

ROI_{income} = Total profit over life of investment / Property purchase price

$ROI_{capital\ gains}$ = (Property sale price – Property purchase price) / Property purchase price

The projected ROI can be difficult to estimate due to the large size of the properties, their remoteness and a lack of information on farm performance, seasonal conditions and commodity prices, which make it difficult to assess future income. As one valuer described, these features make it 'quite challenging to apply capitalisation rate for investors and give them indicators that are utilised commonly in the corporate investment world' (Lane 2017, n.p.). This means that the ROI from farm income and the ROI from capital appreciation are calculated using existing data, making station records an increasingly important component of farm value, and driving corporatisation processes in which family farm businesses increasingly need to mirror investment reporting standards (see Langford 2019).

The ROI from capital gains is based on the increasing land prices in the region and are higher and more volatile than those from farm income (see Figures 4.3 and 4.4). There are substantial differences between properties with corporate ownership and the larger and smaller family farmers. While

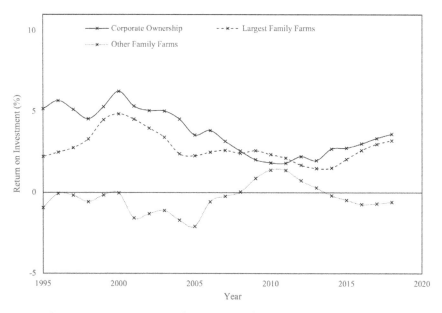

Figure 4.3. Return on investment from income of Australian pastoral zone beef farms. 5-year simple moving average. Image created by the author using data from MLA (2021). © Zannie Langford. Data have since been moved and reorganised, and are now available (with different aggregation options) at https://www.agriculture.gov.au/abares/data/farm-data-portal

since 2000 all properties have appreciated at an average rate of 3.8–3.9% per annum, corporate properties have earned an average ROI from farm incomes of 3.3%, the largest family farmers of 2.6% and the remaining family farmers of –0.3% (see Figure 4.3). The smaller family farmers typically make a loss if their enterprises are assessed as an asset, which interviewees suggested to be a result of factors such as their operation of properties for nonfinancial reasons and management of properties in ways designed to reduce tax liabilities rather than increase profits. It also implies that these properties are overvalued relative to returns generated from them, suggesting that for these farmers, the ROI does not capture the value of the property. In the Gulf country of Queensland, Martin (2019, 131) contrasts the family operator's 'commitment to the land' with 'an understanding of property as fungible, and essentially interchangeable with any other financial asset'. He quotes one long-term Gulf resident describing the station on which he grew up as 'the deepest root' (Martin 2019, 134) and emphasises the connection to the land and the region. From this perspective, the 'true value' of a property lies in its materiality and a diverse range of affordances not captured by the ROI.

Despite this, the practice of assessing property value using ROI-based

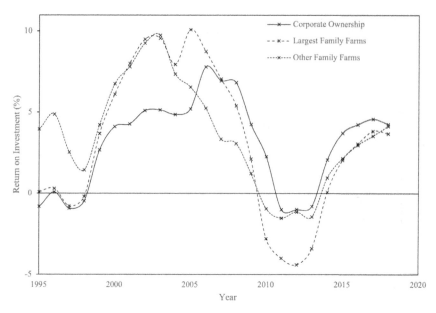

Figure 4.4. Return on investment from capital appreciation of Australian pastoral zone beef farms. 5-year simple moving average. Image created by the author using data compiled from MLA (2021). Data shown from 1995–2020, after which time data disaggregated by ownership type became unavailable. © Zannie Langford. Image created by author using data from Meat and Livestock Australia (2021). Data has since been moved and reorganised and is now available (with different aggregation options) from https://www.agriculture.gov.au/abares/data/farm-data-portal/

measures is becoming more widespread with the increasing influence of actors who view land as a financial asset. Pastoralists often need access to finance, and sources of both debt and equity finance increasingly require stations to be organised in a way that makes an ROI calculable. While pastoralists are often accustomed to viewing station value as derived from the characteristics of the land, livestock and development (as a commodity), investors and bankers view the property as a stream of future income (as an asset), and encourage farmers to develop reporting systems that enable ROI-based valuations. Although this seems obvious, many family-owned properties in remote Northern Australia either do not keep or do not wish to disclose records of their business income and, as a result, bankers in the region maintain very close relationships with their clients in order to assess their asset value and ability to service debt (see Langford, Brekelmans and Lawrence 2021). In this context, bankers exert pressure on farmers to develop certain reporting systems in order to access finance – a process of valuation driven by a view of the land as an asset. One banker described the tension between these different views of station value – his own need to know the financial details of the property, and a pastoralist's assertion that the value of the property can be assessed by a consideration of its physical features and cattle stocking rate:

> In the Northern Territory we sell a cattle station as a walk-in walk-out business, but if I'm selling it to you, I'm not going to show you my books. You name me another business that can be sold on a walk-in walk-out basis without the books. Without three or five-years financial records. What they say to you is, 'I've got twenty thousand head of cattle, this is my herd break-up, I've got so many cows; work out what you think it's worth. You do the math'. If, as an investor, you are looking to invest in these businesses, you're not going to invest in something like that. You want to know what the EBITDA[3] is. No different to me as a banker as with financing. I need to know what your earnings before interest and tax and depreciation are, so I can work out what you can service. But that is the traditional method of selling stations.

An alternative approach to accessing finance is to seek an equity investor in the pastoral business, a desirable but somewhat elusive alternative to bank finance. Pastoralists who reorganise their business reporting systems in order to attract investors are engaged in an act of valuation in the sense that they both demonstrate the value of the business by recording those features needed to calculate an ROI, and create value for investors by making it possible to measure the business value, monitor it from afar and organise its place in a portfolio (for a case study exploring the experience of a cattle farmer undertaking a capitalisation process, see Langford (2019), and for a discussion of these two understandings of valuation processes, see Vatin (2013)). This shows how valuation devices influence the activities of pastoral station managers as they develop reporting systems that are compatible with the ROI (for a related discussion, see Ducastel and Anseeuw (2017)). The needs of the investor that farmers respond to – such as the need for a system recording business management in a way that enables an investor to calculate investment returns – are devices that shape the assetisation of the business.

This section has described ROI-based valuations that develop assessments of station value based on farm income. However, the ROI also includes a consideration of the future sale price of the property, in which the BAV – as the valuation device used by professional land valuers – features, as will be discussed in the next section.

Speculative Development

In choosing how to develop stations, the calculative device used to value stations matters. Developments that target farm income-based measures must weigh up the cost of building and maintaining infrastructure against the increased income they expect to gain from it – developments must 'pay for themselves' over a certain lifespan through the increased income they generate. Conversely, developments targeting increased capital gains on an imminent sale do not need to justify themselves against increases in income if they can capture an increase in property value greater than the cost of development. This creates space for strategic combination of the ROI and the BAV to realise higher returns on investment. As Kornberger (2017) notes, valuation devices influence not only what we buy on the consumption side, but also what is sold on the production side, since businesses can change what they produce to better fit valuation devices. In this sense, there is a shift from competing in productive spheres to competing in valuation spheres, in which different actors may exert strategic agency to improve the way their product performs according to different valuation devices. In Northern Australia, producers develop pastoral stations through the use of fencing and watering points to increase the utilisation of the station's vegetation and, by extension, the number of cattle they can support. This approach increases the carrying capacity of the property, leading to a direct increase in the property price as measured by the BAV. This increase in station value is often greater than the cost of developments, as one corporate pastoral company described:

> One thing that we would look at if we were to buy a property is what sort of future potential does it hold in terms of value of that property. We would look at how much utilisation it currently has and how much scope there is to develop additional land there, and by that I mean by putting on more watering points, which then allows you to run more cattle on that property, and by putting those additional water points, when the properties get independently valued each year, those valuers look at the land on a carrying capacity basis, so how much in an average season can this property hold in terms of cattle numbers. So that means any development that we do is increasing the value of that property, and what we're finding is that we can develop the property at a cheaper rate per hectare than what that hectare can end up being worth, so we make that margin, if you like, on the development activities.

These productive investments in station development are directly targeting the BAV valuation device in order to realise higher ROI from capital gains. Unlike property developments undertaken targeting farm incomes, which must weigh up the cost of building and maintaining infrastructure against the increased income they expect to gain from it, developments targeting the BAV in anticipation of capital gains on an imminent sale do not need to justify themselves productively, but only against increases in property value as calculated using the BAV. Thus investors may be able to earn substantial capital gains through property developments that target the carrying capacity, even if the costs of maintaining additional cattle and infrastructure on marginal lands lead farm profits to remain the same or even decrease.[4] These developments could paradoxically reduce farm incomes while increasing farm values. Since business records are not publicly disclosed, it is not possible to tell whether recent pastoral development investments are justified by an increase in returns, and there is the potential for this speculative approach to development to compromise the sustainability of the industry.

Similarly, it remains to be seen how professional valuers – who are responsible for verifying these increases in value – will respond to such developments, given the contested nature of the BAV as a measure of value. One professional valuer described such a case in which they had refused to value the property at the BAV-informed higher rate without being provided with business records (to enable an assessment of the value using the ROI), saying that 'it's up to the person that developed it to prove that it works'. In this case, the valuer and the property developer expressed conflicting understandings of land value informed by differing moral reasoning: the developer located their morality in their development expenditure (for related discussions, see Kish and Fairbairn 2018; Sippel 2018; Ouma 2020), and the valuer in their concern for the stability of the industry. In a context where volatile land prices have had severe negative impacts on many pastoralists in the region due to some unsustainable bank financing practices[5] and the changing lease payments[6] they cause, some valuation specialists see a role for their advice in reducing overpayments for properties and therefore in moderating land markets. As one professional valuer stated:

> as valuers, you want to make sure that fires are [contained]. In the end that makes our job easier, you go: 'That's a well-informed purchaser. That's a good sale. *The market's not getting out of whack.*' (Emphasis added)

This sentiment positions the valuer as not merely reflecting the market, but also regulating it, by preventing above-market sales from escalating into unsustainable land value increases. These negotiations highlight the ways in which various actors exploit and contest valuation processes in pursuit of different outcomes.

Land Value and Industry Sustainability

The valuation practices described here shape the way in which pastoral land is organised, used and traded in Northern Australia. The BAV treats land as a commodity in a process of valuation-qua-marketisation (see Muniesa et al. 2017, 130) in which the pastoral property is described and ranked according to its physical characteristics. The station's value is not totally disconnected from its earning power, since the feature by which it is defined – the carrying capacity – is a rough measure of its earning potential. However, it is an indirect and approximate indication of earning potential, where the station is valued as the sum of its parts (such as the land, buildings, cattle and fencing) rather than as a stream of future income. The increasing use of the ROI, by contrast, represents a process of valuation-qua-capitalisation in which the pastoral station is viewed as a stream of future revenue. The ROI translates the diverse array of land's characteristics 'into something that makes sense in terms if future cash flows' (Muniesa et al. 2017, 21), a process that sees the nature and temporality of a business's value redefined according to the expectations of investors.

What are the implications of treating land as a commodity or asset in this way? First, treating land as a commodity increases its availability to speculation, and the BAV is widely viewed as contributing to high and volatile land prices in the region as a result of the potential disconnect between the BAV price and the income of the property. Purchasing a property without station records requires buyers to have in-depth specialist knowledge of station management to interpret BAV land valuations and estimate the profitability of the investment. Professional land valuers provide some assistance to purchasers by supplementing their valuations with in-depth comments around the basis of the valuation and caution for its use. Yet it remains that station prices can often diverge substantially from their long-term profitability as a result of financial and weather cycles, and this introduces volatility into land markets that can be challenging for producers in the region. Even pastoralists who are not interested in buying or selling properties are affected by shifting land prices through changes to their lease payments, the financing they are offered by banks, and cattle prices.

Conversely, valuing land as an asset by standardising value against the income it generates is viewed favourably by local government actors and industry professionals in the region, as it is seen to reduce this speculative behaviour through a focus on business financial sustainability. As Birch and Muniesa observe: 'Assets can be bought and sold, yes. But the point is to get a durable economic rent from them, not to sell them in the market today' (2020, 2). Bankers and investors seeking equity partnerships drive processes in which pastoral properties are assetised to provide clear reporting on key features of interest to investors seeking to calculate an ROI. This often involves increased data collection and improved management of station financial records. This is not a new process and is not driven exclusively by financial investors, but often by farmers as they seek to access finance. In addition, professional land valuers are increasingly producing land valuations that, while nominally based on BAV calculations, draw in some part on the

ROI to inform their interpretation of the price data on which BAV valuations are based.

However, assets are also subject to speculation and, as Kornberger (2017) notes, it is possible to compete outside the sphere of production, in the sphere of valuation, by designing goods and assets in ways that target valuation devices rather than seeking to maximise profitability. This is occurring in Northern Australia, where pastoral companies – typically those backed by large institutional investors with the capacity to spend substantial funds on trading and developing properties – are undertaking station development programmes designed to increase the station's Beast Area, and therefore its value. This is profitable for investors, who make a capital gain on such developments regardless of whether they increase or decrease station profitability. For example, adding infrastructure such as fences and watering points to remote parts of a property would increase the number of cattle that can live on the property, and therefore its BAV valuation – regardless of whether the costs of maintaining these improvements and mustering the cattle from a remote area outweigh the increased income. This type of speculative development 'reflects the assessment of future earnings that accrue to the owner, rather than rising productivity' (Birch and Muniesa 2020, 7).

These divergent, overlapping and competing approaches to valuation are implicated in the financialisation of the industry in unexpected ways. If financialisation is considered to be increased profit-making from financial rather than productive channels (Krippner 2011), the financialisation of the Northern Australian cattle industry could be located in the speculative trading of properties for capital gains rather than their long-term productive operation. This process is facilitated and resisted by actors using BAV and ROI valuation processes in different ways. Professional valuers increasingly use the ROI to connect station value to its productive uses in order to reduce the potential for speculation; yet, pastoral companies simultaneously combine the ROI and the BAV in an attempt to generate capital gains through speculative developments. This suggests that although the industry appears to suffer from financialisation as evident in its high and volatile land prices, it is not simply the entrance of financial investors who drive this process, but their engagement with local actors and calculative devices across unique and varied geographies.

The financialisation of Northern Australian pastoral land has been associated with high and volatile land prices in the region, which have been attributed to speculative behaviour by nonspecialist investors. However, closer attention to the processes of valuation through which these land prices are made reveals that a range of local and nonlocal, human and nonhuman actors contribute to the assemblage of these values through diverse, sometimes competing and sometimes complementary work. Valuation professionals use the

BAV to construct valuations of land based on their physical characteristics, yet supplement these assessments with detailed comments warning that the 'true value' of the land is better estimated using the ROI. Pastoralists develop reporting systems to enable bankers, investors and professional valuers to measure their station value using the ROI, while simultaneously asserting nonfinancial connections to the land. Investors buy properties based on ROI-based calculations, and then seek to sell them using BAV-based valuations, strategically using these competing valuation processes selectively to profit from speculative development activities. This reveals that valuation devices play a key role in the financialisation of Northern Australian land, but not in a clearly reducible way; rather, land values are assembled by the interactions of a diverse range of actors undertaking unique valuation processes in pursuit of individual goals.

Notes

1. Frank Peacocke is the director of valuation firm Herron Todd White in the NT and the valuer chosen to undertake valuations for all NT properties for the government's 2015 assessments.
2. One response to the high and volatile property prices has arisen in the NT, which is moving away from a market-based system of valuation to determine lease payments, in a highly controversial move that will assign property values using not market rankings, but a general 'regional index'. The amendment was justified by the government on the grounds that 'its benefits, such as its simplicity and lack of volatility, outweigh its imperfections' (Economic Policy Scrutiny Committee (EPSC) 2018: 19). Although it reduces the impact of market volatility on prices, it does not conceptually change the process of valuing land using the BAV.
3. Earnings Before Interest, Tax, Depreciation, and Amortisation.
4. Cattle health is a major driver of station profitability, since it is not the number of cattle itself that drives farm income, but the number of calves they produce (for breeding properties). Unsustainable stocking rates can therefore actually decrease the number of calves that are produced if food is not sufficient for cattle to reach conception weight.
5. Including overextending debt due to both incompetence (Weller and Argent 2018) and intentional manipulation of land valuations (e.g. Ludlow 2018; Neales 2018).
6. For example, increases of up to 441% in the NT in 2009 (EPSC 2018).

Chapter 5

THE MORAL ECONOMIES OF DEBT

Financialisation in the Banks

Chapter 4 explored the ways in which land values are negotiated in practice by a range of actors. This chapter looks more closely at the process of debt administration, in which these land values are converted into lending to farmers and investors. Debt is the traditional method of financing agricultural development and is a key part of financing investments in land. It is used by farmers to develop their properties, invest in expansion and manage the additional costs of drought. Financialisation is often viewed as a shift away from bank financing to other forms of capital; however, banks themselves are subject to processes of financialisation that affect the way they lend and, as crucial mediators between Australian farmers and global capital markets, are a key site for understanding how financialisation changes the way in which farms are financed. This focus is particularly important for understanding how rural lending is shifting in response to changing global circumstances.

In late 2017, the Royal Commission into Misconduct in the Banking, Superannuation and Financial Services Industry (hereinafter 'the Commission') was announced to investigate widespread reports of misconduct in the financial services industry. The Commission's Letters Patent described the mandate of the Commission (among other things) as to inquire into:

> Whether any conduct by financial services entities (including by directors, officers or employees of, or by anyone acting on behalf of, those entities) . . .

might have amounted to misconduct . . . [or] fall below community standards and expectations . . . whether any findings in respect of [these] matters . . . are attributable to the particular culture and governance practices of a financial services entity or broader cultural or governance practices in the relevant industry or relevant subsector . . . or result from other practices, including risk management, recruitment and remuneration practices, of a financial services entity or in the relevant industry or relevant subsector. (Commonwealth of Australia 2017, 2)

Round 4, Topic 1 (hearing days 30–35) dealt with farm finance. The Commission received 410 submissions on agricultural lending. Eighty-five of these related to issues in land valuation practices, including practices such as deliberately overvaluing farmland in order to enable lending of larger amounts (thereby increasing the banker's loan portfolio) and then later revaluing properties at a lower price, often resulting in a breach of the loan-to-value ratio (Commonwealth of Australia 2019, 37); encouraging farmers to take out larger loans to fund expansion, stock or equipment, only to shortly after default the loan; the use of in-house valuations by staff lacking the appropriate expertise to undertake these; and a failure to negotiate with distressed clients and/or forced sale of assets below market value. Over sixty-five submissions related to modification of lending conditions, such as amounts, expiry periods and verbally agreed offers of loans. Over sixty submissions described misleading, fraudulent and inappropriate conduct such as document falsification, intimidating or threatening behaviour, or coerced signing of documents. Over fifty-five submissions described issues accessing banking services and support, including ignored requests for assistance, excessive delays, a lack of understanding by banks of farming realities, enforced default after short-term cashflow problems and the enforcement of unreasonable timeframes for loan repayments.

In its review of the evidence provided by the submissions and during the hearings, the Commission ultimately concluded that there were issues in the ways in which banks valued the land, and the way in which banks dealt with distressed agricultural clients (Recommendations 1.11–1.14). In addition to some legal changes, the Commissioner urged banks to pursue a culture of collaboration with farmers in administering their loans, to 'apply their own hardship policies' and to ensure that distressed agricultural loans 'are managed by experienced agricultural bankers'. These recommendations are difficult to enforce, but suggest a view of rural lending as a moral economy, and of moral engagements to be an essential component of their functioning. In this chapter, I explore how these debt markets are shifting in response to financialising circumstances, and what this means for the moral economy of debt.

Bank Lending to Agriculture

Private finance has historically been reticent to lend to agriculture as a result of the risks associated with managing agricultural assets. As a result, the state has played a key role mediating financial investments in agriculture through credit provision, contract enforcement, supporting marketing boards, mediating conflicts and intervening in financial markets (McMichael 1984; Martin and Clapp 2015; Larder, Sippel and Argent 2018). However, since the 1980s there has been a reduction in state support for agriculture in order to encourage Australian markets to restructure in pursuit of agricultural efficiency, and as a result farmers have had to rely on commercial debt offered on less favourable terms (Larder, Sippel and Argent 2018). Banks have adapted to changing global circumstances by modifying their lending behaviour, and this can introduce volatility into land markets if banks behave in a way that exposes agricultural industries to global financial markets. This can occur in three key ways.

First, bank lending may be procyclical, meaning that banks wish to expand their lending portfolio during global economic expansions (Athanasoglou, Daniilidis and Delis 2014). Banks that do not have a history of lending to Northern Australian agriculture may perceive profit-making opportunities in the region and enter the market offering low-cost loans in order to build a client portfolio. Existing banks may then compete by reducing their lending rates or requirements. This has the effect of making credit cheaper and easier to access during periods of global economic expansion. Similarly, during economic slowdowns, banks may increase interest rates and decline additional lending to pastoralists that may be needed to fund property purchases, infrastructure or operating costs. This can be particularly problematic if short-term loans are needed to manage agricultural or weather cycles, as an inability to access credit during these times can undermine the viability of a farm operation for an extended time period. Procyclical lending behaviour such as this introduces the volatility of global capital markets into Northern Australian agriculture, a shift that may be seen to be associated with a bank-driven financialisation of agriculture.

Second, changing demand for pastoral investments internationally can drive fluctuations in land values. Northern Australian pastoral properties are often very large and may be worth millions of dollars, and the largest, corporate stations in particular have been subject to extreme price volatility in recent years (see Figure 5.1). This volatility is related to both weather and investment demand, and affects the circumstances of pastoralists, even if they have no intention of selling their property. For example, their property value may be assessed at $1,000,000 during a period of strong property prices and the bank may offer them a $600,000 loan

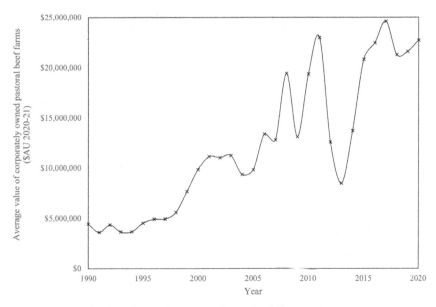

Figure 5.1. Land value of Australian pastoral zone beef farms with corporate ownership. Image created by the author using data from MLA (2021). © Zannie Langford. Data have since been moved and reorganised, and are now available (with different aggregation options) at https://www.agriculture.gov.au/abares/data/farm-data-portal

based on a 60% lending ratio. However, if the same property is revalued at $800,000 a few years later during a property price collapse, at the same lending ratio the bank would now only be comfortable lending the pastoralists $480,000 and may seek repayments or decline additional short-term lending needed to meet operating costs, creating a difficult, but predictable, problem for pastoralists.

Third, property values shift with changing local circumstances. A drought in a region may lead to hardship, resulting in decreased demand for properties and a depressed land market, which will again affect the pastoralists' lending position. This is a particular problem because it is often during drought that pastoralists are in need of additional lending to manage increased operational costs, such as the cost of purchasing supplementary feed. If banks are unwilling to work with bankers and provide finance where needed to overcome drought, pastoralists may be forced to make management decisions that undermine the viability of the operation in the long term. In addition, if banks cannot flexibly accommodate this aspect of pastoralism, they may seek to foreclose on pastoralists and sell the property during the drought. A short marketing period for these properties can lead to properties being sold far below their previously assessed value, further depressing property market valuations and increasing the volatility of the market.

Pastoralists and bankers may have competing needs. Banks may develop adversarial lending behaviour if they respond to opportunities and challenges in global markets without prioritising the long-term viability of the industry. Lending may be extended on somewhat speculative grounds, with riskier loans being made during periods of economic expansion and then being modified or foreclosed upon during periods of drought or of limited credit availability. As a result, 'procyclicality has transformed banks from mitigation mechanisms to amplifiers of changes in economic activity' (Athanasoglou, Daniilidis and Delis 2014, 58). Despite these incentives for opportunistic lending behaviour on the part of banks, it is not the case that rural bankers merely transmit these market signals. Closer attention to the work of rural lenders, who are tasked with mediating bank–farmer connections in practice, reveals them to be important mediators of rural lending markets.

Relationship Lending in Northern Australia

From an economic perspective, setting up a loan between a bank and a farmer is a contracting process in which the banker must assess the capacity of the farmer to repay the loan (Moss, Kropp and Bampasidou 2018). In this transacting process, the banker faces the problem of 'asymmetric information', where the farmer has a greater knowledge about the farm and its financial sustainability than the banker and may seek to withhold information that would reduce the willingness of the banker to lend. From this perspective, the banker and the farmer are adversaries, and rural debt markets are formed through transactional lending negotiations in which each seeks to maximise their return from the negotiation. When bankers use 'relationship lending' and create close working relationships with their clients, this is viewed as an economically rational strategy for reducing this asymmetric information (Fiordelisi, Monferrà and Sampagnaro 2014; Beck et al. 2018), particularly for long-term clients (López-Espinosa, Mayordomo and Moreno 2017) and large borrowers (Akhavein, Goldberg and White 2004; Hilkens et al. 2018). Farmers who participate in these relationships are also said to benefit, for example, from increased access to credit during difficult periods such as drought or periods of low economic growth (Berg and Schrader 2012; Bolton et al. 2016; Beck et al. 2018).

However, these close banker–client relationships are often more than economically rational behaviour. The recent edited volume *Markets in Their Place: Context, Culture, Finance* offers a view of market formation through geographically situated and morally informed negotiations that underpin markets in practice (Prince et al. 2021). The concept of moral economy is helpful in understanding how moral judgements shape economic behaviour and market formation in a range of fields. Carrier (2017) notes that the concept is widely used to explore how broader societal values shape consumer expectations of economic behaviour, in which a range of 'trancendent value[s]' (Carrier 2017, 22) shape expectations of what is 'right'. These transcendent values express 'a social group's explicitly normative frameworks outlining the "proper" organization of society . . . They contain ideological elements and are spatially situated in concrete material contexts' (Wolford 2005, 245). However, as Carrier (2017) argues, these values not only inform economic behaviour, but are also shaped by them. A pragmatic approach to the study of moral economies can reveal how markets are formed in local spaces by focusing not just on how these broader values shape economic activity, but how morality *itself* is shaped through economic transactions. The nature of the relationship between a banker and a client – whether they meet in an office, on a farm or in a client's home; whether they discuss their families alongside their business; whether they can confide their concerns and whether the nature of their business means they need to trust each other's judgements – these factors contribute to feelings of mutual obligation and affect the way that each behaves towards the other. Focusing on these processes of interaction can reveal how moral economies are generated in practice, as well as how they are performed and reinforced through continued interaction.

In the pastoral lands of remote Northern Australia, debt has generally been administered by rural agrifinance specialists (hereafter referred to as 'bankers'). Rural bankers in pastoral Northern Australia typically live in the region alongside their clients and as such are embedded in these local communities, as well as within a virtual professional network with its own processes and calculative tools. Bankers drive long distances to their clients' farms to discuss business plans, and to assess the value and business performance of the property and the management skill and risk tolerance of the pastoralist. They must consider a wide range of human and nonhuman factors, including property soil type, weather patterns, infrastructure, access to watering points and livestock, which interact with calculative tools such as bank lending ratios and valuation devices to produce a property as a commoditised space. In this context, rural bankers exert considerable agency in deciding whether to lend, how much and on what terms, drawing on specialist knowledge of the region, the industry and the farmer, to make judgements that blend qualitative and quantitative elements. As one cattle industry representative put it:

> In rural lending, you need to have an understanding and an empathy of what's happening on that property. You really do need to understand the cycles,

there's wet years and there's dry years, there's good cattle prices there's bad cattle prices . . . there does need to be a bit of leeway because people might need to borrow money to build the capacity of that asset.

Bankers must assess the farmer's plans, risks and likelihood of success based on both their physical operations and management expertise. As one banker described, for this task it is necessary to visit clients on farm 'to see the operations, to get a better handle on the operation and on the family dynamics'. Importantly, they must assess the farmer's management ability 'to try and pick out the better farmers' such that 'we wouldn't do a deal without going and meeting a farmer on farm'. Bankers need to be able to make important decisions on whether or not to extend further capital and, in cases of extremely distressed loans, whether to foreclose. Many bankers are themselves from pastoral backgrounds, and this is often considered to be essential expertise for operating in remote Northern Australia. Specialist agricultural banks often emphasise this knowledge on the part of their lenders. Rabobank, for example, claims to be 'By farmers, for farmers' (Rabobank 2023, n.p.), emphasising that: 'Our rural managers take a hands-on approach, working alongside you to grow your business' (Rabobank 2023, n.p.). Similarly, Elders Rural Services assert that 'our network of agribusiness specialists . . . are ready to assist you with all aspects of your farm business' (Elders 2023). During the Royal Commission, the Commissioner inquired at several points whether banks had provided sufficient and appropriate agricultural advice to their clients, indicating that this is viewed as part of bank lending to agriculture.[1]

In the context of New Zealand dairying, bankers developed strong working relationships with their clients as 'an important client-retention strategy [that] allowed them to compete successfully with other banks, and retain customers in situations where other banks may offer cheaper loans' (Hilkens et al. 2018, 87). A similar phenomenon was observed in my research – as one banker put it, 'money is money, your money is the same as my money, so the difference I suppose with us is the value we can bring to the client – the customer experience they get'. It is evidently important that rural bankers get to know their clients on a personal level, alongside developing a working knowledge of their business and the industry in which they operate. Bankers living in Northern Australia generally agreed that their role required them to develop and maintain relationships with their clients. As one banker explained, 'I get out and about and be interested, which I genuinely am', and 'aim to have meaningful conversations with the client throughout the journey, throughout the year'. Developing this knowledge and these relationships was viewed by bankers and farmers alike as part of behaving morally in this industry – in Carrier's (2017, 22) words, these are the 'transcendent value[s]' that shape how bankers are 'supposed' to behave. However, these relationships are themselves spaces in which mutual obligations are formed, and relationship lending is not only symptomatic, but also generative of moral economic activity.

Generating a Moral Economy

One of the key features affecting lending behaviour in Northern Australia is the remote geographies and limited markets for agricultural consultants. Bankers can be thought of as 'embedded advisors' because they provide farm management advice alongside their other services such as the provision of loans (Klerkz and Jansen 2010). These features act to valorise local expertise as a key service provided by bankers. One banker described that it was their local experience and expertise that enabled them to compete with clients, even when their bank's products were more expensive than those of their competitors:

> You tend to develop with your client a trust . . . you may not be the cheapest in the market but you understand their business better. I've been up here doing this type of work for more than ten years. Most of my counterparts from other firms and banks, they churn over every two or three years. I'm still here doing it. That *means something*. It may be worth it for the client to have a point two or point five of a percent [interest rate] differential just to have me there because I've been there for so long and I've always been able to deliver.

It was common for bankers in Northern Australia to feel strongly invested in their clients and to see their business advice as a key part of what they offered their clients. Some bankers spent substantial time with their clients and were emotionally invested in their business goals, as one banker described:

> We spend a lot of time with our clients, really understand their business, and we get around the kitchen table with them and become part of the family, and become part of their business I suppose. I like to think we are a pretty crucial partner to them. And to be a successful partner in any business, you need to be open and transparent with them. So we are that way with our clients, and hopefully they are with us as well. They should feel comfortable picking the phone up and talking to me on Sunday night, or whenever it might be. If they've got concerns, get it out and talk about it with us. We don't want to have surprises. I generally think that is the case, that clients will call me and say 'Oh, I'm really worried about such and such', but if you leave it till the problem has happened, that's no good for anybody.

An important feature of these relationships is that they are not unidirectional. Bankers emphasised mutual obligation and care, noting that 'very few clients leave us, so *they're very loyal, as we are to them*'. In putting their personal energy into these relationships, they came to expect to be valued and respected by their clients. As one banker put it:

> If all you want is a cheap rate, go somewhere else. If you don't want any service, if you don't value what I bring to your business, I don't want to deal with you. It's not a true partnership, you're just looking for a funding source. If all you want is a funding source get on the internet. The big four banks will bloody fund you, not a problem. But they'll also not take any time to *understand* you.

Bankers both offered and expected personal relationships with their clients, emphasising trust, loyalty and mutual care as key features of the banker–client relationship. Their close relationships with their clients were not performed merely to fulfil moral obligations, as one might obligingly double-check figures out of a sense of care, but in and of themselves became spaces in which feelings of care and trust were generated. These relationships arose out of the necessity of operating lending businesses in remote Northern Australian geographies, but became spaces in which moral economies were not only performed but also generated.

The case of pastoralist Melville Ruddy, heard in Round 4 of the Commission (on the topic of 'Experiences with financial services entities in regional and remote communities'), exemplifies farmer expectations of banker–client relationships. Ruddy had entered into a loan with his bank and altered his business model under the assumption that the bank would work with him, and alter the conditions of his loan, to support the financial sustainability of the business, but this support was not forthcoming. He described his confusion and disappointment with the lack of support from the banker who had contracted the loan:

> I was looking for a long-term relationship with [him] . . . It was confusing. Like, you – you know, when you're sort of in the drought and cattle prices are totally depressed and you can't sort of go and talk to anyone, they're in Brisbane . . . I'm used to having a bank manager ring up, he comes out and sees me, we have a cup of tea, we have a drive around and we come to a decision about things, you know. That's how it's been all my life, since I was 23.[2]

Ruddy's experience offers insights into the importance of close banker–client relationships. Ruddy had elected to transition to a different breeding model, a decision that would reduce his cashflow for a number of years. This transition would require the ongoing lending support of the bank during this time. When Ruddy assessed his business options, he had sought advice from his banker as to whether they would support him during this period. Hilkens et al. (2018, 94) refer to this as 'binding advice', since Ruddy required the financial support of the bank and could not proceed without it. In situations such as these, the bank – and the advice of the banker – actually shapes the trajectory of business development. Ruddy perceived the lack of the relationship with the banker as a barrier to his obtaining support from the bank during the drought. His decision to change business models had been based on trust that the banker would exercise care for the property. In this scenario, the practical and interpersonal aspects of the banker–client relationship are inseparable, and the Royal Commission noted that this represented a situation in which banker behaviour had not met community expectations.

Research on relationship lending has emphasised the benefits it provides to banks by increasing the information they have about their clients in order to reduce their costs of lending (Moss, Kropp and Bampasidou 2018). However, relationship lending may also benefit farmers during times of drought if they have access to a banker who has faith in their management ability, as this banker may be more likely to support them during difficult times (Bolton et al. 2016; Beck et al. 2018). As Hilkens et al. (2018, 88) describe, farmers 'perceived that building personal relationships with their banker would increase the banker's trust in their capability and therefore the bank would more likely provide them financial support when they needed it'. My research noted similar themes, with one farmer stating that bankers 'know amongst their book of clients who's being doing well even when times have been tough'. This appeared to be supported by evidence from bankers; as one banker described, the 'benefit of being in the same place for a length of time is you get to know the people in the region. I have a fair idea of who the better operators are [and] who has what property'. This knowledge allows bankers to differentiate between properties that are distressed due to mismanagement or an unsustainable business model, and those that are distressed due to circumstances such as drought that are outside the pastoralist's control and require short-term support to overcome. One banker noted that for those clients with whom they had a close working relationship, lending decisions could be made quickly and efficiently:

> for those guys that communicate, are free and open with their business planning with us, [my bank] will bend over backwards for them. If they need an extra half a million dollars until they get the next big cattle sale away in three or four months' time, not a problem! That's a bloody two-hour decision process.

For farmers, banker approval and understanding during difficult times can be a source of emotional as well as practical support. There is a desire from many farmers to identify as a 'good' farmer (Aitkin 1985; see also Hunt et al. 2013), and in remote situations where there may be limited sources of reassurance during times of financial distress, bankers can provide an importance source of support. In his testimony to the Royal Commission, Melville Rudy emphasised his distress that: 'We were made to feel guilty, that our farms were u[n]viable' (Ruddy 2018, 3). In my research, bankers expressed a similar sentiment, working to be thought of as a 'good banker' through developing trusting and loyal relationships.

Close relationships between the banker and the client are therefore important for both practical and emotional reasons. In Northern Australian pastoralism, an industry characterised by high levels of remoteness, low populations and unpredictable weather patterns, bankers and clients work closely together to develop lending plans. Their relationships exceed those that are strictly necessary for practical reasons because in their ongoing enactment over many years, they lead to the formation of those 'mutual obligations' that underpin moral economies (Carrier 2017). These mutual obligations shape the way in which bankers respond to financialising bank policies, as I will discuss in the next section.

Moral Responses to Financialised Markets

During my research, the bankers I spoke to suggested that it was common practice for banks to expand the scale and geographic reach of their lending activities into Northern Australia during periods of economic expansions, and then to reduce their activities during credit shortages. This type of lending behaviour is procyclical, since it means that banks shift their lending approaches in ways that match global cycles and transmit them into rural Australian markets. This expands the influence of global financial patterns and logics into new geographies, a pattern associated with financialisation (Pike and Pollard 2010). During periods of increased credit availability in the region, pastoralists find it easier and cheaper to access loans from new sources. This puts pressures on banks already operating in the region to offer loans at cheaper rates or for larger sums of money. One banker expressed the opinion that this lending behaviour by banks was not necessarily in the clients' interests, since it may be justified by criteria other than a consideration of the pastoralist's risks and repayment ability:

> Banks obviously look at risk differently than some of our clients do. If the bank says yes, that's a good deal, we'll lend you the money, [it] doesn't mean it's a good business decision for the customer. The bank looks at risks that are appropriate for the bank, and not necessarily from the client's perspective.

The bankers I spoke to described being aware of lending procyclicality and often feeling under pressure to participate in these lending cycles by increasing their lending and/or reducing their lending criteria. One long-term resident agricultural banker told me with some concern about his experiences of operating within these cycles:

> When the market was hot . . . things were going really good, property and cattle were both strong prices and there was a bit of activity happening. There were banks in the region trying to drum up business everywhere. But as soon as things got a bit wobbly, they're gone. They're offering really cheap rates to people, it's not sustainable and you just know at some point they will start ratchetting up fees and margins. That's probably the hardest time I found in this area, was that period, and it's happening again now where we're seeing them come up and they're writing deals and they're pushing the boundaries. And you come to me and say you want to borrow money and I say 'I don't really feel comfortable with that!' and if I dare show any resistance or any lack of enthusiasm towards you borrowing the money the guy says 'Oh, well if it's going to be too hard doing this deal with you guys, I'll go to another bank, and they'll do it, and they'll do it at a cheaper rate, and they'll probably do it no questions asked!'

These long-term resident agricultural bankers were deeply concerned about the sustainability of the loans they offered. Living in the region meant that they would be there five or ten years after loans had been given out and would personally need to deal with the consequences of unsustainable loans. This was contrasted with bank lenders who entered the region for shorter periods of a few years. As one agricultural banker put it:

> I've seen it happen years ago with a manager out pumping money to the community like you wouldn't believe, as in lending to farmers, he wins all these awards and he moves off to wherever he goes, and the next guy comes in and has got to come and clean up all the mess. I don't think that's *right* . . . I personally avoid that situation . . . I want to sleep at night as well.

In moral economic relationships, guilt often plays a key role in preventing negative behaviours (Rose 2011). In this case, the banker felt a sense of personal obligation to his clients, a sense of care for their long-term wellbeing, and avoided engaging in risky behaviour out of a sense of guilt. Long-term resident agricultural bankers develop ongoing relationships with their clients, which meant that they felt invested in the outcomes of the pastoral business. As one banker put it: 'I want the best for the customer, whether it's buying this property or getting this deal done for them, or maybe it's not. Maybe the customer doesn't know it yet and you've got to help them with the decision, maybe it's a bit too risky for them.'

Interestingly, these bankers did not see themselves as merely facilitating bank–client connections, but as moderating them. They associated conservative lending criteria with an ethos of care for the client and felt responsible for the business sustainability. As one banker described it:

> We understand that even in good times, yes it might look good, but there's going to be bad times around the corner. We hope that there's not, but there always will be something happen. So some people will say we are very conservative, [but] I like to think that we understand the business better, we're not just here for the good times, we're here for the long time. We want to be able to look after [our clients] through the good and the bad. So when there's a hiccup like the GFC or a drought, we can still support our clients to get through that.

According to some bankers, this loyalty to clients was associated with specialist agricultural banks, which they felt were more suited to the risk profiles and timeframes of farming. One banker at a specialist agricultural bank felt that the bank they worked at had policies that were flexible enough to allow him to spend time building connections and, by focusing on banking top performing clients, did not put undue pressure on them to extend loans that they felt would be risky. As they described, 'they want me to get growth, and want me to meet certain targets, but I've never felt too threatened if I didn't meet those targets . . . they realise I'm still putting the effort in'. This banker was passionate about that role and had stayed with the same bank over a very long period of time, feeling that it enabled them to conduct their work in a meaningful way. As they described it: 'That's what appeals to me, why I still work here, what gets me out of bed in the morning. I don't know if I could have that same passion if I was working in another organisation.' This suggests that bank policies and ways of measuring banker performance may enable the development of close working relationships to different extents. Others felt that the loyalty was not so strongly influenced by bank policy as by the relationship with the individual banker. One pastoralist, when asked if there were benefits to banking with an agricultural bank, answered: 'Oh . . . not really. I think it comes down more to the manager that you've got.' These differing perspectives highlight the potential of the interaction of bank policy with individual agency to assemble lending patterns in diverse ways.

The theme of interaction with individual banker judgements also arose during the hearings for the Commission. The Commission heard evidence from a number of former bank clients about situations in which they felt that banks had not taken the expected level of care in administering their loans. Cases were discussed in which rural bankers had increased their client book by contracting excessively risky loans, sometimes in conjunction with property overvaluations to enable higher loan amounts. These cases were often motivated by bank incentives. The Commission noted this potential for bankers to exploit the high level of authority that they have in assessing and approving loans, referring to an earlier report, which noted that rural bankers have 'an uncomfortably high level of formal authority in the qualitative aspects of loan approval and management', which 'puts a significant degree of risk into the loan portfolio' (McGrath Nicol 2009, 40). Recommendations were made to alter policy in order to reduce this level of authority by separating land valuations from loan decisions, restricting banks from charging default interest in drought-declared areas and implementing a national scheme of debt mediation (Commonwealth of Australia 2019). In addition to these policy recommendations, the Commission also emphasised the importance of agricultural banking expertise, noting that distressed agricultural loans should be managed by 'experienced agricultural bankers' and that banks dealing with distressed loans should 'recognise and apply their own hardship policies' (Commonwealth of Australia 2019, 102).

These differing approaches to oversight of loans – at the national, bank and individual banker levels – highlight a tension between the need to prevent rural bankers from exploiting their roles, while also creating space for their expertise and individual moral judgements to mediate debt markets. The Royal Commission highlighted situations in which greater oversight within the bank could have prevented farmer hardship. Some of the bankers I spoke to agreed with the importance of such oversight, with one banker acknowledging the risk of getting 'too close to a client' and the usefulness of having input from others in the bank who may 'see it a bit differently to what you do on the ground'. Having said that, many of the same bankers also complained about bank policies designed to increase oversight that in fact only had the effect of increasing their workload without supporting their decision-making in meaningful ways, such as additional administrative burdens. There is also a limit to what can be officially legislated and it is important to avoid simplistically assuming that greater oversight will lead to better outcomes for bank clients: as this research has demonstrated, the qualitative judgement and in-depth local expertise of rural bankers is an asset and essential to making decisions about lending and assessing risk. Policies that reduce the authority of these experienced bankers also limit the usefulness of their expertise and the benefits of relationship lending, which are central to agricultural debt markets. Instead, by observing the conditions under which moral economic lending behaviour is generated, it may be possible for banks to support the development of loan portfolios.

Bankers as Key Intermediaries between Finance and Farming

This chapter has explored the work of Northern Australian bankers, many of whom have lived and worked in the region for many years and have developed long-term relationships with their clients. The unique remote geographies of Northern Australia lend themselves to the formation of close relationships as bankers drive long distances to meet their clients on the farm and develop specialist knowledge of pastoral properties that enable them to assess the sustainability of these businesses. These relationships are key to rural lending in the region, and are widely seen by bankers and pastoralists as essential to the moral operation of rural debt markets. The important parts of these relationships – a cup of tea or a phone call on a Sunday night – are not things that can be contractually enforced, yet pastoralists and bankers alike see these things as key parts of rural lending markets. Mutual care and loyalty are key elements of this moral economy, and bankers demonstrate their moral behaviour through care for clients and basing lending decisions not only on the bank's needs, but also those of the clients.

These day-to-day interactions are not only symptomatic of moral economic behaviour, but are also generative of it. It was clear in my research that these relationships, born out of the unique Northern Australian geographies and the quirks of the pastoral industry, were in themselves key sites for the generation of this sense of morality through the formation of caring interpersonal relationships. Research on relationship lending has found that close banker–client relationships can increase access to credit during an economic downturn as bankers continue to lend to clients whose businesses they know well. This study extends this research by showing a case in which relationship lending can also *decrease* access to credit during an economic boom, where lending is perceived by the banker to be irresponsible and contain a high degree of risk for the client, as bankers perform their care for their clients through retaining conservative lending criteria. This may have the effect of dampening the procyclical bank lending behaviour, thereby reducing the influence of global markets in Northern Australian lending markets. In this way, bankers exert their agency to moderate the effects of financialisation without consciously engaging with it, but through a sense of care and beliefs about what constitutes the moral operation of markets.

Like other chapters in this book, this chapter highlights how the engagements of various human actors shape patterns of financialisation in unexpected ways. Individual banker agencies in this case could contribute to or resist financialising patterns of rural lending, and their choices depended on their life histories and their relationships with people in the region. The diverse geographies of Northern Australia shape these relationships, in some cases (and at some banks) leading to long-term resident bankers in remote regions and, in others, to short-term placements of bankers from other cities. Bank policies similarly affect these relationships by shaping the amount of authority bankers hold and the amount of time they are able to spend with clients. Attention to these features has policy implications, as it suggests that bank policy will affect different bankers in different ways, for some bankers increasing their care and responsibility, while for others offering opportunities for short-term personal gain. This highlights the importance of close attention to the local spaces in which financialising patterns are negotiated.

Notes

1. See Transcript of Proceedings, *Royal Commission into Misconduct in the Banking, Superannuation and Financial Services Industry* [28 June 2018].
2. Transcript of Proceedings, *Royal Commission into Misconduct in the Banking, Superannuation and Financial Services Industry* [28 June 2018, 3443–44].

Chapter 6

HOW TO GET AN INVESTOR

Introducing the Farmer-Investor

Chapter 5 explored the ways in which pastoral farms in Northern Australia engage with debt to finance their operations, and how the unique geographies of Northern Australia both shape and are shaped by moral economies of rural lending. While debt remains an important source of finance in remote Northern Australia, it is increasingly viewed by government and industry as inadequate to finance the development of Australian agrifood industries (ANZ 2012; Heath and Tomlinson 2015; Department of Agriculture and Water Resources 2018). Debt is often not appropriate for the timeframes and seasonal variation of agricultural production (Goodhart 2010). Farmers who use debt bear both the risks of production – such as drought – and the financial risks of changing interest rates and shifting land values that can severely compromise the sustainability of their operation (Smith 2015). As a result, debt lending is viewed as being both insufficient and unsuitable for funding investments in improving farm productivity and developing global supply chains (Heath and Tomlinson 2016). A 'capital gap' of $600 billion to 2050 was identified to fund necessary improvements in farm productivity in Australia (ANZ 2012), generating concerns about the need for other types of investment in agriculture and fuelling a discourse of 'finance to the rescue' (Magnan 2018, 113).

As a result of this shift, farmers are increasingly being encouraged to pursue equity partnerships with sophisticated investors. Unlike investor-driven models of financial investment in which the investor purchases a farm business and either leases it to a farmer or hires a farm manager to operate it, equity partnerships see the farmer as a part-owner of the business. These models are viewed as an ideal outcome for Australian agribusiness, since they simultaneously offer investors access to specialised farming skillsets, and offer farmers access to capital for development, expansion and risk sharing (see also Sommerville and Magnan 2015). State support for farmers to access financing increasingly targets these models by supporting farmers to 'consider their investment options and business structures and develop the skills and expertise necessary to work with external investors' (Department of Agriculture and Water Resources 2018, iii). Farmers must become 'investment ready' (Larder et al. 2018) and restructure their operations to appeal to external investors. For this task, they need financial as well as farming skillsets, and are increasingly encouraged to 'conceive of themselves as investors in relation to their farm' (Larder, Sippel and Argent 2018, 405). Today's ideal farmer 'not only understands and strategically plans their position within global markets but . . . also seizes global investment opportunities and incorporates the needs and values of their financial partner' (Larder, Sippel and Argent 2018, 405).

In Australia, Pritchard, Burch and Lawrence (2007) described a new category of farmers that they referred to as 'farm family entrepreneurs', who developed new business structures that were not clearly identifiable as either family or corporate businesses. Cheshire and Woods (2013) offered a study of 'globally engaged farmers', who travelled internationally and undertook extensive skilled work developing global supply chains. I added to these with a study of a 'capitalised farm family entrepreneur', who not only developed corporate structures and reporting but also engaged a financial partner with a majority ownership (Langford 2019). These studies highlight how entrepreneurial family farmers are engaging with activities beyond the farm gate, remodelling themselves as financial subjects (Preda 2005; Hall 2011) who must combine specialist farming and financial expertise. However, despite the widespread support for this approach to financing, there are relatively few examples of family farmers who have successfully attracted equity investors. In this chapter, I describe the experience of one family farm business who successfully negotiated a private equity partnership with a large foreign pension fund. The exceptional experience of this family offers insights into the realities of private equity partnership formation that have important implications for policy formulation.

Who Wants an Investor?

During my research in Northern Australia, I attended a number of public forums. At one such event, the discussion turned to farm financing, and a number of farmers in the room raised the issues they were having accessing the finance they needed to operate their businesses and develop their operations. They wanted to know how they could get an investor in, and where they could learn how to go about finding an investor. Afterwards, I spoke with a representative of a youth farming network and asked them about this interest in equity investment. They responded emphatically:

> Oh, everyone is desperate for it, that's what everyone wants. Anytime you run a workshop they want to hear from people who have successfully attracted equity partners and then they want to know: 'Well, how do I do that?'

Attitudes to equity finance vary substantially between farmers, who are a heterogeneous group with a diverse range of perspectives and aspirations (Weller, Smith and Pritchard 2013; Woods 2014; Nuthall and Old 2017). Farmers respond to differing perceptions of risks and benefits in a range of ways, such as by initiating global partnerships (see Cheshire and Woods 2013) or by resisting change through protest (see Woods 2014). An openness to equity investment appears to be a particularly common attitude among young farmers who may have trouble accessing debt due to a lack of savings and may be open to new business strategies. The appeal of equity finance in this case is a sharing of risk and an ability to access larger sums of money than would be available from leveraging debt. One agrifinance specialist observed that farmers with this attitude 'think getting an investor in is free money'. By contrast, other farmers were much more concerned about the risks of equity investment, such as the potential to lose control over their business. As one agrifinance specialist put it, 'farmers tend to go into agriculture because they want to be the masters of their own destiny. They don't *want* a partner'. The theme of maintaining control of the business through separation of productive and financial management was common for many farmers. As one cattle farmer stated:

> If it was me, I'd want someone who's here for the long term, and someone who is happy to be the money and not tell me how to run things . . . maybe if they had good finance and corporate governance people or something then they'd provide that, but they would stay out of the production side of it.

There was a perception that corporate cattle enterprises were run by 'overpaid executives with no real knowledge of how the business operates at the grassroots [level]' – by financial actors who were 'out of touch' (Sippel, Larder and Lawrence 2017, 261) with farming realities. Many farmers simultaneously desired equity investors in their business and maintained that these investors should 'stay out' of farm management decisions.

Although this desire for investment appeared to be widespread, few farmers had succeeded in actually finding an investor with whom such a relationship could be developed. Farmers need to find investors whose interests and goals align with their own, with whom farm management and development plans can be agreed upon, with whom control over financial and productive decisions can be amicably negotiated, and with whom decisions about processes and timeframes for farm management, development and expansion can be agreed upon. As one farm consultant explained, 'it's not a swipe right, swipe left kind of thing. Actually finding the right match between an investor and a farmer is a long process'. As few investors are capable of, or open to, obtaining the agricultural skills needed to manage an agricultural investment, the onus often falls on farmers to become 'investment ready'. One professional with extensive experience in both farming and financial management lamented that many farmers:

> had grand ideas around 'I'm going to go and get myself an investor and put them into my business', but they really didn't have the commitment to actually making the necessary changes to actually make it possible for an investor to invest in their business. The most basic, fundamental reporting systems that you need to have. I mean, you start talking about them to some people who do genuinely hold ambitions to raise capital, and they just don't even get that that's a key requirement.

The difficulties of becoming 'investment ready' are widely recognised in industry and government documents (see, for example, ANZ 2012; Department of Agriculture and Water Resources 2018) and emerged as a theme in my interviews with consultants, government professionals, rural lenders and farmer organisations. Notably, though, these discussions of the benefits and risks of equity partnerships rarely went beyond speculation: very few people knew anyone who had successfully created such a partnership, and most people referred to only a small number of examples of successful partnerships to support their opinion.

In particular, I heard repeatedly of the success of one of these partnerships, in which a farming family had entered into an equity partnership with a large foreign pension fund and had since gone on to very successfully expand and develop their business. I contacted the business to request an interview to learn about their experiences constructing this partnership. The CEO of the company very generously undertook repeat interviews to explain the history of their partnership, the challenges they faced, and the way they see the resulting business. This CEO was the adult son of a pastoralist couple who had gradually developed the business using debt. In the next section, I retell the story of this family farm business, drawing heavily on the words of the family member who negotiated its construction. Their exceptional experience negotiating this partnership at very high cost, over many years, and requiring extensive financial and agricultural skill highlights the reality of equity partnership development and the limitations of the model for a wider cohort of Australian farmers.

Becoming 'Investment Ready'

The farm business that I describe first began seeking an equity partner just prior to the 2007–8 financial crisis. At this time, the business was a large, multigenerational family cattle enterprise with substantial savings, managing several times more cattle than the average of the largest family farms in Australia's pastoral zones (using MLA (2021) definitions). The family had gradually expanded their business by leveraging their savings using bank debt; as my informant described, 'we traditionally raised debt to expand our business, did that over a very long period of time, my parents in particular were very successful in that'. This had resulted in incremental growth, since the potential to develop properties and expand a business using bank finance is limited, since it is fundamentally linked to the underlying assets of the family (see also Pritchard et al. 2007). The family originally began seeking an equity partnership to enable faster growth of the business, as they described:

> we wanted to buy larger-scale assets as opposed to, you know, the incremental gain that came from acquiring small assets, where you essentially expanded based on your capital that was available to you by debt funding ratios.

The important point here is that the farm family were not motivated to seek equity investment by debt stress or a lack of capital, as seemed to be the case for other farmers in the region. Rather, they were in a strong financial position with a sound plan for expansion that exceeded the risk appetite of bank lenders at the time. It was the entrepreneurial desire combined with a willingness to take risks that motivated the owners to seek an equity partner.

The farm business was originally connected with a small financial advisory firm by their bank, who they worked with for two years to develop an investment prospectus and marketing materials with which to approach investors. The farm business described this period as one of growth and change, in which they had a growing awareness of the management and reporting systems necessary to engage with external investors, and began to reorganise their operations to meet these needs. As they described: 'I'm sure you've heard people talk about getting investment ready . . . part of that was actually learning about the do's, don'ts, requirements, non-requirements of attracting an investor . . . we were continuously improving.' They described formalising

112 • Assembling Financialisation

a range of processes from employment contracts to budget forecasts and developing new systems for monitoring and recording details of the business. The roles of family members in the business were formalised during this time, with two family members taking on official employment in the business management. As they described:

> Looking back, where we started to where we finished were a long way apart . . . that was the time of our life when we went from having three old phones on the desk to a Commander system. That [was the] change from being a private business, where you're just making do with what you've got, to actually investing in things to make you a more sophisticated enterprise capable of managing and expanding using other people's money.

This period lasted for two years, in which they continued internally reorganising their management and:

> morphing into a far more sophisticated enterprise in terms of our overall administration, our management, most basic things that could be done better from employment contracts to financial management, budgeting forecasting, budgeting forecasting actuals, filing system servers, all this type of stuff that we had to get in place. Policies and procedures, so on, and so forth.

After this two-year period working with the small financial advisory firm, the family found that they had incurred substantial expense with little success in attracting an investment partner. As they noted:

> we actually then stopped, and we had to make a decision as a family, did we want to keep putting money into this process? Because . . . most people don't realise just how much money and commitment it takes to actually raise capital. So we had to make a decision after a couple of years, and we sat down as a family and said, 'Do we want to pursue this?'

As a large cattle business looking to expand into new properties, they realised they would need an investment partner willing and able to finance the purchase of properties worth millions of dollars and invest in the development of those properties, and that this would require a substantial investment partner 'who had a long-term view of the market'. They realised that the small firm they had engaged 'didn't have the global network to actually raise us the capital' and that a different approach would be needed to successfully locate an investment partner. They describe deciding to proceed and how:

> we actually, we developed on our own back, using our own private consultant, essentially an information memorandum about ourselves, with a baseline investment proposal, just taking some quasi properties, and we took that

to the financial advisory space . . . we ended up presenting our company to about ten different financial advisors, from very small to the largest in terms of including two of the 'big four'. And to cut a long story short, we ended up engaging [one of the big four accounting firms]. And that was the real turning point for us.

They described working with this firm as giving them access to a range of much larger investors, such that 'that's where paying money for . . . the best advisors with a global network [is worthwhile]'. Working with this firm for a further three years, my informant met with a wide range of potential investors. As they described:

> I travelled overseas multiple times, meeting various different investors. God knows – I never added it up – how many different parties I met. Did a lot of work, a lot of shaping, reshaping, presentation decks, investment memorandums, that type of stuff, because you tend to meet different investors along the way who have a slightly different way of doing it.

My informant met with investors largely in financial spaces rather than on-farm, and through both face-to-face and virtual meetings. This required the individual to acquire substantial financial expertise, becoming a farmer-investor who combines specialist farming and financial expertise. Several features of the business and farm family made this possible. First, the substantial skill of my informant, who took on a role as the CEO of the company, who described having 'a natural interest in sophisticated systems' and who took a leading role in reorganising the business and pursuing financial expertise over many years. Second, the CEO's sibling, the company's Chief Operating Officer (COO), who was a skilled farm manager and who, while the CEO was frequently travelling to meet with investors, 'was trying to optimise and keep the business absolutely powering ahead and showing good returns to make us highly marketable, saleable, or investable'. Third, the wealth and stability of the cattle business prior to the capital seeking process, as a result of the long-term efforts of the informant's parents in building the business, which made the expense and time of the investment-seeking process possible.

The core of the investment proposition of the farm business was not so much the existing assets of the business, which are not substantially different from those of other productive cattle enterprises, but the skill and farm management expertise of the family. As they described, agriculture 'is absolutely a foreign space for most of these investors'. My informant was effectively selling a business expansion proposition that drew on their specialist knowledge of cattle production in the unique environment of Northern Australia, and using which a nonspecialist investor could profitably buy and sell very large cattle properties, build a growing cattle enterprise and intensify the business through infrastructure development. They proposed not the static sale of a single farm, but a partnership in which the investor would finance a plan of expansion and development. This involved 'identifying potential assets to expand with, and trying to keep them live or partially live while [we were] trying to raise the capital' such that they were trying to 'raise capital for something [we didn't] actually have'. This is a process associated with capitalisation or, more narrowly defined, assetisation (Birch 2017; Muniesa et al. 2017), in which a shift occurs from valuing something as a commodity – whose value is derived from the sum of its parts – to valuing something as an asset, whose value is derived from its projected income generation potential. This process was driven largely by the farm enterprise themselves as they reorganised their systems to anticipate investor needs.

Negotiating a Partnership

Over the three years that the farm business worked with the consulting firm seeking equity investors, they engaged in initial negotiations with numerous potential investors, in some cases proceeding so far as to enter exclusive periods. However, they ultimately chose not to proceed with these investors for various reasons, both professional and interpersonal. In particular, the informant emphasised the importance of being 'culturally aligned' and described how they had pulled out of some negotiations because 'you know, if it doesn't feel right, its generally not right'. By the time that the farm business met with the pension fund with whom they ultimately formed the partnership, they had spent substantial funds and undertaken many years of work, and reported being exhausted by the process:

> we ended up meeting [the pension fund]. We were quite fatigued of the process at that stage, to be honest, but we'd spent so much time and money and effort on it at that stage it was sort of like, where do you start and stop? . . . [But] to my family's absolute credit, we were in the market long enough to find a really great partner.

They then entered into a negotiation process with the pension fund, in which a range of features of the structure of the new business were negotiated – namely, how much control the farmer retains in managing the business, the division of ownership between the investor and the family, and the processes for making financial decisions, including, in particular, the terms on which the investor could exit the partnership. In these decisions, the farmer seeks to set up a sustainable long-term structure that offers them control over farm management decisions and the capacity to develop a sustainable long-term business structure. The investor seeks to optimise the returns they earn from income and to negotiate an agreement that will allow them to exit the partnership – and earn the returns on their investment – at an acceptable time. The interests of the farm business and the sophisticated institutional investor did not always align, and in some cases required the amelioration of competing priorities. To negotiate a beneficial arrangement for the farm business, they required substantial resources and technical ability. Although investors may have previously undertaken such negotiations, farmers forming private equity partnerships are very likely to be doing so for the first time, such that expert advisors are essential to address this imbalance. As my informant described, 'you obviously need advisors on your side and lawyers to ensure that you're trying to negotiate as aggressively as possible to make sure that you are in control' and to 'protect yourself going into a deal'.

In this case, the accountancy firm arranged for the provision of appropriate expertise. The farm business emphasised the importance of getting 'the best advice in the market', suggesting that it is advisable 'to pay a couple of hundred thousand dollars more for the right advice because they will save you millions in the way they structure a deal for you'. They suggested that 'one of the Achilles' heels of agriculture, and the ability of agriculture to attract more large, viable, stable streams of equity funding, is . . . resistance to paying good money for good advice'. This highlights the importance of intermediaries such as lawyers and finance professionals in structuring investment in agriculture. It is worth examining the work that such professionals do – the assumptions they make, the calculative devices they employ, the tools they use and the information they draw upon, as these features influence the way that investment enters – and leaves – Australian agriculture, and the outcomes that it has for local places.

Having said that, the farm CEO nonetheless played a key role in negotiations, and the success of the partnership was largely a result of the substantial skill they developed during the equity-seeking process. They described how they had to learn to operate effectively in financial spaces:

> I had a teleconference once with twenty-nine people on it. Twenty-nine people! Three different law firms, two of the 'big four' accounting firms, ourselves, and [the pension fund] represented on the call . . . I don't know if you're into horses, but we talk about 'loping' horses, they 'lope' horses, they 'lope' and canter them slowly around in circles before they show them to take the edge off them. I was pretty much loped to death by that stage! It was just part of the process, it was just, 'Whatever! Another day of teleconferences!'

In these negotiations, it was the farmer rather than the investment firm who moved between rural and financial spaces, often virtually, and who had to learn to blend specialist production and financial knowledge. These features highlight the importance of farmer agency to these negotiations, and the limits to the replication of this model more broadly across Australia.

In addition, the consultancy firm handled many aspects of the negotiation and had a significant influence on the structure of the final business. This firm drew on global networks of investors, organised meetings, balanced the interests of different clients and used a range of templates, reports and calculative tools to structure their work (see Higgins 2006; Henry 2017; Henry and Scott 2017), all of which shaped the final structure of the partnership. The work was undertaken by people in the organisation who had individual experiences and moral judgements related to their work and exerted agency in different ways within it (see Ho 2009; Ortiz 2014). These aspects of the partnership formation remain unexamined in this case study – they are 'black boxed' (Ouma 2016), yet they are powerful shapers of farmer–investor engagement. Given the key role that these human and nonhuman actors play in shaping investment forms, further attention to these details would be useful in understanding the factors that shape financial investment in farmland.

The Capitalised Farm Family Business

After concluding the somewhat adversarial negotiations, the investor and farm manager began working together. They described the disjunct between these two phases:

> as a private enterprise when you're negotiating against a [multi]billion-dollar firm with highly sophisticated lawyers, investment bankers and everything else, and then you've got to pivot at the end of all of that and go into a business partnership where you've got great relationships, [this] is an extraordinary feat.

My informant expressed a great deal of enthusiasm for the working relationships they then developed with the pension fund. Although they had initially been ambivalent about the source of the investment, in practice they found that having strong working relationships were extremely important to the operation of the business, for both effective professional communication and for their enjoyment of their role. As they described:

> You've got to find a good partner in life, and we're very lucky in that we found someone that was culturally aligned, and it just works beautifully . . . What's the point of doing it otherwise, right? I mean there's enough stress in day-to-day business without having to deal with someone who actually doesn't understand or *get* you.

How to Get an Investor • 117

They described the outcome of the partnership as 'a wild success', saying that the equity parentship gave them access to large amounts of capital for expansion, through the purchase of additional properties, and development, through additional infrastructure such as fencing and watering points. This enabled them to 'buy the land, buy the livestock, have an operating business and simultaneously, as aggressively as possible, develop that land'. This fulfils the ideal scenario expected from equity partnerships, in which capital is sought to develop the industry (Heath and Tomlinson 2015).

I have suggested that this form of family–finance partnership can be characterised as a 'capitalised farm family entrepreneur' (Langford 2019, 484). This is building on the work of Pritchard et al., who in 2007 suggested that farms were not always clearly identifiable as family or corporate-owned, but that these categories overlap, creating new and unique hybrid structures. The case study presented here, of a family farm that transformed into an equity partnership with an institutional investor, is exemplative of a similar hybridity, this time of family, corporate and financial farm ownership.

In a follow-up interview conducted sometime after the initial story had been told to me, I asked the CEO whether they still considered their business to be a family business. Clearly somewhat frustrated by what must be a common question, they stated that:

> I explain us as an Australian-owned company, run by a family, funded by foreign capital, that's how we explain ourselves . . . [two family members] are executives in the business, we are running the business and we are the original family . . . So when you ask the question, do we still think we are a family business, *yes we absolutely do approach this as a family business and we try to operate it like it is a family business to the extent possible being a large business.*

To them, operating the business as a family meant an integration of productive and financial management. As my informant described, 'I can still go and change a pipe fitting if I need to, I can strain a fence, but I can also run the business at the executive level', which they contrasted with corporate models in which businesses were made by executives who had limited production expertise. Although they had previously emphasised the importance of formalising family roles in the business, it was clear that the nuclear family played a key role in negotiating the structure of the business, with decisions made 'as a family'. When asked which of these the CEO represented, they replied that they represented all these interests simultaneously, conceding that:

> It sounds like a very politically correct answer, but it's actually just a matter of fact. We [the CEO and the COO] do represent the best interests of the

company and by doing so we automatically are representing the best interests of [the family] and the [institutional investor].

This shift was enabled by a perceived alignments of the objectives of the family, the company and the institutional investor, which in turn was formalised by a business structure that prioritised the longevity of the company over quick speculative returns. Here, the role of the family is as owners of *and investors in* the new capitalised business, reflective of emergent farmer–investor subjectivities. The business neither remains as a traditional family farm business, nor is it fully separated from family ownership and control, suggesting emergent forms of farm business hybridity.

Farmer Agency in Financialisation

As such, it is worth asking how common are such new financially funded hybrid structures, and how likely is it that they will continue to emerge? Given the policy support for this model of development (Commonwealth of Australia 2015; Department of Agriculture and Water Resources 2018), there are important implications revealed by this case study. First, the case of this farm family challenges the historical view that family farmers are uniformly subsumed by large corporate interests and that those who continue to farm 'have been unwittingly enrolled into transnational networks on terms that render them powerless against multinational corporations' (Cheshire and Woods 2013, 240). Rather, as a number of studies have shown, innovative and entrepreneurial farmers endeavour to adapt to changing circumstances by proactively working to organise supply chains beyond the farm gate (Johnsen 2004; Pritchard et al. 2007; Magnan 2012; Cheshire and Woods 2013; Weller, Smith and Pritchard 2013; Williams 2014; Woods 2014). This case study highlights how exceptional farmers who are able to valorise their niche farming expertise are in a position to 'to work within and benefit from a financialized food system' (Williams 2014, 407), exploiting options created by broader processes of globalisation and financialisation (see also Magnan 2012; Cheshire and Woods 2013; Sommerville 2018).

The family farm business I describe here was able to mobilise substantial financial resources accumulated through the incremental and long-term development of a successful family business in pursuit of an equity partnership that enabled the family to much more rapidly expand and develop the business. The process of equity seeking was undertaken over many years and at substantial expense, and required a member of the farm business to develop extensive financial expertise on top of their existing productive expertise. What they sold to the investor was their knowledge of agricultural production and their ability to strategise in relation to the buying and selling, and development of properties. What the investor offered was access to a large pool of capital to enable them to, first, take advantage of property cycles, in which farm prices can undergo extreme changes, and, second, develop these stations quickly to enable improved productivity. This created a temporal shift in the management of the business, in which the farm business is able to move much more quickly to take advantage of seasonal shifts in the industry. The business is a significant player in the Northern Australian pastoral industry, and their activities have a noticeable effect on the organisation of the industry. This highlights how the work of one family can noticeably affect the patterns of financialisation in Northern Australia.

The exceptional experience of this family also highlights the limits of this approach to financing for a wider cohort of Australian farmers. Most family cattle farms in Northern Australia are much smaller, have less financial resources and may not have the capacity or interest to undertake these extensive and difficult processes. My informant emphasised the significance of 'the journey, emotionally and personally, for myself and my family', and likened their experience to undertaking 'a PhD in capital raising' undertaken over many years, with no clear model to follow. In addition to these resource constraints, my informant felt that many farmers were also unwilling to make the changes required to attract an investment partner in relation to relinquishing control of some aspects of the business. As they described, 'they say "oh, it would be a great idea to get more foreign investment in the industry" . . . but until the industry becomes less emotive about their ownership structures, I don't see it happening on any great scale'. They felt frustrated that 'people who are actually willing to make the sacrifices and cede technical control to another party is very limited' and suggested that it was this unwillingness to cede control that excluded many farmers from private equity markets.

This evidence suggests that farmer agency plays an important role in shaping the form of financial investment in Australian land – farmers who are willing and capable of undertaking equity-seeking processes are in a position to gain substantial influence over resources that enable the development of large businesses of a form that they see as different in nature from other corporate enterprises. Similarly, farmers who are unwilling or incapable of undertaking these processes can reject opportunities to form hybrid farm structures, which may lead to foreign capital being enrolled in Australian farms on different scales and in different forms. Equity partnerships, while widely promoted as an emerging solution to the capital needs of Australian farming, appear in practice to be difficult to negotiate. Those exceptional farmers who can navigate this process are well placed to influence the development of Australian rural spaces, while other farmers may exert their agency to resist the formation of these partnerships, which may reduce investment in

Australian land or redirect it to other forms of investment, such as own-lease out models or investments in other parts of the supply chain. What is clear is that farmer agency plays an important role in assembling the financialisation of Australian agriculture.

Chapter 7

'UNLOCKING' THE INDIGENOUS ESTATE

Remote Indigenous Business Development Strategies

One of the defining features of new efforts towards Northern Development is the growing involvement of Indigenous corporations in the establishment of agricultural business ventures. Historically, Indigenous people have featured in agricultural development efforts largely as sources of labour, particularly in the pastoral industry and in missionary-led efforts to develop market gardens. Today, however, there is increasing legal recognition of Indigenous land rights and aspirations of Indigenous corporations to use these new entitlements as development assets. Legal recognition of Indigenous land rights has been possible since 1976 in the NT and 1993 in Queensland and WA. Since then, Indigenous Australians have successfully claimed legally recognised rights to a land area representing over 30% of Northern Australia – some 700km^2 (Australian Government 2015a, 16). However, for many Indigenous people, these land rights have not resulted in significant improvements in welfare and access to opportunities, and many remote Indigenous Australians are still unable to access essential goods and services (Dale 2014, 11). Remote living Indigenous Australians have very poor overall health outcomes (Australian Government 2020; Australian Institute of Health and Welfare 2022) and there is a severe lack of employment skills and opportunities which means that only one-third of remote Indigenous Australians are employed in market-based jobs (Gray and Hunter 2011).

As a result of this, Indigenous land-based business development has been described as 'the next phase of land rights in Australia' (Australian Government 2015b, 6), as Indigenous groups work towards '"unlocking" the Indigenous estate' to enable them to 'enjoy the rightful entitlements, opportunities and benefits that the return of country and its management brings' (Indigenous Land and Sea Corporation (ILSC) 2021, 4). The Indigenous business sector has grown rapidly over the last decade; however, much of the growth has been concentrated in certain industries where incentives have been created by the Indigenous Procurement Policy (Langford 2023). Remote businesses, while fewer in number, often provide wider social benefits.

For example, regional and remote businesses registered with Supply Nation, a national database and certifier of Indigenous business, are more than twice as likely to hire Indigenous workers as businesses located in major cities (Langford 2023). Remote businesses are therefore seen as a way to provide employment and training opportunities to remote Indigenous people, alongside generating wealth for their Indigenous owners (Commonwealth of Australia 2021). Of particular interest are natural resource-based businesses that provide both employment and opportunities to work 'on country'[1] in roles that are perceived to overlap with cultural values and responsibilities (Fleming, Petheram and Stacey 2015; Austin and Garnett 2018). However, Indigenous corporations seeking to develop agricultural businesses face the same environmental challenges as other corporations in Northern Australia, as well as additional costs associated with the provision of other social benefits to remote communities. Much of the Indigenous estate is extremely remote, with limited infrastructure and long distances from markets. These lands are therefore not the prime farmland usually targeted for investment by financial entities. Such entities typically seek an enterprise with established profit streams and a comprehensive management solution in which to invest funds. Indigenous corporations must therefore be highly strategic if they wish to develop profitable agricultural activities.

There are three approaches to agribusiness development that are commonly pursued by remote Indigenous businesses in order to overcome these high production costs.[2] First, Indigenous businesses may pursue a strategy of import substitution. In this case, they seek to produce foods for consumption by the local community. The high cost of importing foods to remote communities means that fresh food in remote areas is often very expensive. As a result, locally produced food can be sold at a higher price in nearby retail markets than if it were exported to urban locations, and has the additional advantage of reduced transport costs. Food production for local consumption is therefore one approach to managing high production costs in remote areas. There is of course a trade-off here, where the price of locally produced foods, if too high, has minimal benefits for local consumers, and if too low may undermine business profitability; Indigenous corporations pursuing this strategy therefore need to balance business sustainability with other welfare goals. It is worth noting here that this approach, while advocated at a policy level (see e.g. Communicable Diseases Network Australia (CDNA) 2021), has been met with limited success in the context of fruit and vegetables (see Fitzgerald 2016b), although the local supply of meat has had some success (Pearson and Liu 2016).

The second approach is to produce high-value niche products, which can be sold at high prices in urban and international markets, particularly if these leverage Indigenous branding opportunities. This approach involves the production of small volumes of high-value goods in which Indigenous communities have a competitive advantage, by virtue of either being the only suppliers of those goods or by capitalising on Indigenous branding to increase the appeal of the products. In the agricultural sector, a well-known example is the Kakadu plum, a fruit that grows wild across several Indigenous regions in Northern Australia and has gained notoriety in recent years for its high Vitamin C content and distinct flavour (Gorman 2021). There are other examples of wildlife-based enterprise development – for example, sea cucumbers (Fleming, Petheram and Stacey 2015), crocodile eggs (Corey et al. 2018) and buffalo mustering (Austin and Garnett 2011) – and this type of work is appealing to many remote Indigenous people (Zander et al. 2014). Indigenous corporations can develop profitable enterprises based on this approach due to their monopoly control over key resources, use of Indigenous branding and marketing to access higher prices (Jarvis, Maclean and Woodward 2022), but are often reliant on additional grant funding that is available based on the social benefits of employment.

The third approach is to undertake industrial-scale agricultural production. This approach gains its competitive advantage from pursuing economies of scale that reduce the variable costs of production and marketing, while benefiting from the low value of remote land. Targeting of economies of scale is a common theme across Northern Australian development efforts and has mostly been met with limited success. This approach often requires high levels of initial capital investment and uses large areas of land, creating a need for financing. The high-capital, high-risk nature of these enterprises generally necessitates equity finance (as opposed to debt, which is suitable to lower-risk ventures).[3] This is the approach that sees Indigenous corporations pursuing private investment and is the subject of this chapter.

Assetisation as a Development Approach

Chapter 3 explored the ways in which Northern Australian agriculture is being framed as an investment proposition, espousing a view of development as a 'partnership' between investors and governments (Australian Government 2015a, 2–3). Government development efforts include a substantial focus on attracting investors, in which investors are allocated responsibility for determining what and where development should take place. A similar process can be seen occurring on Indigenous land in Northern Australia. The Northern and Central Land Councils (the Native Title Representative Bodies and Service Providers[4] (NTRB-SPs) responsible for the majority of land in the NT) are pursuing this approach. They identified a need for intermediating bodies that would facilitate partnerships between Indigenous groups and investors, as the then CEO of the Northern Land Council (NLC) described in 2016:

> what is the process of developing the identified opportunity? How would an investor or operator approach a partnership with Aboriginal landowners? Are there any specific legal or regulatory requirements? How would the costs of engagement in the project be calculated? What are the timeframes involved? Is there, in fact, any roadmap to guide investors and operators? And finally, who is managing the process [and] who is the contact point for information, assistance and organization? (Lange 2017, n.p.)

Since this time, a range of partially and totally government-funded intermediating bodies have been tasked with performing this role. These include the appointment of private sector bodies to support projects on Indigenous Land (such as the Land Development Corporation), the performance of this work by government departments (in Arnhem land), the use of consultants by Indigenous corporations in Queensland and WA, and the establishment of new private development organisations in the NT (such as the Aboriginal Land Economic Development Agency (ALEDA) and the funding of research projects (such as the North Australian Indigenous Land and Sea Management Alliance (NAILSMA) Business on Country programme). These bodies are engaged in processes of assetisation, in which particular parcels of land are targeted as potential investment opportunities. The simplest assetisation processes involves basic leases over land, while more involved assets include joint ventures on Indigenous land. There is even the case of the development of a managed fund of Indigenous agribusinesses, representing an advanced stage of assetisation. Some of these bodies are engaged across the whole asset-making process, while others are involved only in certain stages. Assetisation is best thought of as a continuum, where investor and local control depends on the extent, and type, of asset-making work undertaken (see Figure 7.1). The form that Indigenous land-based assets take depends on a range of factors, including the aspirations and financial and technical capacity of the asset-maker, and the desires of the investor. These assets are being constructed in unique environmental and cultural settings, often involving

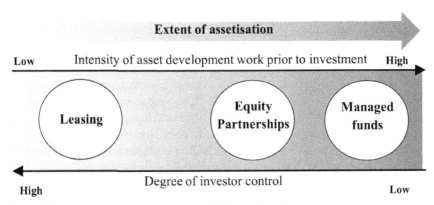

Figure 7.1. Assetisation as a continuum. © Zannie Langford

extended processes of negotiation between a large group of stakeholders, including Traditional Owners (TOs) and other resident Indigenous people, investors and professionals such as banks, valuers, government funders, farm managers, agricultural consultants, government land and water management individuals, Indigenous corporations and Indigenous overseeing bodies such as land councils and NTRB-SPs.

These diverse stakeholders have a range of imaginaries of 'what land is, can, and should be' (Sippel and Visser 2021, 271) and their negotiations can produce various results (Magnan 2012, Sommerville and Magnan 2015). The processes of assetisation described in this chapter are still ongoing; few have resulted in investment deals. As such, it is not possible to assess the outcomes of this approach to development and the ways in which they are likely to shape, and be shaped by, remote communities with which they interact. Instead, this chapter offers insights into a particular moment in Indigenous economic development in which the potential for asset-making is being explored and tested. Negotiations over investment opportunities and structures represent a space of 'friction' where 'heterogeneous and unequal encounters can lead to new arrangements of culture and power' (Tsing 2005, 5). The work described here may result in the development of powerful 'scripting devices' for organising the assetisation of Indigenous land across Northern Australia more broadly (Latour 1992). Such pathways, once formed, become accepted processes by which later negotiations are expected to proceed, both facilitating and limiting future processes of assetisation. They 'make motion easier and more efficient, but in doing so they limit where we go. The ease . . . they facilitate is also a structure of confinement' (Tsing 2004, 6). Indeed, some of these approaches developed in one area have already been applied by other Indigenous groups. However, it is also possible that the processes described here may fail to result in significant investments and could represent a moment in financialised development trends that comes to be of little historical significance. As discussed in the early chapters of this book, large-scale agricultural development projects have historically had limited success in Northern Australia, so their inevitability of their occurrence is far from assured. It is nonetheless worth examining the processes of assetisation being undertaken to explore this approach to Indigenous development. Investment-led approaches to rural development (such as impact investment for development) are growing in popularity (Suehrer 2019) and it is likely that the processes through which such investments are negotiated in Northern Australia will affect future development pathways.

Asset-Making in Practice

In order for land to be able to be held as an asset, it needs to have certain characteristics that render it both profitable and fungible. Land does not naturally have these characteristics – rather, significant sociotechnical work goes into creating and maintaining them. Visser (2017) proposed a typology of asset-making, in which he described five characteristics of land that must be met in order for farmland to become an investible product with attached streams of future income. His five typologies are: potential for profit, liquidity, scarcity, standardisation and legitimisation. I proposed an additional typology for social enterprises: impact (Langford, Lawrence and Smith 2021). The establishment of these components is necessary to transform land into an asset, and failure to establish any of them may undermine the viability of the asset. This framework can be usefully applied to frame examination of asset-making processes being undertaken on Indigenous land in Northern Australia.

Potential for Profit: Marketing Development Potential

Creating an asset from remote Indigenous land first requires that the potential to profit from the land be established. This is a nontrivial task in very remote areas of Northern Australia where there has been limited past development of successful, profitable agribusiness. The profitability of the land is dependent on a range of biophysical, economic and social characteristics. First, it must be capable of producing something, which typically requires a combination of suitable soil types, availability of water for irrigation, appropriate weather patterns and low levels of risks associated with biosecurity, natural disasters and pests. In addition, there should be available expertise in the cultivation of land with these characteristics and species of plants that are able to grow in these environments. Once these biophysical characteristics have been met, it is necessary to establish the economic viability of production. Factors such as proximity to markets, available transport infrastructure, power access, irrigation infrastructure and costs of inputs, and price of the goods in regional and international markets affect the economic viability of a proposed development. Finally, there are a range of social factors relating to the surrounding community, such as the availability and interest of a suitable labour force and their skill base and training needs. Meeting these requirements is nontrivial: much of the Indigenous estate includes marginal lands that are not prime targets for agricultural production – in many cases, it was this marginal suitability for production that made it possible for Indigenous rights to be granted (NAILSMA 2019; Pedersen and Phillpot 2019). Second, much of the Indigenous estate is very remote. In many areas it is common for road access to be cut off during part of the year, transport tends to be very expensive, and power and other enabling infrastructure are often limited. Finally, there is typically a limited availability of a suitable labour force, and training needs tend to be very high, even for relatively low-skilled jobs. In addition, local populations often require greater flexibility around labour hire arrangements, which can make it difficult for business owners to secure the reliable workforce required to operate an agricultural business. These environmental, economic and social factors do not lend themselves to the development of profitable businesses that would provide the secure income streams required by investors (see Leyshon and Thrift 2007). As a result, business development on remote Indigenous lands is highly dependent on individual entrepreneurship. The 'Developing Northern Australia' programme approach to development involves marketing the region to investors, who are tasked with identifying opportunities for greenfield developments (Australian Government 2015a). Indigenous asset-makers typically draw heavily on the discursive work done as part of this programme to market their opportunities to potential investors. In particular, there is frequent use of four tropes promoted by the Northern Australia development agenda: the region as an area of 'underutilization', the region as Australia's 'gateway to Asia', the availability of 'free' water, and the notion of a 'clean and green' environment. In addition, the use of Indigenous branding is promoted as a potential value-adding opportunity.

Underutilisation

The Australian government's 'value proposition' for Northern Development is 'Northern Australia: Emerging opportunities in an advanced economy' (Austrade 2015, 1), implying a similarity between rural Northern Australia and emerging economies that many agricultural investments have targeted. This portrays the region as containing unrealised value that can be quickly

128 • Assembling Financialisation

extracted through the application of capital. Private commentators have also commented on this potential, calling the Northern Australian cropping development a 'special case' in which substantially 'undervalued' land is available in an advanced economy such as Australia (Byerlee and Deininger 2011; 2013). The promise here is that investors can profit through gaining control of land at a price that is substantially below its value. While Indigenous land is inalienable and thus cannot be bought, it may be possible to profit from increases in the value of businesses operating on the land (if the land can be put to productive use) and through monopoly control (without ownership) of land (as occurs for pastoral leaseholds). However, such narratives ignore the challenges associated with developing farms in remote locations such that 'a diverse array of land types in a great many places is homogenized and aggregated under a new label: their underutilization' (Li 2014, 592). There has been less development of technologies, genetics and farming strategies in Northern Australia and as one farm consultant put it, potential investors and new farmers need to have a 'budget for learning' the new environment. This complicates narratives of Northern Australia as a setting for profitable speculative investments.

A 'Gateway to Asia'

The proximity of Northern Australia to Asia and its 'booming middle income markets' (Australian Government 2015a, 57) is widely promoted as a selling point for the region. According to the White Paper, it is Australia's 'gateway to Asia' (Australian Government 2015a, 169) and its 'closest connection with our key trading markets and the global scale changes occurring in Asia' (Australian Government 2015a, 1). The physical proximity of Asia is emphasised in these efforts, which note that 'south east Asia and southern China are within three to five hours flying time from Darwin', 'the north operates in similar time zones to the most dynamic economies in Asia' and that 'the region is integrating fast' through Free Trade Agreements (Australian Government 2015a, 1). However, as one government official observed, this discourse is at present just 'spin', because currently most of the horticultural produce from Northern Australia is transported by road to cities in Southern Australia before being flown overhead to Asian markets. Despite the physical proximity of Northern Australia to Asia, produce from this region typically travels further to reach Asia, since the North does not currently have large enough export volumes to make direct transport viable. Despite this, marketing materials frequently include imagery highlighting the proximity of Northern Australia, and Darwin in particular, to Asia.

'Free' Water

Another key 'value proposition' of the North is the large amount of rainfall it receives annually. If this water could be stored and distributed, it would provide opportunities for irrigated agriculture on a large scale. The White Paper emphasises this as a major benefit of agricultural production in Northern Australia, noting that annual rainfall represents 'enough water to fill a bucket the size of the Melbourne Cricket Ground to a height of more than 80,000 km, or more than 20 per cent of the way to the moon' (Australian Government 2015a: 40). This certainly sounds like a lot of water, and for producers familiar with the high water prices in much of Southern Australia, the prospect of 'free' water is appealing. In some areas of the NT, investors have been able to gain access to large quantities of free water as a result of the underallocation of groundwater in some regions, which sees water licences allocated at no cost. However, this situation is limited to certain groundwater basins, and it is not universal across the North. In addition, it is important to avoid 'fetishising' certain assets (Visser 2017). Focusing on irrigation water in isolation ignores the range of other factors required to enable production, such as soils, seasonality and actual processes of water capture, storage and distribution. For many locations across Northern Australia, accessing the promised 'free' water is a greater challenge than it immediately appears. Nonetheless, the possibility of water access is commonly used to promote Northern Australia as an investment destination.

'Clean, Green, Premium and Safe' Australia

Third, it is common for investment-seekers to emphasise Australia's reputation as a producer of 'clean, green, premium and safe' agricultural produce (Austrade 2015, 14). This involves emphasising both the purity of remote Northern environments and their biosecurity benefits. For example, the Tiwi Islands investment prospectus emphasises the 'pristine ground water and surface water', the availability of 'greenfield land that has not previously been developed' and the area's 'bio-security due to the isolation from the mainland' (Land Development Corporation 2017, 20). Similarly, a non-Indigenous initiative, the Humpty Doo Barramundi farm, emphasises its location 'alongside the majestic Adelaide River in Australia's remote Northern Territory' and its 'award-winning saltwater wetland system' that 'uses natural grasses to clean the water for recirculation through the farm, delivering optimum quality water for high quality Barramundi' (Humpty Doo Barramundi 2022). Such perceptions of Northern Australia as a pristine wilderness location can be used by businesses to attract higher prices, drawing on Australia's reputation abroad as a producer of 'clean and green' produce

(Cocklin, Dibden and Gibbs 2008). The branding opportunities afforded by this reputation offer a potential source of profitability if they can be used to attract premium pricing. Similarly, the remoteness of Northern Australian locations alongside Australia's well-regarded biosecurity practices suggest a comparative advantage relative to regions affected by diseases – as Austrade's 'investment proposition' material emphasises, 'Australia is free from many exotic pests and diseases prevalent across the tropics. Effective biosecurity has enhanced Australia's reputation as an exporter of high-quality, clean and safe agricultural produce' (Austrade 2015, 14). However, it is worth noting that several of Northern Australia's large agricultural development schemes have failed *because* of interference by pests and wildlife (Ash 2014), a fact that is not emphasised in investment brochures. Rather, investment-seekers draw mainly on perceptions of Northern Australia as a pristine location for production in order to imply potential for profit.

Indigenous Branding

Finally, options to use branding of products as 'Indigenous produced' offer a potential value-adding opportunity, particularly for the supply of niche products to high-value markets, such as bush foods to restaurants (Craw 2008; Moginon, See and Saad 2012). There is a growing body of consumers willing to pay premium prices for food products that offer certifications of environmental sustainability or social benefit (Li and Kallas 2021). However, the use of this branding raises issues such as how Indigenous branding should be used, what qualifies producers to draw on it, what kinds of benefits should accrue to Indigenous people and how these should be distributed (see Drahos and Frankel 2012). One study of Australia's bush food industry found very limited participation in the industry by Indigenous people (Mitchell and Becker 2019), raising issues concerning the ethical use of Indigenous branding. In addition, there are strategic issues relating to how to capitalise on opportunities for Indigenous branding in markets for products not typically associated with Indigenous culture. It may be the case that such branding opportunities are limited to niche markets for products associated with Indigenous culture, and that attempts to employ this branding more broadly may result in limited success.

These five tropes are frequently used to promote the potential for profit of the region – by imagining remote Northern Australian locations as the so-far-undiscovered site of production for growing Asian markets, with free water, an unspoilt landscape and social benefits for resident populations, it is possible to imagine the profitability of the investment proposition. However, to realise actual future streams of income, would-be investors also need to solve a range of nontrivial environmental and socioeconomic challenges. In addition to the use of marketing tools, some Indigenous organisations are working towards 'solving' some of these practical challenges by developing business development planning documents.

Business Opportunity Development

The second thing that some asset-makers and intermediating bodies are doing to establish and communicate potential for profit is to undertake some of the work required to scope out potential for viable businesses. This often involves engaging independent bodies to undertake some of the work required to assess the potential of the land for business development. This less optimistic, more incremental approach typically leads to the identification of opportunities that have already been proven to work in the region rather than 'blue sky' thinking favoured by more investor-led approaches. There is a movement towards the development of an overarching Indigenous 'prospectus' for business development and investment opportunities on their lands. Such a prospectus would facilitate greater Indigenous participation in asset-making processes by both undertaking land assessment work to facilitate investments and by facilitating discussion on the types and conditions of developments that would be desirable. NAILSMA outlined a vision for this prospectus, which would be designed:

> to place Indigenous people in a stronger and clearer negotiating position, where they can determine the conditions under which they will invest their land, knowledge and futures in commercial ventures and, just as critically, the conditions that co-investors will need to meet to access Indigenous assets . . . [it] will provide the opportunities rather than the barriers to northern development, including the identification of selected development and investment opportunities. (2013, 28)

The recent 'Business on Country' initiative has pursued this approach, aiming to 'position traditional landholders to invite investment when they are satisfied that they understand the options available to them' (Archer 2020, 5). In a recent report, the initiative emphasised that 'Business on Country is not "Business as usual"', but will require sustained funding and support (NAILSMA 2020a). The project has developed three land use plans for land rights holders in Queensland – for the Western Yalanji, the planning resulted in an industry focus on cultural tourism, carbon farming, and land and heritage management programmes (NAILSMA 2020b); for the Balngarrawarra, a focus on cultural tourism, carbon farming, environmental and conservation services, and beef enterprises (NAILSMA 2020c); and for the Waanyi and Garawa, a focus on 'land and sea services business – minor earth works and grading', carbon farming and payments for ecosystems services (PES) and 'activities that complement the existing cattle operation on the Garawa land trust' (NAILSMA 2020d). There is not a strong focus on greenfield agricultural development projects by these groups (which is reflective of environmental constraints), but rather a focus on land management service provision and cattle grazing. This represents a more comprehensive asset-making process than those that merely draw on broader tropes about Northern Australian development.

Scarcity

In order for land to take the form of an asset, it must not only be profitable but also scarce enough for demand to outstrip supply such that the asset can appreciate in value (Visser 2017). However, in moves to develop greenfield agricultural projects in Northern Australia, land availability is typically not a key constraint, since agricultural and horticultural developments typically occur on much smaller areas than cattle grazing, which is the current main use of the land. Rather, it is the intersection of irrigation water availability with suitable soil types and environmental characteristics that limit scope for development. Indigenous groups have legally recognised rights to a very large area of Australia, and this is often emphasised by Indigenous organisations and activists in advocating for increased political influence and resourcing – in Northern Australia, Indigenous people have exclusive control over more than 800,000km², about the size of France and the United Kingdom combined. However, much of this land is not environmentally suitable for production (NAILSMA 2019) and Indigenous people have a range of different relationships with different areas of traditional land, which mean that not all areas are appropriate for development.

The work of establishing scarcity of the land is to make visible the environmental, economic, social and cultural factors that make much of the land unsuitable for development, and thus the scarcity of Indigenous land suitable for agricultural development. However, this process requires that artificial lines be drawn between land that is profitable and land that is not, and this process shapes investment landscapes. As Mehta (2010, 2) observes, 'scarcity is not merely a natural phenomenon that can be isolated from planning models, allocation politics, policy choices, market forces and local power, social and gender dynamics', but is a construct assembled by a range of actors involved in asset-making processes. Establishing scarcity requires that a subset of lands 'affordances' – such as soil characteristics, irrigation water availability, weather patterns, terrain and biosecurity features – are selected and valorised. Choosing these characteristics, measuring them in detail over remote land and mapping the way in which they interact on a large scale is a nontrivial task, and for greenfield projects requires the use of many technical assumptions and projections.

One group that has pioneered this approach is the Land Development Corporation working with Tiwi Island Traditional Owners (TOs) to undertake detailed mapping of the Tiwi Islands. The Corporation began with a map of the total area available on the island, and then through consultation with the Tiwi Islands TOs, excluded culturally and socially important sites, and then identified the most favourable areas of the island for certain key agricultural industries such as buffalo grazing, forestry and fruit and vegetable farms, alongside opportunities for tourism, aquaculture and industrial developments. As part of this process, it undertook extensive surveying of the region alongside TOs and extended community consultations. Once it had identified a number of potential development sites, the remaining land was discarded from consideration, creating a limited selection of potential assets. Through this process, the Tiwi Islands, an available area originally claimed to be '10 times the size of Singapore', was transformed into precisely thirty-six plots of suitable agricultural land (Land Development Corporation 2017, 7, 14–15). Other groups have since taken up this approach; as one person seeking to reproduce the Tiwi Islands approach put it, 'fitting that kind of methodology to here'. One intermediary undertaking such activities explained that:

> The true mission here is to *eliminate* areas. You need to discard areas that would be challenging or hard to develop, because you really want to find the best-case scenario. So you really have to be harsh and *look for reasons to eliminate areas.*

Often a very small team of technical staff were involved in the surveying and assessment processes underpinning these selections, and they worked in contexts in which there was limited existing planning and a lack of detailed official data on the environmental characteristics of the land. They sought to provide the basic planning required to support development in 'a pseudo process of what you'd do in town'. The decisions being made about which of land's characteristics are important and constitute its value, lead to the creation of planning documents that structure land's investability in the long term.

Standardisation

Standardisation is a process by which agricultural assets in a range of different locations and with different characteristics are made comparable. It is an important precursor of liquidity since it situates unique parcels of land within a wider market. Standardizing agricultural investments involves processes of ranking and pricing (see Langford 2022). Ranking involves situating land parcels relative to other land parcels within a global land market such that land-based investments become comparable to each other. In undertaking this process, asset-makers 'produce and enable a new way of thinking about "underutilized land" as a singular thing with qualities and potentials that can be rendered commensurable according to different criteria, and made available for comparison (and investment)' (Li 2014, 593). Intermediaries undertaking this work must select important aspects of land (such as soil characteristics or rainfall) and compare these characteristics to other parcels of land, fitting it into the 'universe' of investment opportunities according to these selected indicators, while also obscuring others deemed unfavourable or unimportant.

Standardisation can be further developed through processes of economic valuation that 'transform ... different qualities into a common metric' (Espeland and Stevens 1998, 314) such as a price. Professional land valuers are engaged for this task and are required to situate parcels of Indigenous land within a marketplace for non-Indigenous land. According to one valuer, they undertake this process 'with a fair bit of difficulty' because much of the Indigenous estate is very remote land with unique environmental, social and economic circumstances, making it difficult to identify comparable parcels of non-Indigenous land. In the absence of data for recent comparable sales, valuers are required to speculate about development futures in Indigenous areas. As one valuer described it:

> [I] had to look at what income was available and the chances of economic development [in that location]. But there's no evidence. [It came down to] what do *I* think this little community is going to be valued at?

Understanding these processes of valuation are important because valuation is not merely a process of objectively assessing land value (Çalışkan and Callon 2009), but is a process of both evaluation (assessment of land value) and valorisation (creation of land value) (Vatin 2013). When a professional valuer reaches a determination of a market price for remote Indigenous land, value is created, since the assessments of these professionals hold weight for investors and other financial intermediaries, such as banks. Once a value is assigned, the land (or leases over it) can be traded and compared to other potential investments based on a comparison of this price with area, remoteness and other key features. These two processes of land standardisation – through direct comparison of key features or by seeking a third-party assessment of its price – are used selectively by different intermediaries to situate potential land-based investments within a wider market for land.

Liquidity

A fourth characteristic of assets is that they must be tradeable. Assets vary in their liquidity, with some assets – for example, large pastoral stations or agricultural ventures that require specialist expertise to manage – having low liquidity and being difficult to sell. Indigenous land in Northern Australia is inalienable, such that it cannot be sold. However, where Indigenous groups have exclusive freehold rights over land, it may be possible to lease that land, and these leases can be bought and sold (with restrictions). The largest areas of Aboriginal freehold land are found in the NT, and it is possible to lease this land for up to 99 years under section 19 of the Land Rights Act. Such lease arrangements are subject to the free, prior and informed consent of the community – an agreement for an area of their land to be leased and thereby made liquid for a defined period of time. Reaching such arrangements is a nontrivial process, since they involve the temporary alienation of a portion of communal land for many years and, as such, establishing this consent, and through it the fungibility of the land, is a key task for asset-makers. As one asset-maker described it:

> The Land Council had always been really reticent about fully interpreting Section 19 and allowing these leases to be unencumbered because the minute they do that, if a project then falls over, a bank, who has a mortgage over – not the land, but over the lease and the business – can assign that to whoever they like, and it might be someone that the TOs don't want on their country . . . [But] the Northern and Central Land Councils decided that with proper consultation, if people make a good decision, fully informed, free prior informed consent – if people decide that's what they want to do, they will allow it. They'll fully interpret the Section 19 of the Land Rights Act . . . which is a breakthrough. It actually means that these leases are fungible.

As a result, these intermediaries are often heavily involved in information and negotiation programmes that make the granting of consent possible. The degree of work involved in this varies across different Indigenous TO groups with different internal governance structures, and in some areas is more complex and contested than others. It also raises important questions about what constitutes free, prior and informed consent for different people (Lange 2017). Several groups indicated that the process of consulting with TOs could take years. During this time, they must also answer important questions about the nature of the lease: under what legal arrangement should it be held? Who enforces loan contracts? Who should govern the lease? And how long should the lease be?

Different intermediaries develop different answers to these questions and must balance a range of practical and moral considerations in order to do so.

Leases up to ninety-nine years are possible under NT legislation, and many private sector actors will request a lease of this term. However, such a long lease is unacceptable to many Aboriginal corporations and, as such, some asset-makers are seeking to implement much shorter leases that are long enough to be acceptable to investors and banks, but short enough to enable communities to take over the management of businesses within the foreseeable future. As one asset-maker put it:

> anyone from the outside . . . they'll want fifty years plus [lease term], which means the land is locked up for fifty years. What we're talking about under this . . . arrangement is fifteen, twenty, twenty-five years . . . it's about a generation. [This] gives people time to decide whether they do want to operate in their own right at the end of that lease. They might decide that they don't, but they have a choice, and they can be in control of their own destiny. So that's about choices, you know.

For such asset-makers, driving the asset-making process, rather than simply responding to investors, was perceived to give them greater control over the development trajectories of the communities they worked with and enabled a genuine form of consent for land liquidity.

After the fungibility of Indigenous land has been established, Indigenous asset-makers must also consider the liquidity of the land-based asset in the same way as non-Indigenous asset-makers. Remote land can be difficult to sell as there are fewer potential buyers of unique agricultural ventures in remote areas. In addition, investors and local communities can have competing interests in this area, since investors seek a high level of liquidity to provide them with the flexibility to sell at a time suitable to them, while communities and local partners have an interest in preventing the sale of their land-based assets to unknown buyers at unpredictable times, since such sales can undermine the viability of the business if the new buyer does not maintain the business development and management strategy of the seller. As one non-Indigenous asset-maker described it:

> any investor who is putting good money into a business is going to structure [their] transaction documents and [their] shareholders agreement to ensure that [they] can actually have an exit at a time suitable to [them]. So you obviously need advisors on your side and lawyers to ensure that you're trying to negotiate as aggressively as possible to make sure that you are in control of the exit strategy. The exit strategy is critical for anybody.

Local partners therefore need to pursue investment structures that provide them with a level of control over the future uses of the assets they develop. This does not necessarily need to involve a controlling ownership stake – as one non-Indigenous asset-maker observed, 'you don't necessarily have to have a controlling interest to control a company . . . there's different ways to structure a deal . . . control comes in many different forms'.

One approach to this problem of liquidity is to develop a company with local representation on the board. Another innovative strategy is being undertaken by the Aboriginal Land Economic Development Agency (ALEDA). ALEDA seeks to develop a managed fund of twenty agribusinesses (six in the pilot phase) across Indigenous land in the NT. While still in development, the plan is that TOs will own part of the fund, the Northern and Central Land Council will own part, and the remainder will be open to investors, which could include private investors, government funds, banks or Aboriginal royalty associations (Centrefarm and TopEndfarm 2019). Although currently funding is being sought from grants and loans, it is anticipated that equity investments will be sought in the future. The managed fund structure would allow investors to trade their stakes in the fund (with some restrictions) without compromising the long-term viability of the individual businesses, thereby establishing greater liquidity for these assets than they would as stand-alone businesses. It has the additional benefits of combining private investment with public grant money (thereby increasing potential-for-profit) and minimising risk through the pooling of a number of different businesses in different industries and geographical areas. This is the first fund of its kind to be proposed on Indigenous lands, and its novel structure has been developed through consultation with key financial intermediaries and consultants, government funding bodies and TOs. This extended asset-making process is being pursued to facilitate investment while balancing community and private sector needs – seeking to make investment both possible and beneficial to communities.

Legitimacy

Asset-makers must also establish the legitimacy of the asset that they construct since investors are increasingly sensitive to negative publicity that they may receive for investing in assets that are perceived to negatively impact communities. As described above, for freehold land, legitimacy is entangled with liquidity since consent is required for land to be leased. In Australia, NTRB-SPs play a central role in overseeing Indigenous development plans. For freehold Indigenous land in the NT, NTRB-SPs oversee development plans and consult with communities to ensure that genuine consent is forthcoming from an appropriate proportion of community members. For Native Title holders (who have rights to land that is not freehold, but over which Indigenous groups have some legally recognised exclusive or non-exclusive rights), NTRB-SPs are similarly involved in negotiating benefits packages when developers seek to change the use of the land in a way that impacts these rights. This is common in the development of mining operations and was also recently undertaken for an area of Legune Stations, where Seafarms sought to develop a large aquaculture operation (now defunct).

The role of NTRB-SPs in overseeing such developments sees them regularly subject to criticisms from TOs wishing to develop areas of land, mainly for the slow pace at which their involvement proceeds. Despite this, they are key intermediaries tasked with establishing the legality and legitimacy of investments and do so through extended negotiations with TOs and communities, driven by a desire to ensure favourable outcomes. Asset-makers who participate in this process seek to have an area of land removed from the political arena. They wish to reach a satisfactory agreement, certify its legitimacy and protect it from future contestation. However, as Li (2014, 591) notes, 'legitimacy can wax and wane', and TOs who were satisfied at one point in time may not remain so as projects develop and their perceptions of costs and benefits change. Legality does not necessarily ensure legitimacy (Visser 2017), and development on communal land is inherently political. NTRB-SPs absorb some reputational risk on behalf of investors by approving certain arrangements and are therefore key intermediaries in the establishment – and communication – of legitimacy to investors. In undertaking negotiations, NTRB-SPs must balance community needs with investor needs, seeking to support development where favourable outcomes for both parties can be achieved. However, it is difficult to predict the actual outcomes of development efforts and, over time, as these developments progress, it may take ongoing effort to maintain the legitimacy of operations through balancing business outcomes with the diverse needs of community members and TOs.

Impact

The five typologies of asset-making described above fit within a typology proposed by Visser (2017). However, for socially orientated enterprises that target investors with nonfinancial as well as financial targets, there is arguably an additional component of asset construction: that of social and/or environmental impact. Many of the intermediaries described in this chapter are targeting not only financially focused investors, but also social impact investors who may be willing to accept lower returns if social benefits accruing from the project can be demonstrated. Impact builds upon, but extends beyond, legitimacy, since it is not merely the absence of contestation, but also the demonstration of tangible benefits. As Busch et al. (2021) argue, it is important to differentiate between genuine impact investments, which have social outcomes as a primary goal of the project, and financially focussed investments that incorporate environmental, social and governance (ESG) aspects within a broader profit-focused approach. Confusing legitimacy with impact runs the risk of 'impact washing' (Busch et al. 2021), in which all investments with ESG components are considered to be impact investments. Nonetheless, both types of investments typically require acceptable financial returns on investment.

Social impact investment markets vary in their sophistication and the degree to which they have developed tangible, measurable indicators of impact. In Northern Australia, measures for demonstrating social impact are at this stage still mostly qualitative. In general, benefits such as employment opportunities, training opportunities, service provision or infrastructure development are targeted, which can represent an important social benefit in remote places with small labour markets and high training needs. However, in practice actual benefits are difficult to specify in advance and need to be negotiated with investors on a case-by-case basis. Since few of the initiatives discussed here have reached the investment-seeking phase, most do not yet have explicit criteria for measuring social impact due to the uncertainty of the types of developments that might occur. This depends on the degree of assetisation work being undertaken independently by the asset-making organisations (see Figure 7.1 above) with some groups – such as those taking the 'prospectus approach' – leaving the negotiation of actual benefits to a later stage in the project. By contrast, others are developing fully established businesses in which to seek investment, and in doing so need to define the benefits that will accrue (such as the number and type of employment and training opportunities). For such projects, defining and demonstrating impact is important for both attracting finance, and for ensuring that businesses actually generate benefits for communities. As one interviewee noted:

> it's a grassroots strategy, it's not a government imposed top-down thing, you know? And that's what we believe will make it successful. It's coming from the mob [Indigenous people] themselves, you know?

This requires an assessment of the trade-off between providing social benefits and business financial viability. One asset-maker observed that in remote areas, the costs of developing businesses and providing social benefits was so high that it 'only makes sense if we get massive concessional finance' to improve the financial viability of the projects. Another argued that there was a gap in the impact investment space where social enterprises undertaking industrial agriculture were not seen as sufficiently in need of government support to acquire it, and nor were they profitable enough to secure private investment. They observed that government funding was targeting only the businesses most in need of support, such that 'under the current system of funding these projects, if you do get them funded, it means that they're not sustainable, they're likely to fall over. And that's not on'. Indigenous organisations therefore vary in terms of the extent that they are engaging in work to define and communicate impact of potential assets, and in many cases struggle with balancing communicating profitability to private sector investments with communicating social need and benefits to public sources of investment.

Finance-Led Development Approaches

This chapter has explored some of the work being undertaken to construct assets based on Indigenous land. This approach to development involves private funds being sought for developments that will generate social and economic gains. In addition to a financialisation *of* development, in which development funds are not invested directly in projects but are devoted to attracting private investment for projects (Mawdsley 2017), it can be considered an approach by Indigenous corporations to participating in financialisation *for* development (Langford, Lawrence and Smith 2021). This is a response to a lack of progress on many important social and development indicators that sees Indigenous organisations searching for new approaches to development. As this chapter discusses, it involves work to actively assemble assets for financial investment in pursuit of local development goals. However, in doing so, it expands the reach of global finance into remote geographies in ways that have been associated with financialisation. Paradoxically, asset-makers who may politically oppose this financialised approach to development participate in it through asset-making work. As the then Northern Land Council CEO Joe Morrison put it:

> are we letting governments off the hook by encouraging royalty holders to spend their own money on amenities and programs to benefit their own communities? Whether that's the case or not, we know that it's not worth waiting around for governments to deliver. (Morrison 2016, n.p.)

A lack of sustained, direct public funding for development projects sees individuals searching for approaches to development such as those described here. However, asset-making for industrial agriculture is just one approach to rural agricultural development. As described above, other approaches have seen success, including in food import substitution for cattle (Pearson and Liu 2016) and vegetables (Fitzgerald 2016b), and niche product development for crocodile eggs (Corey et al. 2018), buffalo mustering (Austin and

Garnett 2011) and furniture (Pearson and Helms 2010; Pearson and Liu 2016). They can be undertaken alongside other land-based businesses such as environmental services (Brueckner et al. 2014) and tourism (Murphy and Harwood 2017). These different approaches have certain costs and benefits, and in many cases it is likely that a combination of approaches would be ideal for remote communities. Some Aboriginal Corporations have experienced success developing a portfolio of businesses that complement each other through the provision of different services and employment opportunities (Pearson and Rota 2010; Langford 2023). While industrial anticultural asset-making offers one potential development pathway, it is not necessarily suitable for all situations, and is best viewed as one possible approach within a wider range of activities. These incremental approaches to the development of small-scale local businesses have seen success in some parts of Australia and should not be ignored through an excessive focus on large-scale investor led developments. Policy efforts to support such incremental developments should not be neglected in favour of high-risk investor-led approaches.

Notes

1. 'Caring for country' is a term that refers to Indigenous peoples' 'traditional' responsibilities for the land and sea – see Altman and Kerins (2012).
2. Note here that this discussion focuses on remote business development, but there is also a wide literature on the role of other uses of land in the lives of remote Indigenous people, particularly for 'on-country' activities such as cultural activities, bush food collection and fishing, which may serve social, cultural and food provisioning roles.
3. Another reason why debt is not typically used is the difficulty of accessing loans using inalienable land rights as collateral (Terrill 2016).
4. NTRB-SPs are organisations appointed by the Department of the Prime Minister and Cabinet to represent native title holders and advocate for their interests. Their staff includes both Indigenous and non-Indigenous professionals.

Chapter 8

COVID-19 AND SEVEN YEARS OF 'DEVELOPING NORTHERN AUSTRALIA'

When I began this research in 2016, there was a lot of hype around the potential for Northern Development through financial investment. Energy levels were high, as was concern by some professionals working in the area. The questions that hung over my interviews were: would this time really be different? Would remote Northern regions be able to attract investors who would develop sustainable businesses, provide employment, boost populations in remote regions and contribute to economic development? Looking back seven years after the White Paper on Developing Northern Australia was first published, much of the hype that surrounded the programme has died away. This is reflective of previous efforts to develop the region. As Archer writes, in Northern Australia:

> episodic bursts of enthusiasm – driven by reports of easily accessed riches from 'unused' resources in vast, productive but nonetheless putatively un-peopled landscapes – have alternated with longer periods of disinterest and neglect. (2020, 3)

It is worth re-examining some of the key components of the Developing Northern Australia initiative to assess the outcomes of this approach in some key priority areas.

Large Agricultural Development Schemes

The Northern development programme had a strong focus on incentivising large agricultural development programmes, as was discussed in Chapter 3. In the NT, such projects were given 'Major Project Status', which gave them increased access to government resources to facilitate investment approval processes. When I began undertaking the research for this book in 2016, the NT government had granted several large agricultural programmes Major Project Status, including Project Sea Dragon, Quintis sandalwood and the Tiwi Islands development opportunities. In the time that has passed since then, both Project Sea Dragon and Quintis have undergone very public financial collapses.

Quintis collapsed in 2017 after a short-selling company released a report comparing the company to a Ponzi scheme (Poljak 2018). The share price plummeted, and the company was placed in receivership, before recapitalising in 2018 with $145 million from BlackRock Advisors, LLC and its affiliates (Morse 2018), which have restructured the business. Quintis continues to manage significant plantations in the Ord River; however, its NT properties appear to be struggling, with a recent major development of 800 ha of sandalwood trees on a property near Mataranka in the NT – which was developed with a significant free water allocation of 5.8 GL – on the market with the expectation that the new owner will need to clear the underperforming trees at their own cost (Brann 2022). This raises questions as to why such a large area of sandalwood was planted in an untested growing area, why Quintis were allocated such a large quantity of water at no cost (although see Sorensen 2017) and why it received so much support and backing from the NT government. Ultimately the financial structure of the company undermined its sustainability by contributing to the fast scale at which properties in the NT were developed.

A similar experience occurred with Project Sea Dragon, which also had major project status at the time I was undertaking research. Project Sea Dragon was to be a $1.5 billion prawn aquaculture development on the border of the NT and WA, with up to 10,000 ha of prawn production ponds and support facilities across Northern Australia. In March 2022, nearly seven years after it was first granted major project status, Seafarms released the results of a review into project feasibility, which had concluded that Project Sea Dragon 'cannot proceed in its current form' and 'will not generate acceptable financial returns, the existing scope cannot be completed for targeted costs or achieve target completion dates, and the project currently involves unacceptable risk' (Seafarms 2022a, 7). The review, undertaken by Mick McMahon, who had recently been appointed the new CEO of Seafarms, and Ian Brannan, Seafarms CFO, noted that in order to compete with rival prawn producers on price, it would need to significantly outperform them on production at Legune station – in a new environment, with unproven, very large 10 ha ponds that have never been tested in Australia. He argued that this was unlikely, given the failure to establish small-scale pilot plots as proof of concept. The review recommended that a much smaller pilot project be undertaken to establish whether the farming operation was possible before investing further in the large-scale development (Seafarms 2022a). McMahon and Brannan both resigned shortly afterwards amid tension in the leadership team (Sinclair 2022). In June, the company released a shareholder briefing saying that it 'continues to believe in the future of Project Sea Dragon and will now undertake a more detailed assessment' (Seafarms 2022b). At the time of writing, the future of Project Sea Dragon remains unclear. However, in the time that it held major project status, it utilised significant public resources, including a $56 million investment in roads by the NT government (Thompson 2022), resources to gain environmental approvals and licences (Seafarms 2022c), and resources from the Northern Land Council (NLC) and the local Indigenous community to negotiate the Indigenous Land Use Agreement over the project area (NLC 2022). A statement by the NLC CEO Joe Martin-Jard noted that:

> The Northern Land Council and the Gadjerrong native title holders have been enthusiastically working with Seafarms on this project for about six years. Native title holders are as invested in this project as any major shareholder . . . We appreciate the recent transparency from Seafarms, although we wish this could have come sooner. Traditional owners and native title holders are straight talkers. They don't want to be sold pipe-dreams. (NLC 2022, n.p)

The failure of these large schemes to realise substantial benefits for NT development arguably qualifies them for inclusion in a long list of previous failed Northern Development schemes (see Chapter 2). It reflects something that many local people told me during my fieldwork – that large schemes were unlikely to work because, as one farm consultant put it, one needs to have 'a budget for learning' the unfamiliar environment. They contrasted the failure of these large schemes with several successful agricultural developments in the region that had been undertaken incrementally by farmers who worked in the region over the long term and developed new approaches to farming in the new environment, most notably the mango industry. Indeed, one respondent explained that the mango industry in the NT had been initiated as a managed investment project that had undergone financial collapse after investors had pulled out of the programme when the mango trees had failed to fruit after five years, as projected. According to the interviewee, the scheme was bought by new managers and its operation continued, and when the trees fruited several years later – a delay related to different environmental conditions in the NT compared to mango-growing regions in Queensland – it marked the beginning of the long and steady development of the industry. Mangoes grew to become the NT's largest horticultural industry with a production value of $128.8 million in 2019 (NT Government 2022). These features so far suggest the limited efficacy of the large-scheme, investor-led approach to agricultural development, but the potential for more incremental approaches.

Private Financing of Infrastructure

The White Paper outlined the intent of the NAIF loan facility to 'provide concessional loans to projects that would not otherwise have been able to be built' and 'have benefits that flow beyond project proponents' (Australian Government 2015a, 86). The intention was to provide a mechanism 'by which strategic "game changing" and "nation building" infrastructure investments in the north can be identified and funded by the public and private sector' (Northern Australia Advisory Group, cited in Australian Government 2015a, 87). It has now been over five years since the NAIF group began its operations, and it is worth considering the portfolio of loans they have approved. Of the total 4 billion committed funding, 2.1 billion of the funds have been allocated to the resources sector (see Figure 8.1), including $714 million for potash projects, $600 million for urea projects, $310 million for mineral sands projects, $220 for rare earth metal mining, $167.5 million for coal mine construction and $66 million for reinvigoration of a gold mine. The next largest sector was energy, with a total of $737 million allocated, $610 million of which was for a project to build a dam and associated infrastructure to use this as a storage facility. $538 million was allocated to the transport sector, for airport, wharf and port upgrades. In addition, $370 was allocated to university campus upgrades. Only three projects relate directly to agriculture – for upgrades to a barramundi farm in the NT ($31.4 million), the construction of an abattoir in Queensland ($24 million) and the construction of a cotton gin at Kununurra in WA ($32 million). Only one project is by an Indigenous proponent, for upgrades to the airport servicing the Ayers Rock Resort ($27.5 million), although a loan to the Arnhem Land Progress Association was also approved, but ultimately not accepted by the proponent.

The Northern Australia Infrastructure Facility (NAIF) has supported mostly energy and resources projects, and, there has been limited NAIF investment in infrastructure that might support expansion of greenfield agricultural projects across Northern Australia, or in projects led by Indigenous proponents or targeting Indigenous communities. Supporting projects in

146 • Assembling Financialisation

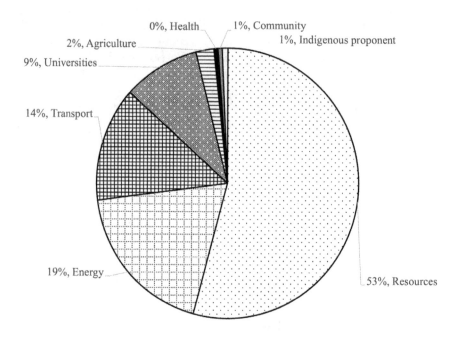

Figure 8.1. NAIF loan value by industry. Image created by the author using data from https://naif.gov.au/what-we-do/case-studies (retrieved 1 May 2003). © Zannie Langford

remote Indigenous communities was certainly an initial goal of the NAIF, which, as one intermediary close to NAIF described, sought to:

> facilitate infrastructure that create jobs, particularly for Indigenous people in remote communities . . . there are a lot of places in remote communities where the businesses have been dependent on a mine, or a refinery for a very long period of time. As you know, a mine or a refinery has a defined life period – they don't last forever. When they move out, if [NAIF] can put something in place that can substitute employment opportunities when the mine moves out, maintain the standard of living in the area, that's the sort of things [that they want to do] in remote communities . . . bring power, water and roads into a community, then, you know, it's easier to then bring in stuff to build with, or houses to build, it improves access, it improves the comfort of living because they know they've got reliable power and clean water. And with that [you can] bring jobs.

The lack of actual NAIF investment in projects with benefits for Indigenous communities likely relates to a range of issues, including the number of projects proposed, the financial ability of schemes to repay loan funding (since the NAIF is a loan rather than a grant scheme, and the costs of developing infrastructure on remote Indigenous land is high – see Chapter 7) and the ability of Indigenous proponents to access more favourable sources of funding (such as grant funding). However, it is worth considering whether the loan facility has really supported projects 'that would not otherwise have been able to be built' and 'have benefits that flow beyond project proponents' (Australian Government 2015a, 86), given the focus on resources and energy projects, which have been two of the few industries that historically have been able to overcome the high costs of remoteness in Northern Australia. There appears to be limited evidence to support such a contention based on the investments made by the NAIF to date, raising questions about the efficacy of the concessional finance approach to supporting development with social impacts.

Australian Land and Water Ownership Post-COVID-19

Much of the research described in this book was undertaken prior to the COVID-19 pandemic. This raises the following question: what has been the impact of the pandemic on farmland investment in Australia? In 2020 and 2021, farmland prices in Australia underwent significant appreciation – the median price per hectare of Australian farmland increased by 12.9% in 2020 and 20% in 2021, continuing a pattern of continuous price increases that has seen property values increase by 123% in the last eight years. Farmland in almost all regions of Australia have seen significant price increases post-COVID, and these increases have been much higher than has been seen over the last two decades (see Figure 8.2).

Actual amounts of foreign owned land in Australia, as recorded in the FIRB register of foreign ownership of Australian land, did not change significantly in 2021 (see Figure 8.3). China continues to own the largest area of Australian pastoral land, with the 2021 register reporting ownership of 8,499,000 ha. This is mostly as a result of Chinese ownership of several very large cattle properties by a handful of investors. The Australian newspaper *The Weekly Times* annually releases a list of Australia's largest landowners, the most recent version of which lists 8,422,000 ha of land with total or partial Chinese ownership, which is held by just thirteen companies (see Table 8.1). The largest of these is Shanghai CRED, a Chinese real estate firm that owns a part share of S. Kidman and Co., as well as a large area of land through its Australian operating arm, Shanghai Zenith. From 2017–22, a number of very large pastoral properties changed hands, including a number of S. Kidman and Co properties (Wagstaff and Miles 2022). These sales have seen an Australian-owned cattle company, Crowne Point Pastoral Company, take over as the largest owner of Australian land. This will likely be visible in

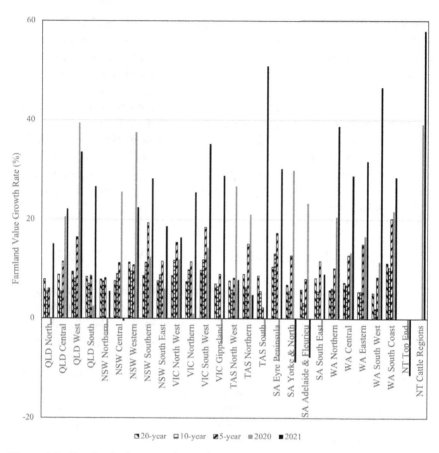

Figure 8.2. Farmland value annual growth rates. Image created by the author using data from Data from Rural Bank (2021; 2022). © Zannie Langford

future FIRB land registers as a decrease in Chinese land ownership. However, it is the result of sales of a few very large properties by large pastoral companies to other large pastoral companies, and so does not represent a significant change in Australia's investment landscape.

Similarly, the 2021 FIRB register of Australian agricultural water entitlements does not show a significant change, except for the growth in Canadian water entitlements, which increased from 295 in 2019 to 810 in 2021, making Canada the largest owner of Australian agricultural water (see Figure 8.4). This is largely the result of the activities of a few very large Canadian investors – PSP Investments, Alberta Investment Management Corporation, Fiera Comox and Auston Corporation (see Table 8.1). The largest of these is PSP Investments, a Canadian government-owned pension

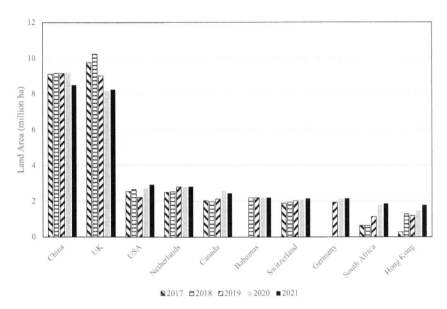

Figure 8.3. Foreign ownership of Australian agricultural land. Image created by the author using data from the Australian Government Foreign Investment Review Board: https://firb.gov.au. © Zannie Langford

fund that is the largest investor in Australian agricultural land with assets of over $5 billion (Wagstaff 2022). PSP has recently bought up several large properties with attached water rights (see e.g. Liveris 2020), as well as water rights in isolation (for example, in 2019 it paid $490 million for 89 GL of water in the Murray Darling Basin (Gray 2019)). It now owns more than 200 GL of water in the Murray Darling Basin (Jasper 2020) as well as 2.5 million ha of land. Other significant foreign investors in Australian land includes US financial services company TIAA-CREF, with a portfolio of Australian agricultural land and water worth an estimated $2 billion (Wagstaff 2022), and Hancock Agricultural Investment Group, with a portfolio of land and water worth an estimated $1 billion (Wagstaff 2022). There are also a number of large Australian-based agricultural investors such as Macquarie Bank and Rural Funds Group that own significant agricultural assets in Australia.

It appears that demand for farmland investment has accelerated since the COVID-19 pandemic (contrary to some predictions – see e.g. Lawley 2020). This is for some of the same reasons that it has been considered a strategic asset class over the last decade: low or negative correlation with traditional assets, competitive returns relative to risk, lower volatility than some other asset classes, and defensive characteristics in some market cycles (Warakirri Asset Management 2020). Warakirri Asset Management, in a publication

150 • Assembling Financialisation

Table 8.1. Australia's largest foreign landowners (data from Wagstaff 2022)

Company	Country of ownership	Area managed (ha)	Details
Cross Pacific Investments	Argentina	548,820	Operated by the Buratovich family
Brett Blundy Retail Capital	The Bahamas	2,054,400	The beef division of Brett Blundy's private investment company
Finasucre	Belgium	9,081	In 2019 paid Hancock Agricultural Investment Group about $60 million for ten macadamia farms around Bundaberg in Queensland
PSP Investments	Canada	2,520,042	Manages the superannuation funds of the Canadian public sector, armed forces and Royal Canadian Mounted Police. The biggest investor in Australian agriculture with about $5 billion in assets through direct investment and joint ventures
Alberta Investment Management Corporation	Canada	91,592	Paid approx. $60 million in 2021 for Lawson Grains, operating ten aggregations totalling 91,592 ha of developed farmland
Fiera Comox	Canada	80,035	Canadian private equity investment firm with billions worth of agriculture and forestry assets across the world
Auston Corporation	Canada	6,338	Australian arm of the Ontario Teachers' Pension Plan Board, which was established in 1991 and administers pensions for 183,000 teachers. Owns almond, apple and avocado farms in SA and Victoria
Shanghai CRED	China	4,515,200	Minority owner, with Gina Rinehart, of the iconic S. Kidman and Co. business
Shanghai Zenith	China	2,052,801	Australian operating arm of Shanghai CRED, a Chinese financial data company
Consolidated Australian Pastoral Holdings	China	1,039,000	Australian-Chinese venture backed by Beijing investment group Archstone
Shanghai Zhongfu/ Kimberley Agricultural Investment	China	490,945	One of Shanghai's largest private real estate developers

Table 8.1. *cont.*

Company	Country of ownership	Area managed (ha)	Details
Australia Aulong Auniu Wang Group	China	115,533	Owned by large Chinese retailer Dashang Group that operates department stores and supermarkets
CK Life Sciences	China	93,308	Hong Kong-listed company, backed by Hong Kong's richest person Li Ka-shing. Australia's second-largest vineyard owner
Hailiang Group	China	50,000	One of China's top 500 groups, controlled by Feng Hailiang and China's ninetieth richest man
Union Agriculture	China	21,260	Subsidiary of Hebei-based Jiahe Brewery.
Moonlake Investments	China	17,800	Backed by Chinese businessman Lu Xianfeng
Oriental Agriculture	China	11,935	Shanghai-based private company
TBG Agri Holdings	China	8,000	Australian arm of Tianma Bearings Group, owned by the Chinese billionaire Xingfa Ma
Quignan Wen	China	4,981	Chinese businessman, Tianyu Wool Industries president
Shandong Ruyi	China	1,012	Chinese textile group
BC Water Pty Ltd	Hong Kong	1,587	Hong Kong-based company
Sarawak Economic Development Corporation	Malaysia	41,500	Malaysian state-owned company
Optifarm Pty Ltd	The Netherlands	32,387	Dutch investment fund with a focus on irrigation assets
Ace Dairy Holdings	The Netherlands	1,030	Mostly owned by Deutsche Bank's DWS Global Agricultural Land and Opportunities Fund and Stichting Pensioenfonds ABP, a Dutch government and education pension fund
Tasman Agriculture Limited	New Zealand	22,000	Owned by major New Zealand farmer Alan Pye
Palgrove Holdings Pty Ltd	New Zealand	13,943	Beef operation founded by Prue and David Bondfield. Comprises the Palgrove Charolais, Charbray and Ultrablack studs. Partnered with the New Zealand Superannuation Fund in 2017 to grow the business

152 • Assembling Financialisation

Table 8.1. *cont.*

Company	Country of ownership	Area managed (ha)	Details
Australian Green Properties Pty Ltd	The Philippines	325,000	Owned by Filipino banker and property developer Romeo Roxas
Pardoo Beef Corporation	Singapore	201,103	Formed in 2015 by Singaporean businessman Bruce Cheung to produce ultra-premium Wagyu beef for Asian markets
Rallen Australia	South Africa	1,152,000	Run by the Sydney-based South African Langenhoven family with a growing pastoral presence in Northern Australia
Consolidated Pastoral Company	United Kingdom	3,143,591	Purchased by British investor Guy Hands in 2020 for $500 million. Previously owned by UK-based investment fund Terra Firma
MH Premium Farms	United Kingdom	70,971	Owned by UK-based Australian billionaire Sir Michael Hintze
Ingleby Farms	United Kingdom	21,344	Owned by British-based Swedish Rausing family. Manages farms in nine countries and across four continents
Romani Pastoral Company	United Kingdom	13,700	Owned by Urs Schwarzenbach, one of Britain's richest people
TIAA-CREF/ Nuveen	United States	288,929	New York-based Teachers Insurance and Annuity Association of America-College Retirement Equities Fund, through its asset management subsidiary Nuveen. It owns approx. seventy properties or aggregations with a land and water portfolio worth approx. $2 billion
Proterra Investment Partners	United States	38,019	Spin-off of Cargill's Black River Asset Management
MRA Merrowie Pty Ltd	United States	34,477	US-based investment institution
Hancock Agricultural Investment Group	United States	44,899	Founded in 1990, Boston-headquartered Hancock Agricultural Investment Group manages about US$4 billion worth of farmland globally. Its Australian investments are worth an estimated [US]$1 billion
Clean Agriculture and International Tourism	Vietnam	732,900	Controlled by the Vietnamese agricultural company TH Group

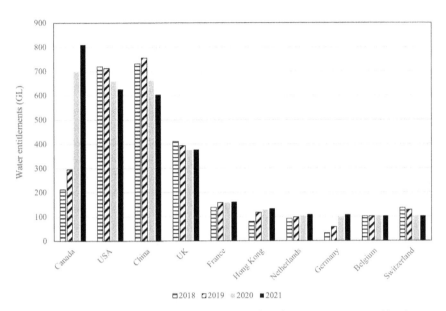

Figure 8.4. Foreign ownership of Australian agricultural water. Image created by the author using data from the Australian Government Foreign Investment Review Board: https://firb.gov.au. © Zannie Langford

entitled 'Is It Time to Consider an Investment in Australian Agriculture?' (Warakirri Asset Management 2020, 2) published in September 2020, noted 'the relatively strong performance of agriculture versus all other asset classes' during the COVID-19 pandemic, which it compared to agriculture's performance from 2008 to 2010 during the Global Financial Crisis. As it stated, 'an investment in agriculture is fundamentally linked to demand for food and staple products. In 2020, as in previous pandemic events, this demand has remained relatively stable and resilient amongst other economic pressures' (Warakirri Asset Management 2020, 2). This reflects the post-2008 focus on agriculture as a 'Return to the Real' (Fairbairn 2014, 782), in which investors targeted 'real' assets such as land, real estate and infrastructure, which are 'physical assets that have intrinsic worth due to their substance and properties' (Chen 2021, n.p.). Although a valuation studies approach would problematise this approach to conceptualising value (see Chapter 4), a focus on 'real' assets as opposed to more complex financial products reflects a focus on investments whose value arises from more durable, visible characteristics. As Sippel (2022, 27) observes, the COVID-19 pandemic is seen to have 'made the case' for agricultural investment. Similarly, financialisation in commodity markets during the COVID-19 pandemic accelerated, particularly in developed regions, although these effects were weaker in agriculture than in other commodities (Bianchi, Fan and Todorova 2020; Sharma 2022).

Despite this overall trend, much investment has been concentrated in developed agricultural industries and locations, and relatively little of this investment has been made in investments that would contribute to the Northern Australian development initiative. Investors typically target large, aggregated businesses with complete management systems in place that will offer defined profits rather than greenfield agricultural projects with uncertain prospects (see Chapter 6). In Northern Australia, the main target for agri-investment has been cattle pastoralism, in which returns are high and established. Investors have partnered with experienced cattle station operators to gain exposure to this asset class – for example, PSP Investments has backed Hewitt Cattle Company, a family-owned company that has since expanded rapidly with this new financial backing, while Brett Blundy entered a partnership with experienced operators Adrian and Emma Brown to gain exposure to the Northern Australian cattle industry. Investors in the industry have typically combined property development with speculative activities (see Chapter 4) in ways that reflect investment patterns in other parts of Australia. However, these investments have provided limited social benefits through new developments, in contrast to the intention of the 'Developing the North' programme. In sum, interest in farmland investment remains high since COVID-19, and there has been an intensification of existing dynamics in Northern Australia, including cattle station investment, trading and development (see Chapters 4, 5 and 6), but this has not translated into wider development impact in the region (Chapter 7).

Pastoral Property Development

As described in the section above, investment in the Northern Australian pastoral industry remains high. In the last few years there have been sales of numerous high-profile properties, many for substantially higher prices than they were bought for. This indicates ongoing potential to profit through capital gains on pastoral properties. In the pastoral industry, opportunities for increasing profitability included intensifying property use (such as through the installation of watering points and fencing (Watson et al. 2013)), improving cattle health and breeding outcomes (e.g. Chilcott et al. 2020; MLA 2022), moving to higher-value production (such as through transitioning to higher-value breeds of cattle (eg. Pardoo Wagyu 2022)), diversification of farming activities (Chilcott et al. 2020) and strengthening risk management procedures (Chilcott et al. 2020). Chapter 4 described in detail how strategic use of different valuation devices made possible a form of speculative development of properties, and Chapter 6 provided a case study of a joint venture between a large institutional investor and a farming family, which made possible both development initiatives and strategic buying of properties. These dynamics continue today with strengthening interest in investing in pastoral land. Indeed, the pastoral industry is one area where a finance-led approach to development appears to lead to more sustainable property management and investment in the development of the industry, albeit in ways that are sometimes speculative. The impact on land management from this approach appears to be positive, since corporate owners are often less likely to overstress properties during drought as a result of their greater financial capacity and frequently own of a set of geographically diversified properties that allow them to move cattle between stations to manage weather cycles (see Chapter 6).

The corporatisation of the industry has proceeded unevenly across Northern Australia, with investment generally targeting the more productive pastoral properties, widening the gap between corporately managed properties and those managed by small family farmers. This creates challenges for small family operators through rising and volatile property values that affect lending capacity (as described in Chapter 5) and also through increased rental payments and changing cattle markets. Small family-run pastoral businesses will need to improve their productivity if they wish to compete with corporate properties, and new farmers seeking to enter the industry are finding it challenging due to high property costs (see Chapter 6). The Northern Australian pastoral industry could therefore be seen as being increasingly financialised, although, as this book has shown, this is occurring in ways that are determined by negotiations between a range of local and global actors.

Indigenous Agricultural Development

During the time I was undertaking research for this book, there were several major Indigenous agriculture projects being developed, such as the Aboriginal Land Economic Development Agency (ALEDA) development of a managed fund of up to twenty agribusiness projects and the Tiwi Islands investment prospectus for agriculture. There were also several locations where Indigenous people were set to receive benefits from agreements negotiated with private companies seeking to develop areas of their land, such as over the Ord River development in Western Australia (Weber 2005), the Legune station Project Sea Dragon development in the NT (NLC 2022) and the proposed Hughenden Irrigation Project in Queensland (Bradbury 2022). Although these are long-term development projects, there has nonetheless been little movement on them over the last seven years. Meanwhile, remote Indigenous communities continue to face urgent wellbeing challenges, some of which intensified during the COVID-19 pandemic.

The pandemic had notable impacts on Indigenous communities and their rural development efforts. Residents of remote Indigenous communities were quickly identified as a group at high risk of severe COVID-19 infection due to high rates of chronic diseases, including among children (CDNA 2021). Travel restrictions for remote areas were introduced early on in the pandemic, and these had the effect of exacerbating issues of remoteness around employment and supply of goods. In particular, the issue of food affordability came to light in early 2020 when news reports emerged of extremely high prices for food and groceries in remote communities, such as an iceberg lettuce priced at $7.89 and a jar of coffee selling for $55 (Fernandes and Cox 2022). A governmental inquiry was launched into food affordability and the potential for price gouging in remote communities (House of Representatives Standing Committee on Indigenous Affairs (SCIA) 2020). The inquiry found evidence of very high food prices 'reflective of the genuine cost of operating supermarkets in remote communities' (SCIA 2020, 2). These prices were purportedly exacerbated by the added pressure on supply chains during COVID-19, but reflected much longer-standing concern around food prices in remote areas. The inquiry made sixteen recommendations, mostly recommending undertaking further monitoring, evaluation and research (recommendations 1, 2, 3, 5, 6, 7, 10, 11 and 15), but also improving distribution links and competitiveness (recommendations 4, 8, 9 and 16), increasing access to grant funding for remote stores (recommendations 13 and 14) and improving local food production (recommendation 12) (SCIA 2020). The food market in remote areas has therefore remained a target for development.

Meanwhile, domestic tourism to remote areas increased during COVID-19 (e.g. Grounds and Prosser 2021; Herron 2021; Marsellos 2022; Treloar 2022), creating additional employment and income-generation opportunities for some remote tourism businesses. However, it is not clear to what extent Indigenous people benefited from this change in different areas, and, overall, employment and training needs in remote areas remain high (Australian Institute of Health and Welfare 2021). The drivers of Indigenous businesses pursuing local agricultural production have not changed significantly during the COVID-19 pandemic, except perhaps to further strengthen the case for local food production – although efforts in this area have had mixed results. So far there have been no strong examples of Indigenous community benefits from finance-led agricultural development efforts. Indigenous participation in agriculture overall remains low, and the main areas where developments have occurred have been in the pastoral industry (see e.g. Kimberley Agriculture and Pastoral Company (KAPCO) 2022), which is well-established in Northern Australia, and in socially focused (rather than financially focused) agriculture (see e.g. Food Ladder 2022). As such, so far there is limited evidence of the efficacy of a finance-led approach to remote Indigenous development, largely due to low levels of investor interest in enterprises that focus on social benefits such as employment and training. There may still be opportunities for partially privately financed agricultural developments; however, it would appear that more substantial public funding is required to support the establishment of remote businesses in areas with high social needs if this is deemed to be an important goal.

Variable Outcomes

Over the eight years since the White Paper on Developing Northern Australia was released, there have been areas of substantial change and intensification in investment activity (particularly in the pastoral industry and in land and water ownership), as well as areas that have struggled to attract investor interest (such as in Indigenous development) and major schemes that have undergone dramatic public collapses (such as in large-scale development schemes). The finance-led approach to Northern Australian development appears to have had little success to date in attracting investment that creates public benefits such as infrastructure and Indigenous employment. Rather, investment is focused on large established businesses and industries with predictable returns, with very limited sustainable investment in the development of greenfield projects. Most investment interest in Northern Australia has been concentrated on the pastoral industry, which is more established and frequently generates favourable returns. Local actors have been heavily involved in the negotiation of the structure of (potential) investments in both established industries and prospective greenfield projects, but it is in the pastoral industry where they hold the greatest influence. In this industry, their region-specific expertise is increasingly valuable to investors, who require their expertise for pastoral property valuations, assessing prospective loans and pastoral station management (see Chapters 4–6). In greenfield project development, where government officials and Indigenous corporations struggle to attract investment (see Chapters 3 and 7), they have been less influential, and it appears that in many areas with high social needs, private finance has so far been largely unwilling to invest in agricultural projects. This contributes important understandings to the ways in which financialisation is negotiated in Northern Australia, as the Conclusion will discuss.

Conclusion

Messy Assemblages

This book has sought to contribute to efforts to ground understandings of financialisation in particular places, as a network of interconnected processes participated in by a range of local and global actors in pursuit of individual goals. The concept of financialisation is important in framing studies of financial investments in land and agribusiness. It has increasingly been used since the early 2000s to describe structural changes in the role and management of finance in national economies. It has been applied at the global and national levels to describe a pattern of accumulation in which profit-making occurs through financial rather than productive investments (Krippner 2005; Arrighi 2010), alongside a shift in decision-making towards serving the needs of shareholders over other stakeholders (Lazonick and O'Sullivan 2000; Crotty 2003; Milberg 2008; Baud and Durand 2012). Studies of the financialisation of land and agribusiness have highlighted the effects that finance has on local producers (Cotula 2012; Scoones et al. 2013; Clapp and Isakson 2018a; 2018b) and in reshaping power relations in food systems (Burch and Lawrence 2009; 2013). However, as was highlighted in Chapter 1, there is a need to examine more closely how financialisation occurs in practice. An emerging literature has focussed on the micro-processes through which financial investments are made and structured (Ouma 2015b; Ducastel and Anseeuw 2017, 2018; Henry and Prince 2018). This includes studies of new financial models (such as equity partnerships and Managed Investment Schemes) through which capital can be placed in agriculture, and the ways in which they organise land and natural resources (Ducastel and Anseeuw 2017; Visser 2017; Ouma 2020).

Recognising the importance of these details and following Williams' (2014) emphasis on the importance of exploring the work of financialisation, this book has engaged with a view of financialisation as *work*, in which it becomes necessary to explore how specific mediators and intermediaries shape the forms of engagement between finance and local industry. Chapter 2 introduced Northern Australia as a case study for exploring this work. In Northern Australia, changing patterns of global capital flows are of particular interest for rural development. Northern Australia is a relatively undeveloped region with limited infrastructure, low populations and limited agricultural development compared to southeastern Australia. Outside of the pastoral industry, Northern Australia does not boast the prime farmland and established farms often targeted by investors. It has a long history of financial investments in land and agribusiness, and for the last seven years has been the focus of a federal government rural development initiative organised around a financialised governance rationality (see Chapter 3). These features make Northern Australia an important site of study for exploring investments in land and agribusiness, since there are both speculative and developmental dimensions to these investments.

This study is grounded in an assemblage ontology, an approach increasingly being used to explore micro-processes of change in agrifood studies (Ouma 2015a; Lewis et al. 2016; Henry 2017; Le Billon and Sommerville 2017; Forney, Rosin and Campbell 2018b). Assemblage approaches offer important contributions to the study of financialisation by highlighting the dynamic processes through which heterogeneous elements come together, are held together and are renegotiated. This approach requires rethinking conceptualisations of financialisation as a continuous and inevitable process, in favour of a view of it as an unstable and contested assemblage constantly in flux. An assemblage and its component parts mutually influence each other in ways that transcend structure-agency dichotomies. This ontology was used to frame this study, employing an exploratory approach in which a wide range of local people working at the intersection of global finance and local spaces were interviewed. Following Tsing (2005, 5), the book focused on moments of 'friction' and explored how human agency, tools and geographies shape negotiations for key actors. It is worth now revisiting the challenges of financialisation in Northern Australia and the ways in which local actors' tools and geographies have contributed to the assemblage of its form.

Identifying Key Challenges in Northern Development

As discussed in Chapter 1, an assemblage approach supports study of the role of a broader range of actors in drawing together assemblages. However, it also requires direction – it is not enough to undiscerningly study components of an assemblage; rather, important mechanisms, relationships and patterns must be identified, and their influence examined (see Forney, Rosin and Campbell 2018a). This involves making 'cuts' to the assemblage (Anderson et al. 2012) to reveal key points of interaction. Each of the five groups of actors described in this book – government officials (Chapter 3), land valuers (Chapter 4), bankers (Chapter 5), farmers (Chapter 6) and Indigenous corporations (Chapter 7) were selected for closer study based on thematic analysis of interviewees in the initial stages of data collection. The people interviewed in this study, when asked about the role of private finance in agricultural development in Northern Australia, identified a range of very specific challenges that were crucial to the understanding of financialisation. These include issues concerning the role of the state in rural development, land market volatility, unsustainable bank lending practices, farm financing and Indigenous economic development. These findings complement key aspects of financialisation identified in the academic literature, with important additional insights being discussed here.

The first theme that was identified in the interviews was that of the role of the state in guiding the direction of agricultural development. Historically, the state has played a key role in shaping the engagement of agriculture with finance (McMichael 1984). It does so by enforcing contracts and bankruptcy laws, providing collateral, undertaking credit provision, supporting marketing boards and intervening in financial markets (Martin and Clapp 2015; Larder, Sippel and Argent 2018). However, the role of government has shifted substantially over the last four decades with a neoliberal reorganisation of the public and private sectors. The Northern Development programme can be viewed as a neoliberal approach to development in which the private sector is encouraged to distribute development resources. However, more than this, a *financialised* governance rationality can also be identified. It is not merely private sector businesses that are allocated the responsibility to guide development; rather, financial investors specifically are named 'to direct' development (Australian Government 2015a, 2). This approach creates challenges at the local level, particularly for the NT government, which is not sufficiently funded to undertake the developments needed to meet the very high social needs of its remote and largely Indigenous population (Dale 2014). In this context, local government officials have little option but to engage with the financialised governance rationality articulated in the White Paper on Developing Northern Australia. As discussed in Chapter

3, government officials engage with and facilitate financialisation through their work, seeking to attract investment to Northern Australia. However, they also work to reduce speculative behaviour and increase investments in long-term productive developments. These government actors are subject to neoliberal and financialised governance programmes directed from the Commonwealth level (through which direct federal funding for development is deprioritised), and also facilitate it.

The second theme identified in the interviews was the increased volatility of land markets and speculation on land by foreign financial interests. Speculation on land and resulting land price volatility is a major issue identified by financialisation scholars (Cotula 2009; Scoones et al. 2013; Borras et al. 2020). In this study, a number of interviewees noted the high and increasingly volatile prices of pastoral land in Northern Australia (MLA 2020) as a challenge for local producers, and speculation on these lands as contrary to local development goals. These changing land markets can be identified as arising from global financialisation, as they are partially the result of increased investment in land from foreign investors. These investors rely on professional land valuations to guide their sales and verify the value of these very large properties; pastoral land valuers are therefore important intermediaries who enable the financialisation of land through evaluating – and valorising – it. However, these land valuers also respond to financialisation and seek to reduce it by modifying their land valuation practices within the constraints set for them by their professional tools. The facilitation, and resistance, of financialisation can therefore again be identified in the work of these intermediaries, as was described in Chapter 4.

The third theme identified by participants was unsustainable bank lending practices, which was the subject of a Royal Commission into Misconduct in the Banking, Superannuation and Financial Services Industry at the time I was undertaking research. The Commission was tasked with inquiring into whether bank lending behaviour may have constituted misconduct or fallen below community expectations, and whether harmful behaviour was attributable to practices within the banks. Banks provide financial services to the majority of Northern Australian farmers, and unsustainable lending practices can create severe hardship. Rural agrifinance specialists mediate connections between their banks and farmers, and some of those who live locally, and are concerned about the sustainably of the region, participate in a moral economy of rural lending in which they work to reduce the impacts of financialisation on their clients, as discussed in Chapter 5.

The fourth theme was farm financing and the emerging challenges faced by farmers seeking access to finance. Financialisation, located in the increasing circulation of capital globally, creates opportunities for farmers to access capital in new ways. The formation of a private equity partnership discussed in Chapter 6 is a response to the difficult circumstances created by neoliberal restructuring and the opportunities created by global financialisation. However, it is also a process of financialisation, as the work undertaken by the farmer in this chapter can be seen as extending global finance capital into new geographies and industries that may not have been possible without the work of this local actor. As such, financialisation is embedded in the very unique and specific work undertaken by this farmer, and in the emerging hybridity of family, corporate, globalising and capitalising farm business structures. This study has demonstrated how it is done, and how particular choices and preferences shape the engagement of finance capital in rural spaces.

The fifth theme identified through the interviews was that of Indigenous development. In remote Northern Australia, Indigenous people face difficult social and economic conditions. Indigenous Australians in remote regions often suffer poor health outcomes and have few employment opportunities (Dale 2014; Australian Institute of Health and Welfare 2015). The remoteness of and lack of infrastructure in much of Indigenous Northern Australia create severe development challenges. These contexts have parallels with development challenges in the Global South, in which the financialisation of development is shifting the way in which remote developing communities access finance. Mawdsley (2017; 2018) discusses the financialisation *of* development as a shift from direct investment in development projects to the direction of development funds towards facilitating private sector investment in these projects. This is thought to be a model for increasing the scale of development funding (Mawdsley 2018); however, it also creates a number of risks for communities (Mawdsley 2017; Staritz et al. 2018). In Northern Australia, similar shifts in government policy have seen funds associated with the Northern Development agenda directed towards intermediaries who work with Indigenous representatives in order to facilitate the attraction of private finance for development, for example, by the Land Development Corporation. This financialisation *for* development occurs as Indigenous communities engage with private sector finance in the hope of organising investments that will deliver social benefits. The work of financialisation can again be identified in the activities of local actors; intermediaries to Indigenous land who, in response to global shifts associated with financialisation, work actively and innovatively to organise financial investments. This work was taken as the subject of study in Chapter 7. Like the pastoralist in Chapter 6, intermediaries to Indigenous land are paradoxically both responding to and facilitating financialisation, as their work makes it possible for finance to flow into new geographies and industries. However, unlike the pastoralist, Indigenous corporations have had little success to date in attracting investment – this highlights the uncertainty of asset-making and the challenges in developing assets in new industries and in areas with high social needs.

The identification of these key development challenges by participants shaped the selection of case studies for this book. 'Locating' (Ho 2009) financialisation in the work of these specific local actors provides new insights into how financialisation is facilitated and contested on a microlevel and can provide some insights into how, in practice, financialisation occurs. The topics target five key issues that reveal intersecting human agencies, tools and geographies whose alignment creates different outcomes for rural development.

Human Agency

The local mediators discussed in this book exercised their agency and preferences in three key ways: their emphasis on the importance of maintaining control over business operations; the desire to prevent speculation on land and resources; and the wish to choose investors with whom to partner.

Maintaining Control

The need to maintain control over operations was a common theme across the interviews, and many respondents discussed their desire to retain control and their efforts to do so. The farmer discussed in Chapter 6 went to great efforts to retain control of the farms' operations. Although they were not willing to disclose details of the structure of the equity partnership and management, they did stress the importance of negotiating control, continually emphasising their desire to direct the way in which their business was managed and developed. This included organisational factors such as what properties they purchased, as well as management factors relating to how the individual operating farm properties were managed. The farmer emphasised that there are a range of ways in which control over operations can be maintained, and that retaining control did not necessarily require retaining a majority ownership share. As they described, 'you don't necessarily have to have a controlling interest to control a company . . . there's different ways to structure a deal'. The farmer in this case went to great lengths and great expense to ensure that they retained control of the operation, particularly over the investor's exit strategy. Controlling the exit strategy is important because it ensures that the investor cannot sell their interest in the business unexpectedly in response to external financial circumstances in ways that could compromise the stability of the business. By controlling the exit strategy of the investor, the farmer was able to control the way that the investor speculated on land. Speculative gains were achieved by the company, which bought and sold land in response to land market fluctuations, and also used the BAV to increase the value of the land through strategic developments. However, the investor could not speculate on the business (by selling it suddenly in response to global market changes) because the farmer enforced restrictions that prevented them from doing so. As such, the farmer managed to retain control over the speculative and productive aspects of business management, changing the way in which financialisation of land occurs.

The theme of control was also evident among intermediaries to Indigenous land, and, indeed, asset-making processes were often explicitly driven by a desire for greater control over rural economies and reduced reliance on government funding. Many intermediaries stressed the importance of these initiatives in giving landowners greater control over the way in which their land is used and developed. Land is frequently mapped to identify potential development sites, and landowners provide input into the decision-making process in the selection of potential sites. In one novel case, a managed fund was being developed to afford greater control over investment exit strategies, paralleling the situation of the farmer in Chapter 6. However, this work should not be simplistically viewed as a contest for control between Indigenous landowners and financial sector entities. It was not necessarily the case that greater control was sought for landowners in all situations. The intermediaries to Indigenous land discussed here were not community members themselves, but often worked in their employ, with government, NTRB-SPs or on their behalf in some other capacity. Their interest was in the development of sustainable long-term businesses on the land, and there were cases where this might be at odds with the need for immediate control over the business by landowners. As such, control is a key component of this assetisation work, but is negotiated by different groups in pursuit of diverse outcomes, as discussed in Chapter 7.

Government professionals similarly sought to negotiate some level of control over the types of investments undertaken and the structure in which they were organised, and substantial efforts were spent attempting to shape the way in which investment proposals were made. The extent to which officials felt this was part of their role varied; some professionals stressed that they chose not to engage with business development work, while another went as far as to say that 'we act more as a business investment developer . . . we are getting ourselves more and more involved to help to shape that project'. For these officials, direct control was not possible, but some level of influence was sought through both formal and informal approaches. Valuation specialists similarly sought to exert control over land markets in order to avoid 'the market . . . getting out of whack'. There are therefore a range of ways in which different local actors sought to retain control of business operations. Different actors have different capacities to exert control in the shaping of financial investments, and these contests are affected by power dynamics (Bortz et al. 2018) and political factors (Keucheyan 2018). The interaction of a range of distributed agencies and power dynamics is a key feature of an assemblage (Fredriksen 2014), which is usefully highlighted by the work of the actors discussed here.

Preventing Speculation

As financialisation is often framed as the increased importance of financial (speculative) profit-making over productive (development-based) profit-making, reducing speculative behaviour can be a direct political response to financialisation (Fairbairn 2014). For the farmer discussed in Chapter 6, reducing speculative behaviour was pursued through retaining control of the exit strategy of the equity partner; it was very important to prevent the investor from selling their part of the business in response to changes in global financial circumstances, as this could reduce the farm business' access to capital and compromise its long-term viability. In this case, speculative gains and productive long-term stability represented competing needs for the investor and the farmer, which needed to be ameliorated during investment negotiation.

For intermediaries involved in setting up leases over Indigenous land, reducing speculative behaviour is sometimes exercised through development conditions on leases. They have an explicit development agenda, which requires intensive asset-making work to develop assets for investment that will create productive outcomes, including local businesses, as well as employment opportunities and incidental infrastructure development. Government officials are similarly focused on development outcomes. They expend substantial effort to explain local conditions to investors in order to ensure that buyers of land are willing and prepared to invest in agricultural development. This work involves guiding investor understanding of the environment to prevent them from undertaking developments that were unlikely to be successful and encouraging them to undertake long-term productive developments. Government officials also work in other ways to reduce speculative financial activity in the region. For currently operating agribusiness, there was a focus on avoiding financial activities such as spot trading that reduced investment in supply chains and compromised the long-term viability of the industry. In the mango industry, which is one of the NT's largest horticulture industries, one government official expends substantial effort encouraging farmers not to sell to commodity traders at the farm gate, as many of these mangoes ended up being illegally smuggled into China. This practice, while making selling easy for growers in the short term, makes it difficult to invest in supply chains over the long term. There are efforts by Department of Primary Industries in the NT government to encourage producers to export out of Darwin, with the goal of achieving better economies of scale (see Chapter 3). As a result, government officials in the Department of Primary Industries encourage producers to build these supply chains, as well as develop other marketing mechanisms (such as the 'Australian Mangoes' brand). This aims to reduce the negative implications of speculative trading in agriculture through building long-term, productive industries, and reflects concerns raised in reports on the effects of financial investment on farmland development (Deininger and Byerlee 2011; Heath and Tomlinson 2016).

Finally, valuers play a key role in moderating land markets to reduce the capacity for land speculation. As discussed in Chapter 4, they use the BAV to assess land values, a tool that is based on comparing properties to recent sales. As a result, the value they assign does not strictly represent the profitability of a property in the way that the ROI does, but reflects the current market and introduces global land price volatility to the region. Valuers expressed concern about the volatility introduced by excessively high land value prices. They saw this volatility as having a negative impact on the region by encouraging speculation, and one valuer described his role as not only reflecting this market, but also moderating it to reduce speculative behaviour. In sum, local actors are concerned about speculative financial activity and are actively working to reduce it. If, as Krippner (2005) suggests, financialisation fosters speculative outcomes (Krippner 2005), the valuers' actions could be interpreted as an attempt to reduce this speculative activity in favour of longer-term, productive developments. This suggests the need for a more detailed and critical approach to evaluating 'the social efficiency of modern finance' (Storm 2018, 302), one that is able to take account of the range of different ways in which the acceptability of financial investments into land and environments are negotiated (Ouma, Johnson and Bigger 2018).

Choosing Whom to Work with

Local actors in this study (farmers, Indigenous organisations, valuers and government) exercised agency by choosing the investors with whom they worked. Although the broader political discourse in Australia suggests that there are xenophobic and nationalistic concerns driving the choice of investor (Sippel and Weldon 2021), this trend did not appear in my research. Instead, farmers and farm consultants openly disparaged resistance to foreign investment as being racist or xenophobic, while government officials said they did not prejudge the nationality of the source of capital 'as long as it works for the Territory'. However, there were instances where mediators exercised clear preferences as to the source of capital. For the farmer who formed the private equity partnership, having an easy and enjoyable working partnership was a key driver of investor choice. By contrast, intermediaries to Indigenous land were less concerned about working relationships, but sought investors with particular characteristics that suited the Indigenous landowners on whose behalf they worked. They were concerned with ensuring that investors were undertaking legitimate activities and eschewed what was identified as 'dodgy' capital. For Sippel (2018, 4), these observations suggest the need for a 'differentiation between different kinds of "capital" and the way they are not only put to "work" but are also morally evaluated'. There are a variety of ways in which 'the moral grounds on which the legitimacy of capital placements into farmland are negotiated' (Ouma, Johnson and Bigger 2018: 503), and these are not as clearly opposed as they often appear in public debates (Smith and Pritchard 2016).

This book demonstrates how local actors exercised their agency through their work negotiating connections between global finance and local agribusiness, working to maintain control over their business and resources, to reduce speculative investment and to select investors with particular characteristics. The next section considers the importance of tools in shaping their work.

Tools

The tools identified as having a significant effect mediating connections between global finance and local agrifood industries in Northern Australia include valuation devices, Indigenous investment prospectuses and government marketing documents.

Valuation Devices

Land prices are a major driver of investment into land and agribusiness in Northern Australia. Capital gains on land value increases have historically made up over 50% of ROI in pastoral properties. As such, without these increases, pastoral properties would be a much less desirable investment proposition. Pastoral land valuation in Northern Australia is widely undertaken using the BAV. As was explained in Chapter 4, the BAV is calculated in two stages. First, the carrying capacity of the land is assessed to determine how many cattle the land is thought to sustainably support. This involves assessing the grazing patterns of a property and comparing it with knowledge of the existing number of cattle. It is a difficult figure to determine, since it is intended to represent a long-term average of the property across a range of weather patterns, but is also influenced by short-term developments such as the installation of water bores, and by gradual changes in land and vegetation quality. Once determined, the carrying capacity is compared to market data for similar properties to attain a market value. The price thus contains both information on the physical nature of the property and on the current land market in the region. However, it is not a measure of business profitability. As such, it creates scope for land values to become inflated to the point that it is not possible for a producer to make an acceptable ROI from income. By contrast, the ROI from capital appreciation is a measure used by investors to determine the percentage increase in the value of their investment earned each year. These two valuation devices provide alternative indications of value and are used by different stakeholders for a range of purposes. Chapter 4 explored the emergence and competition of these two valuation methods. It reported that much of the volatility in current pastoral land markets is due to the use of the BAV, a measure of value that originally emerged as an industry 'rule of thumb' at a time when properties were sold based largely on the number of cattle they were estimated to carry. This tool has stabilised into a powerful assemblage that has a range of effects in different contexts (in some cases encouraging productive investment in water bores, while in others encouraging purely speculative behaviour) and is a major driver of investment patterns in the region. This highlights the importance of this tool in shaping financial engagements in the region.

Indigenous Investment Prospectuses

Indigenous development is a major priority for Northern Australia and in many cases is being attempted through asset-making processes (see Chapter 7). A tool that is being used in a range of locations is the development of mapping procedures for preparing investment prospectuses over Indigenous land. This approach, an example of which was pioneered by the Land Development Corporation working on behalf of Tiwi Island landowners, involves detailed mapping of the biophysical properties of an area. This process requires particular parcels of land for development to be identified through consultation with Indigenous TOs. Next, the Land Development Corporation developed detailed business proposals based on this mapping work and marketed opportunities using an Indigenous investment prospectus. This 'tool' is being used by a range of other intermediaries to Indigenous land across Northern Australia, shaping investment in Indigenous land quite significantly. This process was described by a range of intermediaries, who look to each other for guidance on best practice for how mapping can be undertaken. For example, pioneering intermediaries to Indigenous land, such as the Land Development Corporation, the Aboriginal Land Development Agency, the NAILSMA 'Business on Country' initiative and the Cape York Partnership, are developing new strategies for business development and investment seeking which are likely to emerge as models for Indigenous development more broadly.

Second, the documents themselves become powerful drivers of local development. For example, the prospectus developed by the Land Development Corporation draws artificial lines between profitable and unprofitable investments in ways that involve somewhat uncertain so-called 'qualculative' work (Callon and Law 2005), but gain legitimacy and determinacy as published documents that take on their own agency in shaping investment landscapes. Chapter 7 explored emerging asset-making processes and tools (such as investment prospectuses and mapping devices) currently under development, some of which will stabilise into important and influential actors, while others will dissolve and become destabilised through renegotiation. The processes through which this occurs is a crucial area of future research.

Government Marketing Documents

Chapter 3 explored the way in which the NT government is seeking to operationalise the federal government plan to develop Northern Australia. It examined financialised governance rationalities articulated in government documents such as the White Paper on Developing Northern Australia and highlighted the work of these documents as marketing materials. These and other marketing tools are also powerful objects used to seek investment. One key example of this is a report produced by Austrade that markets Northern Australia as an 'untapped market full of possibility' (Austrade 2015, iii), emphasising the region as being one of underutilisation in which potentially substantial capital gains might be made. Another is imagery often employed in oral presentations and reports to emphasise the NT's proximity to Asia and thus market Darwin as Australia's 'Gateway to Asia' (NT Government 2020, n.p.). This image was frequently employed by government officials and others who sought to emphasise Northern Australia's strategic position in relation to Asia, and was often accompanied by comments observing, for example, that Darwin is closer to Jakarta than it is to Melbourne. These statements are designed to suggest access to rapidly growing Asian markets. However, they do not fully reflect economic circumstances in existing supply chains – as one government official put it, the idea of Darwin as the 'Gateway to Asia' is currently 'just spin'. Regardless, documents such as these present powerful imagery that effectively communicates simple ideas to investors. These ideas about the profitability of the region become tools in asset-making processes (as discussed in Chapter 7), with asset-makers frequently emphasising Northern Australia as underutilised, the 'Gateway to Asia', possessing 'free' water and being 'clean and green', drawing on government-produced marketing documents to support these discursive claims.

These four groups of tools have agency and power in shaping financial investments into land and agribusiness in Northern Australia and demonstrate the importance of investigating nonhuman objects in studies of financialisation. As Russi (2013, 29) observes, financialisation can be located in 'a sharing of calculative practices and informational devices' that simplify investment negotiation work. However, these tools and calculative devices also naturalise decision-making that in fact contains important judgements about the form that investments should take. By simplifying investment facilitation work, they 'script' user behaviour (Latour 1992) such that certain decisions and actions are repeated continuously. In this way, these objects take on agency by influencing the actions of their users. The development of these tools is often based on a range of factors related to the (workplace) cultures in which they are developed (see Mackenzie 2006, 245), and so may not necessarily be designed with local development outcomes in mind. However, as Henry and Scott (2017, 110) observe, 'decisions about how and what to count are political decisions about what counts', and there are value judgements hidden within these tools that shape who benefits from investment. The tools described here vary in terms of the extent to which their design has purposefully considered contemporary development outcomes. The BAV, for example, has evolved over a long time period in a unique geographical context and, as such, has come to be an assemblage influenced by a range of factors, many of which are no longer useful for land value assessment in a financialising land market. By contrast, many Indigenous investment prospectuses are emergent assemblages in ongoing stages of debate and negotiation, and so are being deliberately shaped in the context of contemporary development goals. Over time, these assemblages may stabilise into particular formations that will vary in their usefulness to changing societal circumstances and will be suitable to future development goals to different extents. This highlights the importance of examining such tools of financialisation as assemblages with long histories of development in specific geographical and historical contexts (see Chapter 2). Examining them in this way allows them to be re-examined, and potentially renegotiated, to more purposefully shape the engagement of finance capital with rural spaces.

Geographies

The cultural and physical geographies of Northern Australia have a significant effect on patterns of financial investment. The majority of Northern Australia has lower populations and less intensive production than the agricultural areas of Southern Australia as a result of its rainfall patterns and soil types, as was described in Chapter 2. As a result, the region has relatively little transport and production infrastructure, and is often portrayed as an area of 'underdevelopment' (Australian Government 2015a, 60) in which 'a diverse array of land types in a great many places is homogenized and aggregated under a new label: their underutilization' (Li 2014, 592). These discursive, socioeconomic and biophysical features have major effects on the engagement of private finance with the region, and manifest in a focus on large-scale projects.

Large-Scale Developments

The relative lack of infrastructure and remoteness of Northern Australian lands has led to a focus on large-scale developments that are thought to be able to overcome high transaction costs through economies of scale. Despite the historic failures of large-scale agricultural schemes financed by distant capital (as discussed in Chapter 2), this book has highlighted the ongoing focus on large-scale projects as part of government development efforts. This closely aligns with the needs of large-scale foreign financial investors, who often also seek to invest in large projects. This emphasis on scale creates particular ways of engaging with finance capital. For the farmer who negotiated the equity partnership in Chapter 6, this created an opportunity. As a relatively large family farm business in a strong financial position, they were of sufficient scale to engage a major consultancy firm to work on their behalf and to seek out larger, institutional investors who were described as having 'a long-term view of the market'. The success of their proposal was grounded in their identification of a range of properties for acquisition – expansion plans that would allow their investor to deploy substantial amounts of capital and so meet their scale requirements. Their business development strategy strongly relied on expansion by purchasing properties at low points in the property cycle, such that they earn substantially from capital gains as well as from increased output. As such, the farmer's expertise in farm and financial management, and their ability to identify suitable projects for strategic investment, was a crucial part of what they were 'selling' to investors. Where in more densely populated agricultural areas it might be possible to employ a range of different local consultants to manage buying and selling of properties, in this case the farmer's expertise was a unique asset that gave the farmer a strong position from which to negotiate the terms of the equity partnership. This is in contrast to the situation faced by smaller family farmers, who are often in a weaker negotiating position and are therefore more likely to be enrolled into farming-finance partnerships through other models (such as own-lease out models) in which the farmer provides production expertise, but is not so extensively involved in financial management of the business, as discussed in Chapter 6.

For intermediaries to Indigenous land, remote geographies and development histories (Chapter 2) also substantially influence their work. Of projects that seek private finance capital, small-scale community development initiatives are unlikely to be within the scale that financial investors are seeking. This leads intermediaries to Indigenous land to focus on developing large-scale initiatives in pastoralism, aquaculture or agriculture. This precludes the development of industries that may be particularly beneficial to Indigenous communities, such as those that focus on niche production, import substitution or development of a portfolio of small, locally embedded organisations. Instead, it leads to a focus on large-scale developments and the negotiation of community development outcomes within these projects. Intermediaries to Indigenous land approached this in different ways. Some, such as the Land Development Corporation working on behalf of Tiwi Island landholders, sought to develop opportunities for large-scale investment and to market these to foreign investors. Conversely, the Aboriginal Land and Sea Development Agency is developing a pool of up to twenty smaller agricultural businesses that will become part of a managed fund. Others are targeting social impact investors and incorporating public funding to allow them to meet social needs, while also developing operational businesses. One group that funded an agricultural business through 50% concessional loans and 50% public funding commented that 'that was the right mix – there's no way a commercial investor would touch this sort of thing'. The remoteness is the main determinant of which industries are being targeted in the region, and scale is an important part of the strategy of many of these businesses.

For government officials, there was a clear focus on attracting and facilitating large-scale, long-term investment into greenfield development projects as a major priority. As one government official described, 'the heavy hitters, they're the ones that we want'. Smaller development projects were not a major priority for their work. This explicit orientation towards large-scale projects means that Northern Australian development efforts are strongly focused on creating a few large-scale industries in the region rather than a multiplicity of smaller operations. While other agricultural areas in Southern Australia have seen a gradual pattern of consolidation of properties and a shift towards corporate management, in Northern Australia, this is an explicit goal and the focus of development efforts, raising questions about how, and on whose behalf, rural spaces are being developed.

For valuation professionals, the large scale of pastoral properties makes their value difficult to assess and reaffirms the role of professional pastoral land valuers as market mediators. The power that these professionals enjoy is largely a result of this scale. This effect was observed across all local mediators, in that with so few people living in Northern Australia with expertise in the particular environments and geographies of the region, local actors were able to market themselves as essential intermediaries between global finance and local spaces. As a result, Northern Australian intermediaries valorise their local knowledge to 'affirm their essential role as gateway to the country and its agricultural value chains' (Ducastel and Anseeuw 2017, 201). Farmers may be able to negotiate more effectively as a result of this privileged position. However, the lack of professionals can also have negative implications. This was the case for some intermediaries to Indigenous land, who, lacking a local market of operational expertise, were more reliant on external businesses to provide this management expertise.

These findings demonstrate the central role of Northern Australian geographies in shaping the way in which negotiations over financial investments occur. This supports Visser's (2017) claim that the biophysical environment has great importance in shaping investment outcomes. Financialisation should not be seen as a homogenising and inevitable force, but as an uncertain and reversible process (Visser 2017) assembled by the work of a diverse range of intermediaries (Ouma 2015b). Financial investments are assembled by specific intermediaries who have to 'solve a range of sociotechnical puzzles in order to access, maintain, and/or expand markets' (Ouma 2015b, 5). This is a particular challenge in agriculture, where a diverse range of land and animals need to be organised to fit investment portfolios, a challenge that in some cases undermines efforts to establish investments (Ducastel and Anseeuw 2017; 2018). National and local cultures shape the investment negotiation process, and clashes of cultures can undermine attempts to establish links between investors and businesses in different countries (Muniesa et al. 2017). As such, there is a need to understand financial investments as partially assembled by local spaces in ways that 'agriculturalise' finance (Henry and Prince 2018), and to pay attention to the ways in which this work is undertaken by local actors (Li 2014; 2017). The geographies described in this book add to these studies by showing how Northern Australian geographies are shaping financialisation processes occurring in the region in unforeseen ways. The next section considers the contribution of an assemblage approach to understanding these patterns.

Assembling Financialisation

This book has revealed numerous unexpected ways in which human actors, tools and geographies work to assemble, and disassemble, patterns associated with financialisation. Chapter 1 outlined four key contributions of an assemblage approach to the study of the financialisation of agrifood industries. The next section returns to these to reflect on the contributions they make to understanding financialisation as an assemblage.

Processes of Assembling Heterogeneous Parts

First, assemblage theory emphasises the importance of seeing financialisation as a process of assembling heterogeneous parts. All elements in the assemblage are unique, independent components in constantly shifting relations with each other. They act without any kind of internal coherence or intention to engage with financialisation in any explicitly political way. It becomes unnecessary to search for characteristics of any given actor that might allow them to be classified as 'financialising' or 'definancialising' in nature. Rather, actors are embedded in a range of more complex relations. The importance of this contribution is that financialisation is not seen as an intentional project with a logical pattern of development; instead, it is a pattern that emerges over time through a range of interpersonal struggles that facilitate and resist financialising processes. This aspect of assemblage thinking flags the dynamism and constant renegotiation of relations between global finance and local spaces.

Rather than seeing finance as flowing inevitably into new spaces, this book highlights the work involved in making, and maintaining, global connections. Chapter 6 has shown that although equity partnerships are widely viewed as a potential solution to Australian farm financing challenges, the process of forming these connections is in reality difficult, a long term process and expensive, requiring substantial work on the behalf of farmers to negotiate. Similarly, Chapter 7 has highlighted the uncertain and innovative work involved in creating assets from Indigenous land and resources. It has emphasised that these emergent assemblages were not certain to succeed, but were constantly under development and requiring the attention of entrepreneurial intermediaries. Chapter 3 similarly demonstrates the utility of this aspect of assemblage thinking by highlighting the disparity between government documents on developing Northern Australia, and the actual practical work of government officials who seek to operationalise this agenda. Chapter 4 has highlighted the work involved in constructing land prices and the range of moral projects that contribute to these, again reminding us that these prices are not the natural or inevitable results of market forces, but assemblages that emerge from dynamic relations between a range of actors. Assemblage thinking thus valuably flags the importance of studying the *work* of assembling financial investments.

Exteriority of Relations

Second, assemblage thinking emphasises the importance of relations of exteriority to the assemblage. This aspect reminds us that relations are not fixed and do not define the components; rather, these components maintain their own identity and capacity for action, but actualise and behave differently in different assemblages. This is highlighted in Chapter 6 by the way in which the farmer and the investor maintain their individual goals and priorities in the assemblage of the equity partnership they form, and in the future may separate and enter into new assemblages in which they have the capacity for different actions and effects. The farmer is not defined by their relationship to the investor, but maintains their own set of goals and capacities. Similarly, the remote geographies of Northern Australia are components of assemblages that create different challenges and opportunities in different contexts. For the farmer in Chapter 6, these geographical features meant that they were in a strong negotiating position as they possessed important and uncommon environmental knowledge and farm management skillsets, giving them greater power to negotiate with investors. By contrast, for many of the intermediaries to Indigenous land, these geographies meant that limited local agribusiness expertise was available, and as such they often sought an investor that would also be able to provide this expertise; this often weakened their negotiating position. Another example of the ways that component parts actualise differently in different assemblages can be found in Chapter 4 in the two valuation devices used. These devices were used strategically by different actors in pursuit of capital gains and business development goals. The BAV, for example, which in some assemblages creates price volatility that leads to speculation, for other businesses led to spending on farm development in order to realise capital gains from an increased carrying capacity. As such, this valuation device produced both speculative and productive behaviour through its relations in different assemblages. Assemblage thinking usefully directs attention to this potential for different behaviour of elements in different assemblages, reminding us that component parts cannot be simplistically characterised as facilitating or resisting financialisation, but have a range of capacities that actualise in different ways through complex relations with a range of other actors.

Distributed Agency and Nonlinear Causation

The third key contribution of assemblage theory lies in directing our attention to the distributed agency of assemblages and the nonlinear patterns of causation that arise from them. This contribution frames the focus of the book. While studies of financialisation have tended to focus on the work of financial actors, an assemblage ontology alerts us to the ways that a range of local actors contribute to negotiations across financial and rural spaces. This rethinking of agency as being located in distributed networks (Anderson et al. 2012) creates space to examine spaces of 'friction' (Tsing 2005) in which investments in land are negotiated by a range of local actions. It allows consideration of market mediators such as government officials and land valuation specialists to be viewed as important actors in the financialisation of land. Similarly, those who negotiate investments directly – such as farmers and intermediaries to Indigenous land – are viewed as important actors whose work influences the places that investments occur and the structure of the vehicles through which they are made. This rethinking of agency and power as distributed does not imply that they are equally distributed; instead, it highlights the importance of a nuanced understanding of power as manifested in a range of relationships between heterogeneous parts. For example, the ability of the farmer discussed in Chapter 6 to negotiate with a large pension fund was a result of the specialist farming knowledge they brought which allowed him to strategically use the BAV in ways that were exceptionally valuable to the investor. Similarly, in the asset-making process described in Chapter 7, agency and power were distributed in a network of consultants, investors, farmers, community members, government officials and nonhuman actors such as mapping documents, investment prospectuses, valuation tools and environments. There is no clearly discernible pattern of power and powerlessness; rather, the agency of these components interact in unexpected ways, and they exert power over each other in shifting and competing relationships. Further, an assemblage approach alerts us to the nonlinear causality of assemblages, in which the effects of any given action are not easily discernible in advance, but may create a range of different effects depending on their relations in an assemblage. This is clearly demonstrated in Chapter 4, in which the BAV was strategically used by a range of actors to different ends. While in one context, this valuation tool may lead to a speculative purchase, in another it might lead to infrastructure development on a property. The value of an assemblage approach here is in resisting simple causality explanations in favour of an examination of the range of ways in which causality emerges in a provisionally ordered social field (Li 2007c, 285).

Structure and Dynamism

Lastly, assemblage thinking usefully moves discussions beyond the dichotomy between structured and unstructured processes (Anderson et al. 2012, 175). This is also a core contribution of this book, as it highlights the need to view financialisation not as a homogeneous and inevitable process, but as a pattern that emerges from a diverse range of work. Assemblage theory contributes to this book by showing that while assemblages can stabilise and become durable formations that affect their component parts, their component parts also affect the larger assemblage and are able to renegotiate them in a range of ways. Chapter 3 explored the work of local government actors in seeking to operationalise the federal government's programme to develop Northern Australia. In the White Paper on Developing Northern Australia, Chapter 3 identified a neoliberalising, and *financialising*, governance rationality in which decisions about what to develop, where and how were being explicitly outsourced to private financial actors. This policy approach and the documents in which it was expressed are clearly powerful structural drivers of the investment-seeking work undertaken by local government officials. Yet, these officials contribute to them and resist them in a range of ways that also shape what financialising governance *is* in this particular context. A similar tension is highlighted in Chapter 4, which examined the way that the BAV has developed in a historical and geographical context, and stabilised as an important and highly influential assemblage. But it also shows the ways in which a range of local and financial actors are using the BAV strategically in new ways, and how professional valuation specialists are adapting their use of this valuation tool – for example, by providing extensive commentary on the terms under which its results should be used and where it diverges from the results of other valuation practices. In this way, valuation professionals are not only affected by the BAV, but also play a role in shifting what it represents and how it is used. In Chapter 6, the need to seek equity funding was seen to be driven by decades of neoliberal restructuring of the support that the government provided to agriculture and was also enabled by global financialisation patterns that have created a desire for large investors to diversify their portfolios into agriculture. Yet, the farmer in Chapter 6 was not only passively affected by these larger structural shifts, but also contributed to them and their direction in important ways. The partnership formed by this farmer and investor is well known and widely perceived as an ideal outcome for both Australian agriculture and investment firms; the terms on which this partnership were negotiated may therefore affect the ways in which future equity partnerships are formed. This highlights the way in which this unique farmer may contribute to shifting dynamics of the financialisation of Australian agriculture more broadly. A similar observation could be made of the intermediaries to Indigenous land discussed in Chapter 7. While the asset-making processes that they undertake are emergent and in many cases are yet to lead to the creation of physical businesses, some of the tools and processes through which land is mapped and investment is sought are already beginning to stabilise as they are taken up by intermediaries to Indigenous land working elsewhere. Innovative financial work undertaken by individuals can become influential in the development of 'best practice' interactions that are rolled out across very large areas of land, and shape the ways in which global finance engages with Indigenous land. In each of these examples, the distinction between the 'structured' and the 'unstructured' is unclear. That is, a range of assemblages of varying degrees of stabilisation can be observed, with local actors playing multiple roles in stabilising and destabilising larger structural patterns.

These four features of an assemblage approach have been usefully employed in this book to highlight the utility of such an ontology for exploring financialisation in the micro-processes of negotiation between local actors. The next section concludes by summarising the theoretical and applied contributions that arise from this study.

Conclusion

This book has shown the utility of an assemblage approach in exploring the work associated with financialisation. On a theoretical level, it is argued that the conceptualisation of financialisation as a homogeneous and inevitable process is problematic. An assemblage approach is then employed to explore the range of different actors that work to assemble new patterns of financial engagement with rural spaces. This section concludes the book by reviewing these theoretical and policy contributions.

Theoretical Contributions

The core theoretical contribution of this book is to the concept of financialisation and specifically to understandings of how financialisation is assembled at the local level. Applied to the study of agrifood systems, financialisation raises concerns about the ways that changing financial relations are remaking land and agribusinesses as vehicles for financial speculation, challenging national control over food systems, enabling the emergence of a neorentier landholder base, accelerating shifts towards monopoly control of food supply chains, and placing strain on family farms. These studies of financialisation usefully highlight the range of risks that financially driven agrifood transformations pose for local food systems. However, they say little about *how* these transformations occur and the range of ways they are negotiated in practice. The actual processes through which investments are negotiated remain obscured, and this makes them appear as the natural and inevitable result of wider structural circumstances.

The assemblage approach developed in this book encourages us to explore the work involved in forging connections between finance and agriculture. In particular, it highlights these connections as assemblages of heterogeneous elements in relations of exteriority, in which agency is distributed and causality is nonlinear, in ways that usefully overcome dichotomies between the structured and the unstructured. This approach allows an abstract global process such as 'financialisation' to be grounded in place-based studies in a way that 'localizes the market, demonstrating its embodiment' (Ho 2009, 6). The focus on local actors and spaces framed my approach to the book, with a specific emphasis on the work of local actors mediating investments into land and agribusiness in Northern Australia.

This book has also developed and demonstrated a methodology for undertaking this type of study, in addition to contributing to this emerging field of research. Anderson et al. (2012, 183) suggested that in an assemblage of nonlinear causality, 'the identification of mechanical causality results from "cuts" to the assemblage that reveal only specific interactions'. Key sites of study within an assemblage need to be identified in order to know where to 'cut' so that useful information may be gained. Interviews with a diverse range of local actors enabled the identification of critical issues in the negotiation of financial investments. The result is a focus on individuals who are able to 'modify a state of affairs by making a difference' (Latour 2005, 71). This approach to identifying crucial sites of study is important as it helps to avoid the directionless exploration of complexity (Forney, Rosin and Campbell 2018).

Based on interviews, document analysis and observation of financial practices, this methodology has enabled the exploration of the work involved in mediating financial investments into land and agribusiness in detail. This focus was guided by a diverse range of interdisciplinary literature that highlighted the need to explore the role of human agency, tools and geography in the work of financial intermediation. The result has been that from a large, shifting, disordered assemblage of relations between finance and Northern Australian agriculture, this book has identified five important *sites of work* that are shaping the operation of these assemblages (Chapters 3–7). Theoretically and methodologically, this has contributed to understandings of financialisation as assemblage and the particular ways in which financialisation is assembled in Northern Australia. It has also generated a number of important applied contributions to the field.

Applied Contributions

The studies of farmers, intermediaries to Indigenous land, governments, bankers and valuers described in this book each contribute theoretically to the concept of financialisation and the application of assemblage ontologies. However, as each of them is also an in-depth study of work involved in negotiating financial investments into land and agribusiness, they also offer practical insights into the challenges faced in these spaces and offer suggestions for potential policy responses. The specific recommendations of each are detailed in their respective chapters. In sum, they all reflect a central tension in financialised agricultural development efforts: that the financialisation of agriculture and agricultural development has created circumstances that place pressure on local spaces. Farmers have reduced access to finance, Indigenous communities face a lack of investment in development, and local governments lack budgets for infrastructure development. In response to these pressures, each of these groups of actors have become participants in financialisation, paradoxically supporting these patterns of change as an adaptive strategy to them. In a similar manner to Peck and Tickell's (2002) observations on 'roll-back' and 'roll-out' neoliberalism, financialisation comes to be supported through deliberate government and local actor work. This central tension was highlighted throughout Chapters 3–7 and was commonly raised during fieldwork, suggesting limits to financialisation as a governance and development strategy. Rather, greater attention needs to be paid to how financialisation differentially affects diverse actors to create a variety of local-level outcomes.

Rather than subscribing to oversimplified normative views of finance as either 'good' or 'bad', locally grounded approaches to development and agricultural support should be pursued. The practical insights provided in Chapters 3–7 could inform more grounded policy that is sensitive to the range of unexpected ways that global changes and national initiatives are negotiated at the local level. They highlight the need to avoid the assumption that a financialised approach to development will have predictable outcomes in the range of cultural and economic geographies of Northern Australia, and suggest the need for policies that are attentive to the unexpected ways in which local circumstances affect development outcomes. Attention to these features may contribute to better outcomes for remote Northern Australian spaces and communities.

These practical outcomes also highlight the limits of claims that an assemblage approach to financialisation is necessarily apolitical and unable to generate change. Rather, by suspending judgement of actors and their impacts, it is possible to identify how alignments of human agencies, tools and geographies contribute to, and resist, patterns of financialisation in diverse and often unexpected ways. I argue that imposing preconceived ideas about what finance is and does would not advance, but would hinder an understanding of financialisation as it arises in local spaces, and that this understanding is essential to supporting targeted policy advice.

Summary

This book has examined the work of local actors in negotiating financial investments in land and agribusiness in Northern Australia. Local people exercise human agency and work with particular nonhuman tools across diverse geographies, and this complexity shapes the form of financial investment in agriculture and contributes to the assemblage of broader financialising processes. This book has shown how these actors are both *subject to* pressures of financialisation, which constrain their choices and opportunities (for example, by reducing access to state supported farm and development finance), and respond to and *facilitate* financialisation, through work they undertake to access private finance capital. This work is undertaken in pursuit of individual goals, such as farm and community development, but nonetheless helps to expand the reach of finance into remote geographies. The pursuits of local actors shape the form of financial engagement in rural spaces in Northern Australia, and so can usefully be thought of as assembling broader patterns of financial investment. This evidence highlights financial investments as a social and relational process of negotiation, in which a diversity of human and nonhuman actors work to assemble broader agrifood transformations, facilitating and contesting financialisation in unexpected ways. Financialisation in this sense is viewed both as a broad pattern of global change and as an assemblage of locally embedded work that is unpredictable and often 'messy'. Attention to this work can improve regulatory responses to financialisation by locating it in particular places and processes, revealing its mechanisms such that they may be renegotiated.

REFERENCES

Aitkin, Don. 1985. 'Countrymindedness: The Spread of an Idea'. *Australian Cultural History* 4: 34–41.

Abolafia, Mitchel. Y. 1998. 'Markets as Cultures: An Ethnographic Approach'. *The Sociological Review* 46(1_suppl): 69–85, https://doi.org/10.1111/j.1467-954X.1998.tb03470.x.

Akhavein, Jalal, Lawrence Goldberg, and Lawrence White. 2004. 'Small Banks, Small Business, and Relationships: An Empirical Study of Lending to Small Farms'. *Journal of Financial Services Research* 26(3) (2004): 245–61. https://doi.org/10.1023/B:FINA.0000 040051.30624.e2.

Alston, Margaret. 2004. 'Who Is Down on the Farm? Social Aspects of Australian Agriculture in the 21st Century'. *Agriculture and Human Values* 21(1): 37–46, https://doi.org/10.1023/B:AHUM.0000014019.84085.59.

Altman, Jon C. 2004. 'Economic Development and Indigenous Australia: Contestations over Property, Institutions and Ideology'. *Australian Journal of Agricultural and Resource Economics* 48(3): 513–34, https://doi.org/10.1111/j.1467-8489.2004.00253.x.

Altman, Jon and Seán Kerins. 2012. *People on Country: Vital Landscapes, Indigenous Futures.* Alexandria: Federation Press.

Anderson, Ben, and Paul Harrison. 2010. 'The Promise of Non-representational Theories', in Ben Anderson and Paul Harrison (eds), *Taking-Place: Non-representational Theories and Geography.* Farnham: Ashgate, pp. 1–34.

Anderson, Ben, Matthew Kearnes, Colin McFarlane and Dan Swanton. 2012. 'On Assemblages and Geography'. *Dialogues in Human Geography* 2(2): 171–89, https://doi.org/10.1177/2043820612449261.

Anseeuw, Ward, Mathieu Boche, Thomas Breu, Markus Giger, Jann Lay, Peter Messerli and Kerstin Nolte. 2012. *Transnational Land Deals for Agriculture in the Global South: Analytical Report Based on the Land Matrix Database.* Retrieved 16 March 2023 from https://landm atrix.org/resources/transnational-land-deals-agriculture-global-south-analytical-report-bas ed-land-matrix-database.

ANZ. 2012. *Focus Greener Pastures: The Global Soft Commodity Opportunity for Australia and New Zealand, Issue 4.* Retrieved 16 March 2023 from https://bluenotes.anz.com/posts/20 12/10/greener-pastures.

Archer, Ronald. 2020. '"Business on Country: Land Use Diversification on the Indigenous Estate: Introduction and Summary." North Australian Indigenous Land and Sea Management Alliance. Retrieved 27 April 2023 from https://www.crcna.com.au/resources /publications/business-country-introduction

Araghi, Farshad. 2003. 'Food Regimes and the Production of Value: Some Methodological Issues'. *Journal of Peasant Studies* 30(2): 41–70, https://doi.org/10.1080/030661504123 31311129.

Arezki, Rabah, Klaus Deininger and Harris Selod. 2015. 'What Drives the Global "Land Rush"?' *World Bank Economic Review* 29(2): 207–33, https://doi.org/10.1093/wber/lh t034.

Argent, Neil. 1996. 'The Globalized Agriculture-Finance Relation: South Australian Farm Families and Communities in a New Regulatory Environment', in David Burch, Roy E. Rickson and Geoffrey Lawrence (eds), *Globalization and Agri-food Restructuring: Perspectives from the Australasia Region*. Aldershot: Avebury, pp. 283–300.

———. 2000. 'Whither the Lender of Last Resort? The Rise and Fall of Public Farm Credit in Australia and New Zealand'. *Journal of Rural Studies* 16(1): 61–77, https://doi.org/10.10 16/S0743-0167(99)00025-X.

———. 2011. 'Australian Agriculture in the Global Economic Mosaic', in Matthew Tonts and M.A. Siddique (eds), *Globalisation and Agriculture in the Asia-Pacific*. Cheltenham: Edward Elgar, pp. 7–28.

Armstrong, John, and Helen Armstrong. 2017. 'Submission No. 1 – John and Helen Armstrong, Economic Policy Scrutiny Committee, Pastoral Land Legislation Amendment Act, Gilnockie Station, Northern Territory, Australia'. Retrieved 16 March 2023 from https://parliament.nt.gov.au/__data/assets/pdf_file/0004/464251/Submission-No.-1-John -and-Helen-Armstrong.pdf.

Arrighi, Giovanni. 1994. *The Long Twentieth Century: Money, Power, and the Origins of Our Times*. New York: Verso.

Arrighi, Giovanni. 2010. *The Long Twentieth Century: Money, Power, and the Origins of Our Times*. New York: Verso.

Artis, Amélie. 2017. 'Social and Solidarity Finance: A Conceptual Approach'. *Research in International Business and Finance* 39: 737–49, https://doi.org/10.1016/j.ribaf.2015.11 .011.

Ascher, Ivan. 2016. *Portfolio Society*. Brooklyn: Zone Books. https://doi.org/10.2307/j.ctv14 gphwj,

Ash, Andrew. 2014. *Factors Driving the Viability of Major Cropping Investments in Northern Australia – A Historical Analysis*. Retrieved 20 June 2018 from http://northernaustralia.gov .au/sites/prod.office-northern-australia.gov.au/files/files/NA-food-fibre-supply-chain-appe ndix-3-1.pdf.

Athanasoglou, Panayiotis P., Ioannis Daniilidis, and Manthos D. Delis. 2014. 'Bank Procyclicality and Output: Issues and Policies.' *Journal of Economics and Business* 72: 58–83, https://doi.org/10.1016/j.jeconbus.2013.10.003.

Austin, Beau J., and Stephen T. Garnett. 2018. 'Perspectives on Success from Indigenous Entrepreneurs in Northern Australia'. *International Journal of Entrepreneurship and Small Business* 33(2): 176–201, https://doi.org/10.1504/IJESB.2018.090134.

Austin, Beau J., and Stephen T. Garnett. 2011. 'Indigenous Wildlife Enterprise: Mustering Swamp Buffalo (*Bubalus bubalis*) in Northern Australia'. *Journal of Enterprising Communities: People and Places in the Global Economy* 5(4): 309–23.

Austrade. 2015. 'Northern Australia: Emerging Opportunities in an Advanced Economy'. Retrieved 27 April 2023 from https://www.austrade.gov.au/ArticleDocuments/2814/Nort hern-Australia-emerging-opportunities-in-an-advanced-economy.pdf.aspx.

Australian Bureau of Statistics (ABS). 2018. 'Estimates of Aboriginal and Torres Strait Islander Australians'. Retrieved 24 April 2023 from https://www.abs.gov.au/statistics/people/abori ginal-and-torres-strait-islander-peoples/estimates-aboriginal-and-torres-strait-islander-aust

ralians/jun-2016#:~:text=The%20final%20estimated%20resident%20Aboriginal,of%20t
he%20total%20Australian%20population.

Australian Bureau of Statistics (ABS). 2022. 'Agricultural Commodities, Australia, 2020–2021'. Retrieved 16 March 2023 from https://www.abs.gov.au/statistics/industry/agricultu
re/agricultural-commodities-australia/latest-release#data-download.

Australian Government. 2012. 'Australia in the Asian Century: White Paper'. Retrieved 19 November 2019 from www.defence.gov.au/whitepaper/2013/docs/australia_in_the_asi
an_century_white_paper.pdf.

——. 2014. 'Green Paper on Developing Northern Australia'. Retrieved 26 April 2023 from https://www.infrastructure.gov.au/sites/default/files/documents/green-paper-on-developi
ng-northern-australia.pdf.

——. 2015a. 'Our North, Our Future: White Paper of Developing Northern Australia'. Retrieved 26 April 2023 from https://www.infrastructure.gov.au/sites/default/files/docum
ents/nawp-fullreport.pdf

——. 2015b. 'COAG Investigation into Indigenous Land Administration and Use'. Retrieved 16 March 2023 from https://www.niaa.gov.au/resource-centre/indigenous-affairs/coag-inv
estigation-indigenous-land-administration-and-use.

——. 2015c. 'Agricultural Competitiveness White Paper'. Retrieved 26 April 2023 from https://www.agriculture.gov.au/sites/default/files/documents/ag-competitiveness-white-pa
per_0.pdf.

——. 2017. 'COAG Investigation into Indigenous Land Administration and Use'. Retrieved 27 April 2023 from https://www.niaa.gov.au/resource-centre/indigenous-affairs/coag-inves
tigation-indigenous-land-administration-and-use.

——. 2020. 'Closing the Gap: Prime Minister's Report 2020'. Canberra: Department of Prime Minister and Cabinet. Retrieved 26 April 2023 from https://www.niaa.gov.au/resou
rce-centre/indigenous-affairs/closing-gap-prime-ministers-report-2020.

——. 2022. 'Northern Australia Roads Program and Northern Australia Beef Roads Program'. Retrieved 16 March 2023 from https://investment.infrastructure.gov.au/projects/key-proj
ects/northern-australia-programs.aspx.

——. 2022. 'Office of Northern Australia'. Retrieved 16 March 2023 from https://www.infras
tructure.gov.au/territories-regions-cities/regional-australia/office-northern-australia.

Australian Institute of Aboriginal and Torres Strait Islander Studies. 2022. 'Welcome to Country'. Retrieved 24 April 2023 from https://aiatsis.gov.au/explore/welcome-country
#:~:text=Country%20is%20the%20term%20often,material%20sustenance%2C%20fam
ily%20and%20identity.

Australian Institute of Aboriginal and Torres Strait Islander Studies. 2016. 'Native Title Information Handbook: Northern Territory 2016'. Retrieved 27 April 2023 from https://
aiatsis.gov.au/sites/default/files/research_pub/native_title_information_handbook_2016
_nt_2.pdf

Australian Institute of Health and Welfare. 2022. 'Indigenous Health and Wellbeing'. Retrieved 16 April 2023 from https://www.aihw.gov.au/reports/australias-health/indigen
ous-health-and-wellbeing.

Australian Institute of Health and Welfare. 2021. 'Indigenous Employment'. Retrieved 16 March 2023 from https://www.aihw.gov.au/reports/australias-welfare/indigenous-employ
ment.

Australian Institute of Health and Welfare. 2015. 'The Health and Welfare of Australia's Aboriginal and Torres Strait Islander Peoples'. Retrieved 16 March 2023 from https://www
.aihw.gov.au/reports/indigenous-health-welfare/indigenous-health-welfare-2015/contents
/differences-by-remoteness.

———. 2022. 'Rural and Remote Health'. Retrieved 16 March 2023 from https://www.aihw.gov.au/reports/rural-remote-australians/rural-and-remote-health.

Baines, Joseph. 2015. 'Fuel, Feed and the Corporate Restructuring of the Food Regime'. *Journal of Peasant Studies* 42(2): 295–321, https://doi.org/10.1080/03066150.2014.970534.

Bardon, Jane. 2019. 'Billionaire Businessman Launches Legal Action to Keep Origin Energy Fracking off NT Cattle Station'. *ABC News*, 23 June. Retrieved 16 March 2023 from https://www.abc.net.au/news/2019-06-23/billionaire-businessman-takes-on-origin-energy-supreme-court-nt/11237598.

Baud, Céline, and Cédric Durand. 2012. 'Financialization, Globalization and the Making of Profits by Leading Retailers'. *Socio-Economic Review* 10(2): 241–66, https://doi.org/10.1093/ser/mwr016.

Bauer, Francis Harry. 1964. 'Historical Geography of White Settlement in Part of Northern Australia. Part 2: The Katherine-Darwin Region'. *CSIRO Division of Land Research and Regional Survey*. Canberra, Australia.

Baumeister, Roy F., and Mark R. Leary. 1995. 'The Need to Belong'. *Psychological Bulletin* 117(3): 497–529, https://doi.org/10.1037/0033-2909.117.3.497.

Bayliss, Kate, and Elisa van Waeyenberge. 2018. 'Unpacking the Public Private Partnership Revival'. *Journal of Development Studies* 54(4): 577–93, https://doi.org/10.1080/00220388.2017.1303671.

Beck, Thorsten, Hans Degryse, Ralph De Haas, and Neeltje van Horen. 2018. 'When Arm's Length Is Too Far: Relationship Banking over the Credit Cycle'. *Journal of Financial Economics* 127(1): 174–96, https://doi.org/10.1016/j.jfineco.2017.11.007.

Beckert, Jens, and Christine Musselin. 2013. 'Introduction', in J. Beckert and C. Musselin (eds), *Constructing Quality: The Classification of Goods in Markets*. Oxford: Oxford University Press, pp. 1–30.

Beilin, Ruth. 2018. 'Assemblage and the Epistemology of Practice', in Jérémie Forney, Chris Rosin and Hugh Campbell (eds), *Agri-environmental Governance as an Assemblage*. Abingdon: Routledge, pp. 213–31.

Bell, Stephen. 2017. "Historical Institutionalism and New Dimensions of Agency: Bankers, Institutions and the 2008 Financial Crisis'. *Political Studies* 65(3): 724–39, https://doi.org/10.1177/0032321716675884.

Bennett, Jane. 2010. *Vibrant 'Matter a Political Ecology of Things*. Durham, NC: Duke University Press.

Benedikter, Roland. 2011. *Social Banking and Social Finance Answers to the Economic Crisis*. New York: Springer.

Berg, Gunhild, and Jan Schrader. 2012. 'Access to Credit, Natural Disasters, and Relationship Lending'. *Journal of Financial Intermediation* 21(4): 549–68, https://doi.org/10.1016/j.jfi.2012.05.003.

Bessy, Christian, and Pierre-Marie Chauvin. 2013. 'The Power of Market Intermediaries: From Information to Valuation Processes'. *Studies in Educational Evaluation* 1(1): 83–117, https://doi.org/10.3384/vs.2001-5992.131183.

Betts, Alyssa. 2016. 'Concerns over Water Access after Timber Company Tropical Forestry Services Buys Stylo Station'. *ABC News*, 4 February. Retrieved 16 March 2023 from https://www.abc.net.au/news/2016-02-04/water-licence-for-stylo-station/7139066.

Bianchi, Robert J., John Hua Fan, and Neda Todorova. 2020. 'Financialization and De-financialization of Commodity Futures: A Quantile Regression Approach'. *International Review of Financial Analysis* 68: 101451, https://doi.org/10.1016/j.irfa.2019.101451.

Birch, Kean. 2015. *We Have Never Been Neoliberal*. Ropley: John Hunt Publishing.

186 • References

———. 2017. 'Rethinking "Value" in the Bio-economy: Finance, Assetization, and the Management of Value'. *Science, Technology, & Human Values* 42(3): 460–90, https://doi.org/10.1177/0162243916661633.

Birch, Kean, and Fabian Muniesa (2020). "Introduction: Assetization and Technoscientific Capitalism". In Assetization: Turning Things into Assets in Technoscientific Capitalism, edited by K. Birch and F. Muniesa, 1–41. Cambridge, MA: MIT Press.

Bjørkhaug, Hilde and Jostein Brobakk. 2018. 'Profit, Aid and Ethics in Public Financialization', in Hilde Bjørkhaug, Andre Magnan and Geoffrey Lawrence (eds), *The Financialization of Agri-food Systems*. Abingdon: Routledge, pp. 42–61.

Bjørkhaug, Hilde, Philip McMichael and Bruce Muirhead. 2020. *Finance or Food? The Role of Cultures, Values, and Ethics in Land Use Negotiations*. Toronto: University of Toronto Press.

Blackburn, Robin. 2006. 'Finance and the Fourth Dimension'. *New Left Review* 39: 39–70.

Bolton, Patrick, Xavier Freixas, Leonardo Gambacorta, and Paolo Emilio Mistrulli. 2016. 'Relationship and Transaction Lending in a Crisis'. *The Review of Financial Studies* 29(10): 2643–76, https://doi.org/10.1093/rfs/hhw041.

Bonanno, Alessandro, and Steven Wolf. 2014. 'The Legitimation Crisis of Neoliberal Globalization: Instances from Agriculture and Food', in Steven Wolf and Alessandro Bonanno (eds), *The Neoliberal Regime in the Agri-food Sector*. Abingdon: Routledge, pp. 13–31.

Borras, Saturnino M., and Jennifer C. Franco. 2013. 'Global Land Grabbing and Political Reactions "from Below"'. *Third World Quarterly* 34(9): 1723–47, https://doi.org/10.1080/01436597.2013.843845.

Borras, Saturnino M., Jennifer C. Franco, Tsegaye Moreda, Yunan Xu, Natacha Bruna and Binyam Afewerk Demena. 2022. 'The Value of So-Called "Failed" Large-Scale Land Acquisitions'. *Land Use Policy* 119: 106199, https://doi.org/10.1016/j.landusepol.2022.106199.

Borras, Saturnino M., Elyse N. Mills, Philip Seufert, Stephan Backes, Daniel Fyfe, Roman Herre and Laura Michéle. 2020. 'Transnational Land Investment Web: Land Grabs, TNCs, and the Challenge of Global Governance'. *Globalizations* 17(4): 608–28, https://doi.org/10.1080/14747731.2019.1669384.

Bortz, Pablo G., and Annina Kaltenbrunner. 2018. 'The International Dimension of Financialization in Developing and Emerging Economies'. *Development and Change* 49(2): 375–93, https://doi.org/10.1111/dech.12371.

Boy, Nina, and Daniela Gabor. 2019. 'Collateral Times'. *Economy and Society* 48(3): 295–314, https://doi.org/10.1080/03085147.2019.1672315.

Boyce Chartered Accountants and Su McCluskey. 2016. 'Tax in Agriculture: A Collaborative Research Project for the Agricultural Sector. Publication No 16/019, Australian Government, Rural Industries Research and Development Corporation'. Retrieved 16 March 2023 from https://www.mla.com.au/globalassets/mla-corporate/research-and-development/documents/industry-issues/final_taxinag-dec-2016-.pdf.

Boyer, Robert. 2000. 'Is a Finance-Led Growth Regime a Viable Alternative to Fordism? A Preliminary Analysis'. *Economy and Society* 29(1): 111–45, https://doi.org/10.1080/030851400360587.

Bradbury, Matt. 2022. 'Hughenden Irrigation Project Final DBC V87 – 28 April 2022'. *Jacobs*. Retrieved 16 March 2023 from https://hipco.com.au/wp-content/uploads/Hughenden-Irrigation-Project-DBC-v87-Final-with-Departmental-Statement2-28-April-2022.pdf.

Brann, Matt. 2017. 'WA Government Grant to Kick Start Irrigation Project on Roebuck Plains Cattle Station'. *ABC News*, 31 January. Retrieved 16 March 2023 from www.abc

.net.au/news/rural/2017-01-31/government-grant-for-irrigation-project-roebuck-plains-st ation/8223004.

——. 2019. 'Rice Farming Returns to Humpty Doo Using Australia's Own Native Grains'. *ABC News*, 2 April. Retrieved 16 March 2023 from https://www.abc.net.au/news/rural/20 19-04-02/native-rice-trials-set-for-the-northern-territory/10959786.

——. 2022a. 'Indian Sandalwood Company Quintis Puts Northern Territory Farm on Market'. *ABC News*, 18 August. Retrieved 16 March 2023 from https://www.abc.net .au/news/rural/2022-08-18/quintis-indian-sandalwood-farm-mataranka-for-sale/10133 7754.

——. 2022b. 'Ord Irrigation Scheme to Expand into the NT, AAMIG Selected as Developer'. *ABC News*, 3 February. Retrieved 16 March 2023 from https://www.abc.net.au/news/rural /2022-02-03/ord-irrigation-scheme-expands-into-northern-territory/100801664.

Braun, Veit. 2020. 'From Commodity to Asset and Back Again: Property in the Capitalism of Varieties', in K. Birch and F. Muniesa (eds), *Assetization: Turning Things into Assets in Technoscientific Capitalism*. Cambridge, MA: MIT Press, pp. 203–24.

Brenner, Neil, Jamie Peck and Nik Theodore. 2010. 'After Neoliberalization?' *Globalizations* 7(3): 327–45, https://doi.org/10.1080/14747731003669669.

Brewarrana Pty Ltd v Commissioner of Highways (No. 1) (1973) 32 LGRA 170 at 179–180.

Brueckner, Martin, Rochelle Spencer, Gareth Wise and Bundak Marika. 2014. 'Indigenous Entrepreneurship: Closing the Gap on Local Terms'. *Journal of Australian Indigenous Issues* 17(2): 2–24.

Burch, David, and Geoffrey Lawrence. 2009. 'Towards a Third Food Regime: Behind the Transformation'. *Agriculture and Human Values* 26(4): 267–79, https://doi.org/10.1007 /s10460-009-9219-4.

——. 2013. 'Financialization in Agri-food Supply Chains: Private Equity and the Transformation of the Retail Sector'. *Agriculture and Human Values* 30(2): 247–58, https:// doi.org/10.1007/s10460-012-9413-7.

Bureau of Agricultural Economics. 1968. *The Northern Territory Beef Cattle Industry: An Economic Survey, 1962–63 to 1964–65*. Canberra: Australian Bureau of Agricultural Economics.

Bureau of Meteorology. 2016. 'Weather Maps'. Retrieved 16 March 2023 from http://www .bom.gov.au/australia/charts.

Busch, Timo, Peter Bruce-Clark, Jeroen Derwall, Robert Eccles, Tessa Hebb, Aneas Hoepner, Christian Klein et al. 2021. 'Impact Investments: A Call for (Re)Orientation'. *SN Business & Economics* 1(2), https://doi.org/10.1007/s43546-020-00033-6.

Byerlee, Derek, and Klaus Deininger. 2011. 'Foreign Investment in Farmland: Worries about a Land Grab in Australia Are Unfounded'. *Farm Policy Journal* 8(2): 1–9.

——. 2013. Growing Resource Scarcity and Global Farmland Investment. *Annual Review of Resource Economics* 5(1): 13–34.

Çalışkan, Koray, and Michel Callon. 2009. 'Economization, Part 1: Shifting Attention from the Economy towards Processes of Economization'. *Economy and Society* 38(3): 369–98, https://doi.org/10.1080/03085140903020580.

Callon, Michel. 1984. 'Some Elements of a Sociology of Translation: Domestication of the Scallops and the Fishermen of St Brieuc Bay'. *Sociological Review* 32: 196–233, https://doi .org/10.1111/j.1467-954X.1984.tb00113.x.

——. 1998. *The Laws of the Markets*. London: Blackwell.

——. 2006. 'What Does It Mean to Say That Economics Is Performative?' *IDEAS Working Paper Series from RePEc*. Retrieved 16 March 2023 from https://ideas.repec.org/p/emn/wp aper/005.html.

Callon, Michel, Pierre Lascoumes and Yannick Barthe. 2009. Acting in an Uncertain World: An Essay on Technical Democracy. Cambridge, MA: MIT Press.

Callon, Michel, and John Law. 2005. 'On Qualculation, Agency, and Otherness'. *Environment and Planning D: Society & Space* 23(5): 717–33, https://doi.org/10.1068/d343t.

Campbell, Hugh. 2009. 'Breaking New Ground in Food Regime Theory: Corporate Environmentalism, Ecological Feedbacks and the "Food from Somewhere" Regime'. *Agriculture and Human Values* 26(4): 309–19, https://doi.org/10.1007/s10460-009-9215-8.

Campbell, Hugh, and Jane Dixon. 2009. 'Introduction to the Special Symposium: Reflecting on Twenty Years of The Food Regimes Approach in Agri-food Studies'. *Agriculture and Human Values* 26(4): 261–65.

Campbell, Hugh, and Chris Rosin. 2011. 'After the "Organic Industrial Complex": An Ontological Expedition through Commercial Organic Agriculture in New Zealand'. *Journal of Rural Studies* 27(4): 350–61.

Campbell-Verduyn, Malcolm, Marcel Goguen and Tony Porter. 2017. 'Big Data and Algorithmic Governance: The Case of Financial Practices'. *New Political Economy* 22(2): 219–36, https://doi.org/10.1080/13563467.2016.1216533.

Carolan, Michael S. 2006. 'Sustainable Agriculture, Science and the Co-Production of "Expert" Knowledge: The Value of Interactional Expertise'. *Local Environment* 11(4): 421–31, https://doi.org/10.1080/13549830600785571.

——. 2012. *The Sociology of Food and Agriculture*. Abingdon: Routledge.

——. 2018. *The Real Cost of Cheap Food*, 2nd edn. New York: Routledge.

Carrier, James G. 2018. 'Moral Economy: What's in a Name'. *Anthropological Theory* 18(1): 18–35, https://doi.org/10.1177/1463499617735259.

Centrefarm. 2010. 'Who Are Centrefarm?' Retrieved 27 April 2023 from https://centrefarm.com/who-are-centrefarm/.

Centrefarm and TopEndfarm. 2019. 'The Aboriginal Land and Sea Economic Development Agency (ALSEDA): Submission to the Joint Standing Committee on Northern Australia Inquiry into the Opportunities and Challenges of the Engagement of Traditional Owners in the Economic Development of Northern Australia'. Alice Springs: Centrefarm/TopEndfarm. Retrieved 27 April 2023 from https://www.aph.gov.au/DocumentStore.ashx?id=f18822a1-524b-4823-8175-d81497ab1100&subId=669975.

Celik, Serdar, and Mats Isaksson. 2013. 'Institutional Investors and Ownership Engagement'. *OECD Journal* 2013(2): 93–114.

Cetina, Karin Knorr, and Urs Bruegger. 2002. 'Global Microstructures: The Virtual Societies of Financial Markets'. *American Journal of Sociology* 107(4): 905–50, https://doi.org/10.1086/341045.

Chang, Hui-Shung, and Paul Kristiansen. 2006. 'Selling Australia as Clean and Green'. *Australian Journal of Agricultural and Resource Economics* 50(1): 103–13, https://doi.org/10.1111/j.1467-8489.2006.00330.x.

Chen, James. 2021. 'Real Asset: What Is a Real Asset?' *Investopedia*, 22 May. Retrieved 16 March 2023 from https://www.investopedia.com/terms/r/realasset.asp#:~:text=Real%20assets%20are%20physical%20assets,%2C%20equipment%2C%20and%20natural%20resources.

Cheshire, Lynda, Carla Meurk and Michael Woods. 2013. 'Decoupling Farm, Farming and Place: Recombinant Attachments of Globally Engaged Family Farmers'. *Journal of Rural Studies* 30: 64–74, https://doi.org/10.1016/j.jrurstud.2012.11.005.

Cheshire, Lynda, and Michael Woods. 2013. 'Globally Engaged Farmers as Transnational Actors: Navigating the Landscape of Agri-food Globalization'. *Geoforum* 44: 232–42, https://doi.org/10.1016/j.geoforum.2012.09.003.

Chilcott, Chris, Andrew Ash, Sigrid Lehnert, Chris Stokes, Ed Charmley, Kerry Collins, Chris Pavey, Andrew Macintosh, Amelia Simpson, Renata Berglas, Emma White and Martin Amity. 2020. 'Northern Australia Beef Situation Analysis'. *Cooperative Research Centre for Developing Northern Australia*. Retrieved 16 March 2023 from https://crcna.com.au/resources/publications/northern-australia-beef-situation-analysis-report-cooperative-research-centre-developing-northern-australia.

Christian, Clifford Stuart. 1977. 'Agricultural Cropping in Northern Australia: A General Review', in *Cropping in North Australia*. Canberra: North Australia Research Unit of the Australian National University, pp. 11–34.

Christian, Clifford Stuart, and Alan Stewart. 1953. *General Report on Survey of Katherine-Darwin Region, 1946*. CSIRO Land Research Series No. 1.

Christophers, Brett. 2015. 'The Limits to Financialisation'. *Dialogues in Human Geography* 5(2): 183–200.

Clapp, Jennifer. 2012. *Food*. Malden, MA: Polity.

———. 2014. 'Financialization, Distance, and Global Food Politics'. *Journal of Peasant Studies* 41(6): 797–814.

———. 2017. 'Responsibility to the Rescue? Governing Private Financial Investment in Global Agriculture'. *Agriculture and Human Values* 30(2): 247–58.

Clapp, Jennifer, and Doris Fuchs. 2009. *Corporate Power in Global Agrifood Governance*. Cambridge, MA: MIT Press.

Clapp, Jennifer, and S. Ryan Isakson. 2018a. *Speculative Harvests: Financialization, Food, and Agriculture*. Rugby: Practical Action Publishing.

———. 2018b. 'Risky Returns: The Implications of Financialization in the Food System'. *Development and Change* 49(2): 437–60.

Clapp, Jennifer, S. Ryan Isakson and Oane Visser. 2017. 'The Complex Dynamics of Agriculture as a Financial Asset: Introduction to Symposium'. *Agriculture and Human Values* 34(1): 179–83.

Clarkson, Chris, Zenobia Jacobs, Ben Marwick, Richard Fullagar, Lynley Wallis, Mike Smith, Richard G. Roberts et al. 2017. 'Human Occupation of Northern Australia by 65,000 Years Ago'. *Nature* 547(7663): 306–10, https://doi.org/10.1038/nature22968.

Cochet, Hubert. 2018. 'Capital-Labour Separation and Unequal Value-Added Distribution: Repositioning Land Grabbing in the General Movement of Contemporary Agricultural Transformations'. *Journal of Peasant Studies* 45(7): 1410–31, https://doi.org/10.1080/03066150.2017.1311866.

Cocklin, Chris, Jacqui Dibden and David Gibbs. 2008. 'Competitiveness versus "Clean and Green"? The Regulation and Governance of GMOs in Australia and the UK'. *Geoforum* 39(1): 161–73, https://doi.org/10.1016/j.geoforum.2006.09.009.

Collier, Stephen J. 2017. 'Neoliberalism and Rule by Experts', in Vaughn Higgins and Wendy Larner (eds), *Assembling Neoliberalism*. New York: Palgrave Macmillan, pp. 23–43.

Collins, Ben. 2019. 'Indigenous Cattle Company Building Billionaire-Style Cattle Empire That Puts People before Profits'. *ABC News*, 2 January. Retrieved 16 March 2023 from https://www.abc.net.au/news/rural/2019-01-22/indigenous-cattle-company-double-kimberley-acreage/10612428.

Commonwealth of Australia. 2017. *Letters Patent of the Financial Services Royal Commission*. Retrieved 16 March 2023 from https://www.royalcommission.gov.au/banking/letters-patent.

———. 2019. *Royal Commission into Misconduct in the Banking, Superannuation and Financial Services Industry*. Retrieved 16 March 2023 from https://static.treasury.gov.au/uploads/sites/1/2019/02/fsrc-volume1.pdf.

190 • References

——. 2021. 'Report on Indigenous Participation in Employment and Business'. *House of Representatives Standing Committee on Indigenous Affairs*. Retrieved 16 March 2023 from https://www.aph.gov.au/binaries/house/committee/atsia/Indigenousenterprises/report/full report.pdf.

Communicable Diseases Network Australia (CDNA). 2021. *National Guidance for Remote Aboriginal and Torres Strait Islander Communities for COVID-19*. Version 3, revised 7 December 2021. Retrieved 16 March 2023 from https://www.health.gov.au/resources/pu blications/cdna-national-guidance-for-remote-aboriginal-and-torres-strait-islander-comm unities-for-covid-19.

Connelly, Steve, Tim Richardson and Tim Miles. 2006. 'Situated Legitimacy: Deliberative Arenas and the New Rural Governance'. *Journal of Rural Studies* 22(3): 267–77, https://doi.org/10.1016/j.jrurstud.2005.11.008.

Connolly, William E. 2005. *Pluralism*. Durham, NC: Duke University Press.

Cook, Garry. 2009. 'Historical Perspectives on Land Use Development in Northern Australia: With Emphasis on the Northern Territory'. *Northern Australian Land and Water Science Review*: Full Report, Canberra. CSIRO Sustainable Agriculture Flagship and Northern Australia Land and Water Taskforce, Canberra.

Cordonnier, Laurent, and Franck van de Velde. 2015. 'The Demands of Finance and the Glass Ceiling of Profit without Investment'. *Cambridge Journal of Economics* 39(3): 871–85, https://doi.org/10.1093/cje/beu064.

Corey, Ben, Grahame Webb, Charlie Manolis, Adrian Fordham, Beau Austin, Yusuke Fukuda, Dominic Nicholls and Keith Saalfeld. 2018. 'Commercial Harvests of Saltwater Crocodile Crocodylus Porosus Eggs by Indigenous People in Northern Australia: Lessons for Long-Term Viability and Management'. *Oryx* 52(4): 697–708, https://doi.org/10.1017/S0030 605317000217.

Cotula, Lorenzo. 2009. *Land Grab or Development Opportunity? Agricultural Investment and International Land Deals in Africa*. New York: IIED.

——. 2012. 'International Political Economy of the Global Land Rush: A Critical Appraisal of Trends, Scale, Geography and Drivers'. *Journal of Peasant Studies* 39(3–4): 649–80, https://doi.org/10.1080/03066150.2012.674940.

Cotula, Lorenzo, and Emma Blackmore. 2014. *Understanding Agricultural Investment Chains: Lessons to Improve Governance*. London: Food and Agriculture Organization of the United Nations.

Cranston, Matthew. 2016. 'QIC Buys Cattle Station Business NAPCo in Deal Bigger Than S.Kidman and Co'. *Financial Review*, 6 May. Retrieved 27 April 2023 from https://www.afr.com/real-estate/qic-buys-cattle-station-business-napco-in-deal-bigger-than-skidman--co-20160505-gomvh2.

Craw, Charlotte. 2008. 'The Flavours of the Indigenous: Branding Native Food Products in Contemporary Australia'. *Sites: A Journal of Social Anthropology and Cultural Studies* 5(1): 41–62, https://doi.org/10.11157/sites-vol5iss1id86.

Crotty, James. 2003. 'The Neoliberal Paradox: The Impact of Destructive Product Market Competition and Impatient Finance on Nonfinancial Corporations in the Neoliberal Era'. *Review of Radical Political Economics* 35(3): 271–79, https://doi.org/10.1177/0486613403255533.

D'Abbs, Peter. 1970. *The Vestey Story*. Melbourne: Australasian Meat Industry Employees' Union Victorian Branch.

Dale, Allan. 2014. *Beyond the North-South Culture Wars: Reconciling Northern Australia's Recent Past with Its Future*. New York: Springer.

Daniel, Shepard. 2012. 'Situating Private Equity Capital in the Land Grab Debate'. *Journal of Peasant Studies* 39(3–4): 703–29, https://doi.org/10.1080/03066150.2012.674941.

Davidson, Bruce Robinson. 1972. *The Northern Myth: A Study of the Physical and Economic Limits to Agricultural and Pastoral Development in Tropical Australia*, 3rd edn. Carlton, VIC: Melbourne University Press.

Deininger, Klaus, and Derek Byerlee. 2011. *Rising Global Interest in Farmland: Rising Global Interest in Farmland*. Herndon: World Bank Publications. https://doi.org/10.1596/978-0-8213-8591-3.

Dempsey, Jessica, and Patrick Bigger. 2019. 'Intimate Mediations of for-Profit Conservation Finance: Waste, Improvement, and Accumulation'. *Antipode* 51(2): 517–38, https://doi.org/10.1111/anti.12503.

Department of Agriculture and Water Resources. 2018. *Agricultural Lending Data 2016–17*. Commonwealth of Australia. Retrieved 16 March 2023 from http://www.agriculture.gov.au/ag-farm-food/drought/agricultural-lending-data.

Department of External Affairs. 1912. *Report of Preliminary Scientific Expedition to the Northern Territory*. Melbourne: Department of External Affairs.

Department of Trade, Business and Innovation (DTBI), Northern Territory Government. 2018. *International Engagement, Trade and Investment Strategic Plan 2018–2021*. NT Government. Retrieved 5 December 2020 from https://business.nt.gov.au/publications/strategies/international-engagement-trade-and-investment-strategic-plan-2018-2021.

Department of Trade, Business and Innovation (DTBI), Northern Territory Government. 2019. *Territory Benefit Policy* (Version 1.12). Retrieved 16 March 2023 from https://business.nt.gov.au/publications/policies/territory-benefit-policy.

Department of Trade, Business and Innovation (DTBI), Northern Territory Government. 2022. *International Engagement Strategy 2022–2026*. NT Government. Retrieved 24 April 2023 from https://industry.nt.gov.au/__data/assets/pdf_file/0008/1095497/international-engagement-strategy-2022-2026.pdf.

DeLanda, Manuel. 2006. *A New Philosophy of Society: Assemblage Theory and Social Complexity*. New York: Continuum.

———. 2016. *Assemblage Theory*. Edinburgh: Edinburgh University Press.

Deleuze, Gilles, and Felix Guattari. 1987. *A Thousand Plateaus: Capitalism and Schizophrenia*. Translated by Brian Massumi. London: Continuum.

Deleuze, Gilles, and Claire Parnet. 1977. *Dialogues*. New York: Columbia University Press.

Dewey, John. 1939. *Theory of Valuation*. Chicago: University of Chicago Press.

Donovan, Peter Francis. 1981. *A Land Full of Possibilities: A History of South Australia's Northern Territory*. Brisbane: University of Queensland Press.

Drahos, Peter, and Susy Frankel. 2012. *Indigenous Peoples' Innovation: Intellectual Property Pathways to Development*. Canberra: ANU E Press.

Du Gay, Paul, Yuval Millo and Penelope Tuck. 2012. 'Making Government Liquid: Shifts in Governance Using Financialisation as a Political Device'. *Environment and Planning C: Politics and Space* 30(6): 1083–99.

Ducastel, Antoine, and Ward Anseeuw. 2013. 'Situating Investment Funds in Agriculture'. *Farm Policy Journal* 10(3): 23–32.

———. 2017. 'Agriculture as an Asset Class: Reshaping the South African Farming Sector'. *Agriculture and Human Values* 34(1): 199–209.

———. 2018. 'Facing Financialization: the Divergent Mutation of Agricultural Cooperatives in Postapartheid South Africa'. *Journal of Agrarian Change* 8(3): 555–70.

Duménil, Gérard., and Dominique Lévy. 2004. *Capital Resurgent: Roots of the Neoliberal Revolution*. Cambridge: Harvard University Press.

Duncan, Ross. 1967. *The Northern Territory Pastoral Industry, 1863–1910*. Carlton, VIC: Melbourne University Press.

192 • References

Duncan, Emily, Sarah Rotz, André Magnan and Kelly Bronson. 2022. 'Disciplining Land through Data: The Role of Agricultural Technologies in Farmland Assetisation'. *Sociologia Ruralis* 62(2): 231–49, https://doi.org/10.1111/soru.12369.

Economic Policy Scrutiny Committee (EPSC). 2018. 'Legislative Assembly of the Northern Territory. 13th Assembly of the Economic Policy Scrutiny Committee, Public Hearing Transcript', 2 February. Retrieved 16 March 2023 from https://parliament.nt.gov.au/__d ata/assets/pdf_file/0008/485630/FINAL-TRANSCRIPT-ECONOMIC-POLICY-SCRU TINY-COMMITTEE-Friday-2-February-2018.PDF.

Edwards, Tom. 2015. 'Indigenous Cattle Station in Western Australia Attracts Interest from International Investors'. *ABC News*, 15 December. Retrieved 16 March 2023 from http:// www.abc.net.au/news/rural/2015–12–15/mowanjum-attracts-international-investors/702 7830.

Elder, Peter. 1979. *Northern Territory Charlie: Charles James Dashwood in Palmerston 1892– 1905.* Thesis (B.A. Hons) Australian National University.

Elder-Vass, Dave, and Timothy Rutzou. 2017. 'Social Science and Realism after Assemblage Theory', Retrieved 16 March 2023 from https://www.youtube.com/watch?v=qAPeZfc KtMU.

Elders. 2023. Agriculture Services. Retrieved 26 April 2023 from www.elders.com.au/our-ser vices/agriculture-services/.

Epstein, Gerald A. 2002. *Financialization, rentier interests and Central Bank Policy.* Paper prepared for PERI conference December 7-8, 2001, University of Massachusetts, Amherst. Retrieved 27 April 2023 from https://peri.umass.edu/fileadmin/pdf/financial/fin_Epstein .pdf.

Epstein, Gerald A. 2005. *Financialization and the World Economy.* Cheltenham: Edward Elgar.

———. 2019. 'Financialization, Rentier Interests and Central Bank Policy', in *The Political Economy of Central Banking.* Cheltenham: Edward Elgar, 2019, pp. 380–406.

Erturk, Ismail. 2008. *Financialization at Work: Key Texts and Commentary.* New York: Routledge.

Espeland, Wendy, and Mitchell Stevens 1998. 'Commensuration as a Social Process'. *Annual Review of Sociology* 24(1): 313–43, https://doi.org/10.1146/annurev.soc.24.1.313.

Everingham, Sara. 2017. 'Former CLP Candidate Tina Macfarlane Allocated More Water Than She Could Have Used, Review Says'. *ABC News*, 25 November. Retrieved 16 March 2023 from https://www.abc.net.au/news/2017-11-25/tina-macfarlane-allocated-more-wat er-than-she-could-have-used/9193288.

Eves, Chris. 2016. 'The Analysis of NSW Rural Property Investment Returns: 1990–2014', *Farm Policy Journal* 13(2): 35–43.

Fairbairn, Madeleine. 2014. '"Like Gold with Yield": Evolving Intersections between Farmland and Finance'. *Journal of Peasant Studies* 41(5): 777–95.

———. 2015. 'Foreignization, Financialization and Land Grab Regulation'. *Journal of Agrarian Change* 15(4): 581–91.

———. 2020. *Fields of Gold: Financing the Global Land Rush.* Ithaca, NY: Cornell University Press.

Ferguson, Megan, Kerin O'Dea, Mark Chatfield, Marjory Moodie, Jon Altman and Julie Brimblecombe. 2016. 'The Comparative Cost of Food and Beverages at Remote Indigenous Communities, Northern Territory, Australia'. *Australian and New Zealand Journal of Public Health* 40(S1): S21–S26, https://doi.org/10.1111/1753-6405.12370.

Fernandes, Aaron, and Kearyn Cox. 2022. 'Remote Communities Pay 39 Per Cent More at the Supermarket Checkout Than City Shoppers: Here's Why That's a Problem'. *SBS News*, 17 May. Retrieved 16 March 2023 from https://www.sbs.com.au/news/article/remote-co

mmunities-pay-39-per-cent-more-at-the-supermarket-checkout-than-city-shoppers-heres
-why-thats-a-problem/se08d2zjm.

Fiordelisi, Franco, Stefano Monferrà, and Gabriele Sampagnaro. 2014. 'Relationship Lending and Credit Quality'. *Journal of Financial Services Research* 46(3): 295–315, https://doi.org /10.1007/s10693-013-0176-0.

Fisher, M.J., Garside, A.L., Skerman, P.J., Chapman, A.L., Strickland, R.W., Myers, R.J.K., Wood, I.M.W., Beech, D.F. and Henzell, E.F.(1977). 'The Role of Technical and Related Problems in the Failure of Some Agricultural Development Schemes in Northern Australia', in Francis Harry Bauer (ed.), *Cropping in North Australia: Anatomy of Success and Failure*. Canberra: North Australia Research Unit of the Australian National University, pp. 35–94.

Fitzgerald, Daniel. 2015. 'Major Development Continues at Amungee Mungee Station, One Year on from Purchase'. *ABC News*, 17 April. Retrieved 16 March 2023 from https://www .abc.net.au/news/rural/2015-04-17/amungee-mungee-station-changes/6399430.

——. 2016a. 'Stylo Station Transformed into Indian Sandalwood Plantation by Tropical Forestry Services'. *ABC News*, 22 June. Retrieved 16 March 2023 from https://www.abc .net.au/news/rural/2016-06-15/tfs-stylo-station-development/7511608.

——. 2016b. 'Greenhouse in Remote Arnhem Land Community Aims to Supply Fresh Produce'. *ABC News*, 7 November. Retrieved 16 March 2023 from http://www.abc.net .au/news/rural/2016-11-07/ramingining-greenhouse-providing-local-produce-remote-arn hem/8001902.

——. 2017a. 'Quintis Controls More Top End Groundwater Than Government-Owned Water and Electricity Provider'. *ABC News*, 16 October. Retrieved 16 March 2023 from https://www.abc.net.au/news/rural/2017-10-16/sandalwood-Quintis-controls-largest-am ount-of-water-in-top-end/9018262.

——. 2017b. 'Tropical Forestry Services Buys Profitable Northern Territory Banana, Melon Farm'. *ABC News*, 27 January. Retrieved 16 March 2023 from https://www.abc.net.au /news/rural/2017-01-27/douglas-daly-only-horticulture-farm-bought-by-forestry-tfs/821 7278.

——. 2017c. 'Massive Water Development Underway at Top End Station, with Hopes to Run 140,000 Cattle'. *ABC News*, 11 September. Retrieved 16 March 2023 from https:// www.abc.net.au/news/rural/2017-09-11/massive-water-development-underway-at-walhall ow-barkly/8881416.

Fleming, Ann. 2015a. 'Improving Business Investment Confidence in Culture-Aligned Indigenous Economies in Remote Australian Communities: A Business Support Framework to Better Inform Government Programs'. *International Indigenous Policy Journal* 6(3): 5, https://doi.org/10.18584/iipj.2015.6.3.5.

——. 2015b. *Identifying the Key Social and Economic Factors for Successful Engagement in Aquaculture Ventures by Indigenous Communities*. Darwin: Fisheries Research and Development Corporation, Northern Territory Government.

Fleming, Ann, Lisa Petheram and Natasha Stacey. 2015. 'Australian Indigenous Women's Seafood Harvesting Practices and Prospects for Integrating Aquaculture'. *Journal of Enterprising Communities* 9(2): 156–81, https://doi.org/10.1108/JEC-08-2014-0013.

Flick, Uwe. 2018. *Doing Triangulation and Mixed Methods*. London: SAGE Publications.

Food Ladder. 2022. 'Katherine, NT'. Retrieved 16 March 2023 from https://www.foodladder .org/projects/katherine-nt.

Foreign Investment Review Board (FIRB). 2017. *Register of Foreign Ownership of Agricultural Land: Report of Registrations as at 30 June 2016*. Retrieved 16 March 2023 from https://firb .gov.au/sites/firb.gov.au/files/2016/08/Register_of_foreign_ownership_of_agricultural_ land.pdf.

——. 2018. *Register of Foreign Ownership of Agricultural Land: Report of Registrations as at 30 June 2017*. Retrieved 16 March 2023 from https://firb.gov.au/sites/firb.gov.au/files/2017/09/Register_of_Foreign_ownership_of_Agricultural_Land_2017.docx.

——. 2019. *Register of Foreign Ownership of Agricultural Land: Report of Registrations as at 30 June 2018*. Retrieved 16 March 2023 from https://firb.gov.au/about-firb/publications/register-foreign-ownership-agricultural-land-report-registrations-30-june-1.

——. 2020. *Register of Foreign Ownership of Agricultural Land: Report of Registrations as at 30 June 2019*. Retrieved 16 March 2023 from https://firb.gov.au/about-firb/publications/register-foreign-ownership-agricultural-land-report-registrations-30-june-2.

——. 2021. *Register of Foreign Ownership of Agricultural Land: Report of Registrations as at 30 June 2020*. Retrieved 16 March 2023 from https://firb.gov.au/about-firb/publications/register-foreign-ownership-agricultural-land-report-registrations-30-june-2020.

——. 2022a. *Register of Foreign Ownership of Agricultural Land: Report of Registrations as at 30 June 2021*. Retrieved 16 March 2023 from https://firb.gov.au/about-firb/publications/register-foreign-ownership-agricultural-land-report-registrations-30-june-3.

——. 2022b. *Register of Foreign Ownership of Water Entitlements: Report of Registrations as at 30 June 2021*. Retrieved 16 March 2023 from https://firb.gov.au/about-firb/publications/register-foreign-ownership-water-entitlements-report-registrations.

Forney, Jérémie, Chris Rosin and Hugh Campbell. 2018a. 'Introduction: Agri-environmental Governance as Assemblage', in Jérémie Forney, Chris Rosin and Hugh Campbell (eds), *Agri-environmental Governance as an Assemblage*. Abingdon: Routledge, pp. 1–16.

——. (eds). 2018b. *Agri-environmental Governance as an Assemblage: Multiplicity, Power and Transformation*. Abingdon: Routledge.

Fourcade, Marion, and Kieran Healy. 2007. 'Moral Views of Market Society'. *Annual Review of Sociology* 33(1): 285–311, https://doi.org/10.1146/annurev.soc.33.040406.131642.

Fowler, Courtney. 2021. 'Ord Cotton Industry Lands Loan to Build Local Processing Ginnery in WA's Kimberley Region'. *ABC News*, 19 September. Retrieved 16 March 2023 from https://www.abc.net.au/news/rural/2021-09-19/ord-cotton-gin-a-step-closer-to-reality/100473716.

Fredriksen, Aurora. 2014. 'Assembling Value(S): What a Focus on the Distributed Agency of Assemblages Can Contribute to the Study of Value'. Retrieved 16 March 2023 from https://www.research.manchester.ac.uk/portal/en/publications/assembling-values-what-a-focus-on-the-distributed-agency-of-assemblages-can-contribute-to-the-study-of-value(4c520f93-75f8-409a-aa89-21fd314ea80d).html.

French, Shaun, and James Kneale. 2009. 'Excessive Financialisation: Insuring Lifestyles, Enlivening Subjects, and Everyday Spaces of Biosocial Excess'. *Environment and Planning D: Society & Space* 27(6): 1030–53, https://doi.org/10.1068/d7607.

French, Shaun, Andrew Leyshon and Thomas Wainwright. 2011. 'Financializing Space, Spacing Financialization'. *Progress in Human Geography* 35(6): 798–819, https://doi.org/10.1177/0309132510396749.

Froud, Julie. 2006. *Financialization and Strategy: Narrative and Numbers*. New York: Routledge.

Froud, Julie, Sukhdev Johal, Michael Moran and Karel Williams. 2017. 'Outsourcing the State: New Sources of Elite Power'. *Theory, Culture & Society* 34(5–6): 77–101, https://doi.org/10.1177/0263276417717791.

Gammage, Bill. 2011. *The Biggest Estate on Earth: How Aborigines Made Australia*. Crows Nest, NSW: Allen & Unwin.

Geoscience Australia. 2015. *Land Tenure in Northern Australia*. Canberra: Geoscience Australia.

Geertz, Clifford. 1973. *The Interpretation of Cultures*. New York: Basic Books.
———. 1983. *Local Knowledge*. New York: Basic Books.
Gerritson, Rolf, Peter Whitehead and Natalie Stoeckl. 2018. 'Economic Development across the North: Historical and Current Context of Possible Alternatives', in Jeremy Russell-Smith, Glenn James, Howard Pedersen and Kamaljt K. Sangha (eds), *Sustainable Land Sector Development in Northern Australia: Indigenous Rights, Aspirations, and Cultural Responsibilities*. Boca Raton, FL: CRC Press, Taylor & Francis Group, pp. 53–84.
Ghosh, Jayati. 2010. 'The Unnatural Coupling: Food and Global Finance'. *Journal of Agrarian Change* 10(1): 72–86.
Ghosh, Jayati, James Heintz and Robert Pollin. 2012. 'Speculation on Commodities Futures Markets and Destabilization of Global Food Prices: Exploring the Connections'. *International Journal of Health Services* 42(3): 465–83, https://doi.org/10.2190/HS.42.3.f.
Gibson-Graham, J.K.. 2014. 'Rethinking the Economy with Thick Description and Weak Theory'. *Current Anthropology* 55: S147–S153.
Gibson-Graham, J.K., Jenny Cameron and Stephen Healy. 2013. *Take Back the Economy: An Ethical Guide for Transforming Our Communities*. Minneapolis: University of Minnesota Press.
Glaucus. 2017. 'Glaucus Is Short TFS Corp_Quintis (ASX: TFS _ QIN)'. Retrieved 16 March 2023 from https://www.bonitasresearch.com/company/quintia-ltd-f-k-tropical-forestry.
Goodhart, Charles. 2010. 'Is a Less Pro-cyclical Financial System an Achievable Goal?' *National Institute Economic Review* 211(1): 81–90, https://doi.org/10.1177/002795011 0364100.
Goodman, David, and Michael Redclift. 1985. 'Capitalism, Petty Commodity Production and the Farm Enterprise'. *Sociologia Ruralis* 25(3–4): 231–47, https://doi.org/10.1111 /j.1467-9523.1985.tb00764.x.
Gorman, Julian Tyackie. 2021. 'Exploring Indigenous Enterprise Development and the Commercial Potential of *Terminalia ferdinandiana* (Kakadu Plum) as an Indigenous Agribusiness across Northern Australia', Charles Darwin University (Australia). Retrieved 16 March 2023 from https://www.proquest.com/docview/2584334306?pq-origsite=gscho larandfromopenview=true.
Granovetter, Mark S. 1973. 'The Strength of Weak Ties'. *American Journal of Sociology* 78(6): 1360–80, https://doi.org/10.1086/225469.
Grattan, Michelle. 2016. 'Kidman Sale to Chinese Given Preliminary "No"'. *The Conversation*, 29 April. Retrieved 16 March 2023 from https://theconversation.com/kidman-sale-to-chi nese-given-preliminary-no-58655.
Gray, Darren. 2019. 'Canadian Pension Fund Loads up on Australian Water Rights and Almond Farms'. *Sydney Morning Herald* 3 December. Retrieved 16 March 2023 from https://www.smh.com.au/business/companies/canadian-pension-fund-loads-up-on-austra lian-water-rights-and-almond-farms-20191203-p53gfi.html.
Gray, Matthew and Boyd Hunter. 2011. 'Changes in Indigenous Labour Force Status: Establishing Employment as a Social Norm?' Retrieved 16 March 2023 from https://core .ac.uk/download/pdf/162631564.pdf.
Griffiths v Northern Territory of Australia (No 3) (2016) FCA 900.
Grigg, Angus. 2018. 'The Next Cubbie Station, China's $400 Million Investment in Northern Australia'. *Australian Financial*, 12 October. Retrieved 16 March 2023 from https://www .afr.com/companies/agriculture/the-next-cubbie-station-chinas-400-million-investment -in-northern-australia-20181008-h16dgh.

Grounds, Ellie, and Dan Prosser. 2021. 'Coronavirus Restrictions Turn Outback Birdsville Track into "COVID Highway"'. *ABC News*, 12 January. Retrieved 16 March 2023 from https://www.abc.net.au/news/2021-01-12/birdsville-track-becomes-covid-highway-travell ers-avoid-nsw/13035930.

Gunn, Walter. 1977. 'A Commentary on the Financing and Development of Agricultural Ventures in North Australia', in Francis Harry Bauer (ed.), *Cropping in North Australia: Anatomy of Success and Failure*. Canberra: Australian National University, pp. 177–206.

Gunnoe, Andrew. 2014. 'The Political Economy of Institutional Landownership: Neorentier Society and the Financialization of Land'. *Rural Sociology* 79(4): 478–504, https://doi.org /10.1111/ruso.12045.

Gunnoe, Andrew. 2016. 'The Financialization of the US Forest Products Industry: Socio-economic Relations, Shareholder Value, and the Restructuring of an Industry'. *Social Forces* 94(3): 1075–101, https://doi.org/10.1093/sf/sov108.

Gusterson, Hugh. 1997. 'Studying up Revisited'. *Political and Legal Anthropology Review* 20(1): 114–19.

Hall, Sarah. 2010. 'Geographies of Money and Finance I: Cultural Economy, Politics, and Place'. *Progress in Human Geography* 35(2): 234–45.

———. 2011. 'Geographies of Money and Finance II: Financialization and Financial Subjects'. *Progress in Human Geography* 36(3): 403–11.

———. 2012. 'Geographies of Money and Finance III: Financial Circuits and the 'Real Economy''. *Progress in Human Geography* 37(2): 285–92.

Hartwig, M.C. 1965. 'The Progress of White Settlement in the Alice Springs District and Its Effect upon the Aboriginal Inhabitants, 1860–1894', Ph.D. thesis. Adelaide: University of Adelaide.

Heath, Richard, and Adam Tomlinson. 2016. *A Review of Farm Funding Models and Business Structures in Australia*. Retrieved 16 March 2023 from http://www.farminstitute.org.au/pu blications-1/research-reports/a-review-of-farm-funding-models-and-business-structures-in -australia.

Hein, Eckhard. 2015. 'Finance-Dominated Capitalism and Re-distribution of Income: A Kaleckian Perspective'. *Cambridge Journal of Economics* 39(3): 907–34, https://doi.org/10 .1093/cje/bet038.

Henry, Matthew. 2017. 'Meat, Metrics and Market Devices: Commensuration Infrastructures and the Assemblage of "the Schedule" in New Zealand's Red Meat Sector'. *Journal of Rural Studies* 52: 100–9.

Henry, Matthew, and Russell Prince. 2018. 'Agriculturalizing Finance? Data Assemblages and Derivatives Markets in Small-Town New Zealand'. *Environment and Planning A: Economy and Space* 50(5): 989–1007.

Henry, Matthew, and Mike Scott. 2017. 'What Gets Measured Gets What? The Work of Cycling Indicators in a Local Government Initiative'. *New Zealand Geographer* 73(2): 109–18, https://doi.org/10.1111/nzg.12153.

Herron, Robyn. 2021. 'Outback Tourism to Benefit from COVID-Cautious Travellers and Big Rivers'. *ABC News*, 26 December. Retrieved 16 March 2023 from https://www.abc .net.au/news/2021-12-26/why-tourists-are-turning-to-the-outback-this-christmas/10007 18938.

Hertz, Ellen. 1998. *The Trading Crowd: An Ethnography of the Shanghai Stock Market*. Cambridge England; New York: Cambridge University Press.

Higgins, Vaughan. 2006. 'Re-figuring the Problem of Farmer Agency in Agri-food Studies: A Translation Approach'. *Agriculture and Human Values* 23: 51–62.

Higgins, Vaughan, and Wendy Larner. 2017a. *Assembling Neoliberalism*. New York: Palgrave Macmillan.

———. 2017b. 'Introduction: Assembling Neoliberalism', in Vaughan Higgins and Wendy Larner (eds), *Assembling Neoliberalism: Expertise, Practices, Subjects*. New York: Palgrave Macmillan, pp. 1–19.

Higgins, Vaughan, and Melanie Bryant. 2020. 'Framing Agri-digital Governance: Industry Stakeholders, Technological Frames and Smart Farming Implementation'. *Sociologia Ruralis* 60(2): 438–57, https://doi.org/10.1111/soru.12297.

Higgs, Joy. 2013. 'Professional Socialisation', in Stephen Loftus, Tania Gerzina, Joy Higgs, Megan Smith and Elaine Duffy (eds), *Educating Health Professionals: Becoming a University Teacher*. Rotterdam: Sense, pp. 83–92.

Hilkens, Aniek, Janet I. Reid, Laurens Klerkx, and David I. Gray. 2018. 'Money Talk: How Relations Between Farmers and Advisors Around Financial Management Are Shaped'. *Journal of Rural Studies* 63 (2018): 83–95, https://doi.org/10.1016/j.jrurstud.2018.09.002.

Hinchliffe, Steve, Matthew B. Kearnes, Monica Degen and Sarah Whatmore. 2007. 'Ecologies and Economies of Action: Sustainability, Calculations, and Other Things'. *Environment and Planning A* 39(2): 260–82, https://doi.org/10.1068/a38110.

Ho, Karen. 2009. *Liquidated: An Ethnography of Wall Street*. Durham, NC: Duke University Press.

Hogg, Michael A. 2009. 'Managing Self-Uncertainty through Group Identification'. *Psychological Inquiry* 20(4): 221–24, https://doi.org/10.1080/10478400903333452.

Holmes, James Macdonald. 1963. *Australia's Open North: A Study of Northern Australia Bearing on the Urgency of the Times*. Sydney: Angus & Robertson.

House of Representatives Standing Committee on Indigenous Affairs. 2020. *Report on Food Pricing and Food Security in Remote Indigenous Communitie*s. Parliament of the Commonwealth of Australia. Retrieved 16 March 2023 from https://www.aph.gov.au/Parliamentary_Business/Committees/House/Former_Committees/Indigenous_Affairs/Foodpricing/Report.

Humpty Doo Barramundi. 2022. 'Our Farm'. Retrieved 16 March 2023 from https://www.humptydoobarramundi.com.au/ourfarm.

Hunt, Lesley, Christopher Rosin, Hugh Campbell, and John R. Fairweather. 2013. 'The Impact of Neoliberalism on New Zealand Farmers: Changing What It Means to Be a "Good Farmer"'. *Extension Farming Systems Journal* 9(1): 34.

Husson, Michel. 2015. 'Unemployment, Working Time and Financialisation: The French Case'. *Cambridge Journal of Economics* 39(3): 887–905, https://doi.org/10.1093/cje/bet051.

Indigenous Land and Sea Corporation (ILSC). 2021. *Unlocking the Indigenous Estate Corporate Plan 2020–21 Strategy to 2024*. Retrieved 16 March 2023 from https://www.ilsc.gov.au/wp-content/uploads/2020/10/ILSC-Corporate-Plan-2020-21.pdf.

Inquiry into the Pastoral Land Legislation Amendment Bill 2017 (NT). 2017. 'Economic Policy Scrutiny Committee: Legislative Assembly of the Northern Territory'. Retrieved 16 March 2023 from https://parliament.nt.gov.au/__data/assets/pdf_file/0009/488925/Inquiry-into-the-Pastoral-Land-Legislation-Amendment-Bill-2017.pdf.

InvestAg-Savills. 2011. 'International Farmland Market Bulletin'. Retrieved 16 March 2023 from https://www.farmlandgrab.org/uploads/attachment/original_savills.pdf.

Isakson, S. Ryan. 2014. 'Food and Finance: The Financial Transformation of Agro-food Supply Chains'. *Journal of Peasant Studies* 41(5): 749–75, https://doi.org/10.1080/03066150.2013.874340.

——. 2015. 'Derivatives for Development? Small-Farmer Vulnerability and the Financialization of Climate Risk Management'. *Journal of Agrarian Change* 15(4): 569–80, https://doi.org/10.1111/joac.12124.

Jacobs, Keith, and Tony Manzi. 2020. 'Conceptualising "Financialisation": Governance, Organisational Behaviour and Social Interaction in UK Housing'. *International Journal of Housing Policy* 20(2): 184–202, https://doi.org/10.1080/19491247.2018.1540737.

Jarvis, Diane, Kirsten Maclean and Emma Woodward. 2022. 'The Australian Indigenous-Led Bush Products Sector: Insights from the Literature and Recommendations for the Future'. *Ambio* 51(1): 226–40, https://doi.org/10.1007/s13280-021-01542-w.

Jasper, Clint. 2020. 'PSP Investments, a Canadian Pension Fund, Could Now Be the Largest Owner of Water in the Murray-Darling Basin'. *ABC News*, 18 February. Retrieved 16 March 2023 from https://www.abc.net.au/news/rural/2020-02-18/canadian-pension-fun ds-aussie-farm-buying-spree/11950312.

Jayadev, Arjun, J.W. Mason and Enno Schröder. 2018. 'The Political Economy of Financialization in the United States, Europe and India'. *Development and Change* 49(2): 353–74, https://doi.org/10.1111/dech.12382.

Johnsen, Sarah. 2004. 'The Redefinition of Family Farming: Agricultural Restructuring and Farm Adjustment in Waihemo, New Zealand'. *Journal of Rural Studies* 20(4): 419–32, https://doi.org/10.1016/j.jrurstud.2004.07.002.

Kelly, John Henry. 1966. *Struggle for the North*. Sydney: Australasian Book Society.

Keogh, Michael. 2012. 'Editorial'. *Farm Policy Journal* 9(4): iv.

Keough and Wirth v Department of Natural Resources and Mines 2004 QLC 101.

Keucheyan, Razmig. 2018. 'Insuring Climate Change: New Risks and the Financialization of Nature'. *Development and Change* 49(2): 484–501, https://doi.org/10.1111/dech.12367.

Klerkx, Laurens, and Jolanda Jansen. 2010. 'Building Knowledge Systems for Sustainable Agriculture: Supporting Private Advisors to Adequately Address Sustainable Farm Management in Regular Service Contacts'. *International Journal of Agricultural Sustainability* 8(3): 148–63, https://doi.org/10.3763/ijas.2009.0457.

Kilcullen, Molly, Jennifer Feitosa and Eduardo Salas. 2022. 'Insights from the Virtual Team Science: Rapid Deployment during COVID–19'. *Human Factors* 64(8): 1429–40, https://doi.org/10.1177/0018720821991678.

Kimberley Agriculture and Pastoral Company (KAPCO). 2022. 'What Is KAPCO?' Retrieved 16 March 2023 from https://www.kapco.com.au/#overview.

Kimberley Development Commission. 2019. 'Primary Industries'. Retrieved 27 April 2023 from https://www.kdc.wa.gov.au/our-region/invest-in-the-kimberley/primary-industries/

Kinda, Somlanare Romuald, Nazindigouba Eric Kere, Thierry Urbain Yogo and Musonda Anthony Simpasa. 2022. 'Do Land Rushes Really Improve Food Security in Sub-Saharan Africa?' *Food Policy* 113(102285): 1–11, https://doi.org/10.1016/j.foodpol.2022.102285.

Kish, Zenia, and Madeleine Fairbairn. 2018. 'Investing for Profit, Investing for Impact: Moral Performances in Agricultural Investment Projects'. *Environment and Planning A* 50(3): 569–88, https://doi.org/10.1177/0308518X17738253.

Kittrell, Edward R. 1973. 'Wakefield's Scheme of Systematic Colonization and Classical Economics'. *American Journal of Economics and Sociology* 32(1): 87–112, https://doi.org /10.1111/j.1536-7150.1973.tb02182.x.

Kjellberg, Hans, Alexandre Mallard, Diane-Laure Arjaliès, Patrik Aspers, Stefan Beljean, Alexandra Bidet, Alberto Corsin et al. 2013. 'Valuation Studies? Our Collective Two Cents'. *Valuation Studies* 1(1): 11–30.

Kornberger, Martin. 2017. 'The Values of Strategy: Valuation Practices, Rivalry and Strategic Agency'. *Organization Studies* 38(2): 1753–73.

Kornberger, Martin, Lise Justesen, Anders Koed Madsen and Jan Mouritsen. 2015. 'Introduction: Making Things Valuable', in Martin Kornberger, Lise Justesen, Jan Mouritsen and Anders Koed Madsen (eds), *Making Things Valuable*. Oxford: Oxford University Press, pp. 1–17.

Kotz, David. 2010. 'Financialization and Neoliberalism', in Gary Teeple and Stephen McBride (eds), *Relations of Global Power: Neoliberal Order and Disorder*. Toronto: University of Toronto Press, pp. 1–18.

Krippner, Greta R. 2005. 'The Financialization of the American Economy'. *Socio-economic Review* 3(2): 173–208, https://doi.org/10.1093/SER/mwi008.

———. 2011. *Capitalizing on Crisis: The Political Origins of the Rise of Finance*. Cambridge, MA: Harvard University Press.

Kuns, Brian, Oane Visser and Anders Wästfelt. 2016. 'The Stock Market and the Steppe: The Challenges Faced by Stock-Market Financed, Nordic Farming Ventures in Russia and Ukraine'. *Journal of Rural Studies* 45: 199–217, https://doi.org/10.1016/j.jrurstud.2016.03.009.

Lagoarde-Segot, Thomas. 2015. 'Diversifying Finance Research: From Financialization to Sustainability'. *International Review of Financial Analysis* 39: 1–6, https://doi.org/10.1016/j.irfa.2015.01.004.

———. 2017. 'Financialization: Towards a New Research Agenda'. *International Review of Financial Analysis* 51: 113–23, https://doi.org/10.1016/j.irfa.2016.03.007.

Lagoarde-Segot, Thomas, and Bernard Paranque. 2017. 'Sustainability and the Reconstruction of Academic Finance'. *Research in International Business and Finance* 39: 657–62, https://doi.org/10.1016/j.ribaf.2016.03.002.

Lai, Mun Yee, Catheryn Khoo-Lattimore and Ying Wang. 2018. 'A Perception Gap Investigation into Food and Cuisine Image Attributes for Destination Branding from the Host Perspective: The Case of Australia'. *Tourism Management* 69: 579–95, https://doi.org/10.1016/j.tourman.2018.06.033.

Land Development Corporation. 2017. 'Tiwi Islands Investment Opportunity'. Retrieved 9 January 2018 from https://landdevcorp.com.au/uploads/LDC_Tiwi-Islands_Investment-Opportunity_2017.pdf.

———. 2019. 'Agriculture Development Opportunities'. Retrieved 16 March 2023 from https://developtiwi.com.au/agriculture.

Lane, Tim. 2017. 'The Valuation of Agricultural Assets in Australia'. Grains Research and Development Corporation. Retrieved 25 April 2023 from https://grdc.com.au/resources-and-publications/grdc-update-papers/tab-content/grdc-update-papers/2017/06/the-valuation-of-agricultural-assets-in-australia.

Lange, Vin. 2017. 'An Economic Development Strategy for the NT Aboriginal Land Estate. Presentation at Developing Northern Australia Conference 2017'.

Langford, Alexandra. 2019. 'Capitalising the Farm Family Entrepreneur: Negotiating Private Equity Partnerships in Australia'. *Australian Geographer* 50(4): 473–91.

———. 2020. 'Agri-food Transformations in Northern Australia: The Work of Local Actors in Mediating Financial Investments', Ph.D. thesis. Brisbane: School of Social Science, University of Queensland, https://doi.org/10.14264/uql.2020.698.

———. 2022. 'A "Rule of Thumb" and the Return on Investment: The Role of Valuation Devices in the Financialisation of Northern Australian Pastoral Land in Northern Australia'. *Valuation Studies* 8(2): 37–60, https://doi.org/10.3384/VS.2001-5992.2021.8.2.37-60.

———. 2023. 'The Geographies of Indigenous business in Australia: An Analysis of Scale, Industry and Remoteness'. *Supply Nation Research Report 8*.

Langford, Alexandra, Kiah Smith and Geoffrey Lawrence. 2020. 'Financialising Governance?

State Actor Engagement with Private Finance for Rural Development in the Northern Territory of Australia'. *Research in Globalization* 2(100026): 1–9, https://doi.org/10.1016/j.resglo.2020.100026.

Langford, Alexandra, Alana Brekelmans, and Geoffrey Lawrence. 2021. '"I Want to Sleep at Night as Well": Guilt and Care in the Making of Agricultural Credit Markets', in Russell Prince, Matthew Henry, Carolyn Morris, Aisling Gallagher and Stephen FitzHerbert (eds), *Markets in Their Place: Context, Culture, Finance*. Abingdon: Routledge, pp. 122–40.

Langford, Alexandra, Geoffrey Lawrence and Kiah Smith. 2021. 'Financialisation *for* Development? Asset-Making on Indigenous Land in Remote Northern Australia'. *Development and Change* 52(3): 574–97, https://doi.org/10.1111/dech.12648.

Langley, Paul. 2020. 'The Folds of Social Finance: Making Markets, Remaking the Social.' *Environment and Planning A* 52(1): 130–47, https://doi.org/10.1177/0308518X17752682.

Langley, Paul, Gavin Bridge, Harriet Bulkeley, and Bregje van Veelen. 2021. 'Decarbonizing Capital: Investment, Divestment and the Qualification of Carbon Assets.' Economy and Society 50(3): 494–516.

Lapavitsas, Costas. 2009. 'Financialised Capitalism: Crisis and Financial Expropriation'. *Historical Materialism* 17(2): 114–48, https://doi.org/10.1163/156920609X436153.

Larder, Nicolette, Sarah Ruth Sippel and Geoffrey Lawrence. 2015. 'Finance Capital, Food Security Narratives and Australian Agricultural Land'. *Journal of Agrarian Change* 15(4): 592–603, https://doi.org/10.1111/joac.12108.

Larder, Nicolette, Sarah Ruth Sippel, and Neil Argent. 2018. 'The Redefined Role of Finance in Australian Agriculture'. *Australian Geographer* 49(3): 397–418, https://doi.org/10.1080/00049182.2017.1388555.

Larner, Wendy, Richard Le Heron and Nicholas Lewis. 2007. 'Co-Constituting "After Neoliberalism": Political Projects and Globalizing Governmentalities in Aotearoa/New Zealand', in Kim England and Kevin Ward (eds), *Neoliberalisation: States, Networks and People*. Oxford: Blackwell, pp. 223–47.

Latour, Bruno. 1992. 'Where Are the Missing Masses? The Sociology of a Few Mundane Artifacts', in Wiebe E. Bijker and John Law (eds), *Shaping Technology/Building Society*. Cambridge, MA: MIT Press, pp. 225–58.

——. 1996. 'On Interobjectivity'. *Mind, Culture and Activity* 3(4): 228–45.

——. 2005. *Reassembling the Social: An Introduction to Actor-Network-Theory*. New York: Oxford University Press.

Lavoie, Marc. 2012. 'Financialization, Neo-liberalism, and Securitization'. *Journal of Post Keynesian Economics* 35(2): 215–33, https://doi.org/10.2753/PKE0160-3477350203.

Law, John, and John Hassard. 1999. *Actor Network Theory and after*. Oxford: Blackwell.

Lawley, Chad. 2020. 'Potential Impacts of COVID-19 on Canadian Farmland Markets'. *Canadian Journal of Agricultural Economics* 68(2): 245–50, https://doi.org/10.1111/cjag.12242.

Lawrence, Geoffrey. 2017. 'Re-evaluating Food Systems and Food Security: A Global Perspective'. *Journal of Sociology* 53(4), 774–96.

——. 1999. 'Agri-food Restructuring: A Synthesis of Recent Australian Research'. *Rural Sociology* 64(2): 186–202.

——. 2005. 'Globalization, Agricultural Production Systems and Rural Restructuring', in Chris Cocklin and Jacqui Dibden (eds), *Sustainability and Change in Rural Australia*. Sydney: UNSW Press, pp. 104–20.

Lawrence, Geoffrey. 2015. 'Defending Financialization'. *Dialogues in Human Geography* 5(2): 201–5, https://doi.org/10.1177/2043820615588155.

———. 2017. 'Re-evaluating Food Systems and Food Security: A Global Perspective'. *Journal of Sociology* 53(4): 1–23.

Lawrence, Geoffrey, Carol Richards and Kristen Lyons. 2013. 'Food Security in Australia in an Era of Neoliberalism, Productivism, and Climate Change'. *Journal of Rural Studies* 29: 30–39.

Lawrence, Geoffrey, and Kiah Smith. 2018. 'The Concept of "Financialization": Criticisms and Insights', in Hilde Bjørkhaug, Andre Magnan and Geoffrey Lawrence (eds), *The Financialization of Agri-food Systems*. Abingdon: Routledge, pp. 23–41.

Lazonick, William, and Mary O'Sullivan. 2000. 'Maximizing Shareholder Value: A New Ideology for Corporate Governance'. *Economy and Society* 29(1): 13–35, https://doi.org/10.1080/030851400360541.

Le Billon, Philippe, and Melanie Sommerville. 2017. 'Landing Capital and Assembling "Investable Land" in the Extractive and Agricultural Sectors'. *Geoforum* 82: 212–24, https://doi.org/10.1016/j.geoforum.2016.08.011.

Lee, Roger. 2006. 'The Ordinary Economy: Tangled up in Values and Geography'. *Transactions of the Institute of British Geographers* 31(4): 413–32, https://doi.org/10.1111/j.1475-5661.2006.00223.x.

Lewis, Nick. 2016. 'Governmentality at Work in Shaping a Critical Geographical Politics', in Simon Springer, Kean Birch and Julie MacLeavy (eds), *Handbook of Neoliberalism*. Abingdon: Routledge, pp. 396–407, https://doi.org/10.4324/9781315730660-15.

Lewis, Nick. 2018. 'Cultivating Diverse Values by Rethinking Blue Economy in New Zealand', in John Morrissey and C. Patrick Heidkamp (eds), *Towards Coastal Resilience and Sustainability*. Abingdon: Routledge. https://doi.org/10.4324/9780429463723.

Lewis, Nick, Richard Le Heron and Hugh Campbell. 2017. 'The Mouse That Died: Stabilizing Economic Practices in Free Trade Space', in Vaughan Higgins and Wendy Larner (eds), *Assembling Neoliberalism*. New York: Palgrave Macmillan, pp. 151–70.

Lewis, Nick, Richard Le Heron, Hugh Campbell, Matthew Henry, Erena Le Heron, Eric Pawson, Harvey Perkins, Michael Roche and Christopher Rosin. 2013. 'Assembling Biological Economies: Region-Shaping Initiatives in Making and Retaining Value'. *New Zealand Geographer* 69(3): 180–96, https://doi.org/10.1111/nzg.12031.

Lewis, Nick, Richard Le Heron, Michael Carolan, Hugh Campbell and Terry Marsden. 2016. 'Assembling Generative Approaches in Agrifood Research', in Richard Le Heron, Hugh Campbell, Nick Lewis and Michael Carolan (eds), *Biological Economies: Experimentation and the Politics of Agrifood Frontiers*. Abingdon: Routledge, pp. 1–20.

Leyshon, Andrew, and Nigel Thrift. 2005 [1997]. *Money/Space*. London: Routledge.

———. 2007. 'The Capitalization of Almost Everything'. *Theory, Culture & Society* 24(7–8): 97–115, https://doi.org/10.1177/0263276407084699.

Li, Shanshan, and Zein Kallas. 2021. 'Meta-analysis of Consumers' Willingness to Pay for Sustainable Food Products'. *Appetite* 163: 105239, https://doi.org/10.1016/j.appet.2021.105239.

Li, Tania Murray. 2007a. *The Will to Improve: Governmentality, Development and the Practice of Politics*. Durham, NC: Duke University Press.

———. 2007b. 'Governmentality'. *Anthropologica* 49: 275–81.

———. 2007c. 'Practices of Assemblage and Community Forest Management'. *Economy and Society* 36(2): 263–93.

———. 2014. 'What Is Land? Assembling a Resource for Global Investment'. *Transactions of the Institute of British Geographers* 39(4), 589–602.

———. 2015. 'Transnational Farmland Investment: A Risky Business'. *Journal of Agrarian Change* 15(4): 560–68, https://doi.org/10.1111/joac.12109.

——. 2017. 'Rendering Land Investible: Five Notes on Time'. *Geoforum* 82: 276–78.

Li, Tania Murray, and Semedi, Pujo. 2021. *Plantation Life: Corporate Occupation in Indonesia's Oil Palm Zone*. Durham, NC: Duke University Press.

Liveris, James. 2020. 'Record Price Paid for Iconic WA Farming Property Erregulla Plains'. *ABC News*, 10 February. Retrieved 16 March 2023 from https://www.abc.net.au/news/rur al/2020-02-10/record-sale-for-iconic-wa-farming-property-erregulla-plains/11951022.

Lockie, Stewart, Kristen Lyons and Geoffrey Lawrence. 2000. 'Constructing "Green" Foods: Corporate Capital, Risk, and Organic Farming in Australia and New Zealand'. *Agriculture and Human Values* 17(4): 315–22, https://doi.org/10.1023/A:1026547102757.

López-Espinosa, Germán, Sergio Mayordomo, and Antonio Moreno. 2017. 'When Does Relationship Lending Start to Pay?' *Journal of Financial Intermediation* 31: 16–29, https://doi.org/10.1016/j.jfi.2016.11.001.

Ludlow, Mark. 2018. 'Banking Royal Commission: Bankwest's Inflated Valuations Toppled Qld Farmer'. *Australian Financial Review*, 28 June. Retrieved 16 March 2023 from https://www.afr.com/news/politics/banking-royal-commission-bankwests-inflated-valuations-top pled-qld-farmer-20180628-h11yr0.

Mackenzie, Donald. 2006. *An Engine, Not a Camera: How Financial Models Shape Markets*. Cambridge, MA: MIT Press.

MacKenzie, Donald, and Yuval Millo. 2003. 'Constructing a Market, Performing Theory: The Historical Sociology of a Financial Derivatives Exchange'. *American Journal of Sociology* 109(1): 107–45, https://doi.org/10.1086/374404.

MacKenzie Donald, Fabien Muniesa and Lucia Siu. 2007. *Do Economists Make Markets? On the Performativity of Economics*. Princeton: Princeton University Press.

Mader, Philip, Daniel Mertens and Natascha van der Zwan. 2020. 'Financialization: An Introduction', in Philip Mader, Daniel Mertens and Natascha van der Zwan (eds), *The Routledge International Handbook of Financialization*. Abingdon: Routledge, pp. 1–16, https://doi.org/10.4324/9781315142876-1.

Magnan, André. 2012. 'New Avenues of Farm Corporatization in the Prairie Grains Sector: Farm Family Entrepreneurs and the Case of One Earth Farms'. *Agriculture and Human Values* 29(2): 161–75.

——. 2015. 'The Financialisation of Agri-food in Canada and Australia: Corporate Farmland and Farm Ownership in the Grains and Oilseed Sector'. *Journal of Rural Studies* 41: 1–12.

——. 2018. 'Farmland Values: Media and Public Discourses around Farmland Investment in Canada and Australia', in Hilde Bjørkhaug, Andre Magnan and Geoffrey Lawrence (eds), *The Financialization of Agri-food Systems*. Abingdon: Routledge, pp. 108–32.

Magnan, André, Melissa Davidson and Annette Aurelie Desmarais. 2022. '"They Call It Progress, But We Don't See It as Progress": Farm Consolidation and Land Concentration in Saskatchewan, Canada'. *Agriculture and Human Values* 40: 277–90, https://doi.org/10.1007/s10460-022-10353-y.

Magnan, André, and Sean Sunley. 2017. 'Farmland Investment and Financialization in Saskatchewan, 2003–2014: An Empirical Analysis of Farmland Transactions'. *Journal of Rural Studies* 49: 92–103, https://doi.org/10.1016/j.jrurstud.2016.11.007.

Mann, Susan A., and James M. Dickinson. 1978. 'Obstacles to the Development of a Capitalist Agriculture'. *Journal of Peasant Studies* 5(4): 466–81, https://doi.org/10.1080/03066157808438058.

Marsellos, Brad. 2022. 'Farm Stay Industry Thrives as COVID Changes Travel Trends'. *ABC News*, 20 February. Retrieved 16 March 2023 from https://www.abc.net.au/news/2022-02-20/queensland-farmstays-here-to-stay/100795564.

Martin, Randy. 2002. *Financialization of Daily Life*. Philadelphia: Temple University Press.

Martin, Richard J. 2019. *The Gulf Country: The Story of People and Place in Outback Queensland.* Crows Nest, NSW: Allen & Unwin.

Martin, Randy, Michael Rafferty and Dick Bryan. 2008. 'Financialisation, Risk, and Labour'. *Competition and Change* 12(2): 120–32, https://doi.org/10.1179/102452908X314849.

Martin, Sarah J., and Jennifer Clapp. 2015. 'Finance for Agriculture or Agriculture for Finance?' *Journal of Agrarian Change* 15(4): 549–59, https://doi.org/10.1111/joac.12110.

Massumi, Brian. 2002. *Parables for the Virtual: Movement, Affect, Sensation.* Durham, NC: Duke University Press.

Mawdsley, Emma. 2018a. 'Development Geography II: Financialization'. *Progress in Human Geography* 37(2): 285–92.

———. 2018b. '"From Billions to Trillions": Financing the SDGs in a World "beyond Aid"'. *Dialogues in Human Geography* 8(2): 191–95.

Mawdsley, Emma, Laura Savage and Sung-Mi Kim. 2014. 'A "Post-aid World"? Paradigm Shift in Foreign Aid and Development Cooperation at the 2011 Busan High Level Forum'. *Geographical Journal* 180(1): 27–38, https://doi.org/10.1111/j.1475–4959.2012.00490.x.

McGrathNicol. 2009. 'Project Conserve: Financial Due Diligence Volume 1 – Final Report'. Viewed 22 April 2020. Available at https://financialservices.royalcommission.gov.au/public-hearings/Documents/exhibits-2018/25-june/EXHIBIT-4.8.3.pdf.

McKee, Kim. 2009. 'Post-Foucauldian Governmentality: What Does It Offer Critical Social Policy Analysis?' *Critical Social Policy* 29(3): 465–86, https://doi.org/10.1177/02610183 09105180.

McMichael, Philip. 1984. *Settlers and the Agrarian Question: Foundations of Capitalism in Colonial Australia.* Melbourne: Cambridge University Press.

———. 2009. 'Banking on Agriculture: A Review of the World Development Report 2008'. *Journal of Agrarian Change* 9(2): 235–46.

Meat and Livestock Australia (MLA). 2021. 'Farm Survey Data for the Beef, Slaughter Lambs and Sheep Industries'. Retrieved 13 September 2021 from http://apps.daff.gov.au/mla.

———. 2022. 'Northern Breeding Business (NB2)'. Retrieved 27 April from https://www.mla .com.au/research-and-development/livestock-production/reproductive-efficiency/nb2-nor thern-breeding-business/.

Mehta, Lyla. 2010. 'Introduction', in Lyla Mehta (ed.), *The Limits to Scarcity: Contesting the Politics of Allocation.* New York: Taylor & Francis, pp. 1–8.

Michailidou, Domna. 2016. *The Inexorable Evolution of Financialisation: Financial Crises in Emerging Markets.* London: Palgrave Macmillan.

Milberg, William. 2008. 'Shifting Sources and Uses of Profits: Sustaining US Financialization with Global Value Chains'. *Economy and Society* 37(3): 420–51, https://doi.org/10.1080 /03085140802172706.

Mills, Vanessa. 2019. 'Gina Rinehart's Water Plan for the Fitzroy River under Fire', *ABC News*, 28 May. Retrieved 16 March 2023 from https://www.abc.net.au/radio/kimberley/progra ms/breakfast/water-plan/11156068.

Miles, Tallis. 2022. 'NT's $250m Record Breaker'. *The Weekly Times*, 10 August.

Mirowski, Philip. 2012. 'The Modern Commercialization of Science Is a Passel of Ponzi Schemes'. *Social Epistemology* 26(3–4): 285–310.

———. 2014. *Never Let a Serious Crisis Go to Waste: How Neoliberalism Survived the Financial Meltdown.* London: Verso.

Mitchell, Ruby, and Joshua Becker. 2019. 'Bush Food Industry Booms, But Only 1 Per Cent Is Produced by Indigenous People'. *ABC News*, 19 January. Retrieved 16 March 2023 from https://www.abc.net.au/news/rural/2019-01-19/low-indigenous-representation-in-bush -food-industry/10701986.

Moginon, Debbie Ferdinand, Toh Poh See and Mazni Saad. 2012. 'Indigenous Food and Destination Marketing', in Artinah Zainal, Salleh Mohd Radzi, Rahmat Hashin, Chemah Tamby Chik and Rozita Abu (eds), *Current Issues in Hospitality and Tourism Research and Innovations*. Abingdon: Taylor & Francis, pp. 355–58.

Mooney, Patrick. H. 1982. 'Labor Time, Production Time and Capitalist Development in Agriculture: A Reconsideration of the Mann-Dickenson Thesis'. *Sociologia Ruralis* 22(3–4): 279–92, https://doi.org/10.1111/j.1467-9523.1982.tb01063.x.

Morrison, Joe. 2016. 'Unhappy Anniversaries: What Is There to Celebrate? 8th Nugget Coombs Memorial Lecture 2016'. Retrieved 16 March 2023 from https://www.nlc.org.au/uploads/pdfs/Morrison_8th_Nugget_Coombs_Lecture_2016.pdf.

Morrison, Scott. 2016. 'Preliminary Decision of Foreign Investment Application for Purchase of S. Kidman and Co Limited'. Australian Government: The Treasury. Retrieved 16 March 2023 from https://ministers.treasury.gov.au/ministers/scott-morrison-2015/media-releases/preliminary-decision-foreign-investment-application.

Morse, Cameron. 2018. 'Recapitalisation of Quintis'. Retrieved 16 March 2023 from https://quintis.com.au/corporate/news/recapitalisation-of-quintis.

Moss, Charles B., Jaclyn D. Kropp and Maria Bampasidou. 2018. 'The Financial Economics of Agriculture and Farm Management', in Gail Cramer, Krishna Paudel and Andrew Schmitz (eds), *The Routledge Handbook of Agricultural Economics*. Abingdon: Routledge.

Mouat, Michael, and Russell Prince. 2018. 'Cultured Meat and Cowless Milk: On Making Markets for Animal-Free Food'. *Journal of Cultural Economy* 11(4): 315–29.

Mouat, Michael J., Russell Prince and Michael M. Roche. 2019. 'Making Value out of Ethics: The Emerging Economic Geography of Lab-Grown Meat and Other Animal-Free Food Products'. *Economic Geography* 95(2): 136–58, https://doi.org/10.1080/00130095.2018.1508994.

Muniesa, Fabien. 2012. 'A Flank Movement in the Understanding of Valuation'. *Sociological Review* 59(2): 24–38.

———. 2014. *The Provoked Economy: Economic Reality and the Performative Turn*. New York: Routledge.

———. 2017. 'Ethnography at a Critical Distance: A Postscript to Loungification', in D. O'Doherty (ed.), *Reconstructing Organization: The Loungification of Society*. London: Palgrave Macmillan, pp. 269–76.

Muniesa, Fabian, Liliana Doganova, Horacio Ortiz, Álvaro Pina-Stranger, Florence Paterson, Alaric Bourgoin, Véra Ehrenstein et al. 2017. *Capitalization: A Cultural Guide*. Paris: Presses des Mines.

Nader, Laura. 1972. 'Up the Anthropologist: Perspectives Gained from Studying up', in D. Hymes (ed.), *Reinventing Anthropology*. New York: Pantheon Press, pp. 285–311.

Neales, S. 2018. 'Royal Commission: Rural "Specialist" Bank Sent Farmers to Brink'. *The Australian*, 27June. Retrieved 16 March 2023 from https://www.theaustralian.com.au/business/banking-royal-commission/rural-specialist-bank-sent-farmers-to-brink/news-story/35b136355896be0591a9729d074b633d.

Nelson, Sara H., Leah L. Bremer, Kelly Meza Prado and Kate A. Brauman. 2020. 'The Political Life of Natural Infrastructure: Water Funds and Alternative Histories of Payments for Ecosystem Services in Valle Del Cauca, Colombia'. *Development and Change* 51(1): 26–50, https://doi.org/10.1111/dech.12544.

Newman, Janet. 2017. 'The Politics of Expertise: Neoliberalism, Governance and the Practice of Politics', in Vaughan Higgins and Wendy Larner (eds), *Assembling Neoliberalism: Expertise, Practices, Subjects*. London: Palgrave Macmillan, pp. 87–105.

Noble, Keith, Tania Dennis and Sarah Larkins. 2019. 'Agricultural Development in Northern Australia', in Keith Noble, Tania Dennis and Sarah Larkins (eds), *Agriculture and Resilience in Australia's North*. Singapore: Springer Singapore, pp. 35–67.

Northern Australia Infrastructure Facility (NAIF). 2023a. 'FAQs: Answers to Some of the Common Questions Asked about NAIF, What We Do and How We Operate'. Retrieved 23 April 2023 from https://naif.gov.au/about-naif-finance/faq/.

Northern Australia Infrastructure Facility (NAIF). 2023b. Retrieved 16 March 2023 from https://naif.gov.au.

Northern Territory of Australia v Griffiths (2017) FCAFC 106.

North Australian Indigenous Land and Sea Management Alliance (NAILSMA) 2013. 'An Indigenous Prospectus for Participating in the Sustainable Development of North Australia'. *North Australian Indigenous Experts Forum on Sustainable Economic Development – Second Forum Report*, Kakadu National Park, Northern Territory, 30 April–2 May. NAILSMA Knowledge Series 019/2013. Retrieved 27 April 2023 from https://nailsma.org.au/uploads/resources/KS-020-NAIEF-2-Indig-prospectus-position-paper_0813_171113_144348.pdf.

———. 2019. 'State of the Indigenous Estate: Background Information for Identifying and Evaluating Opportunities for Economic Development on Indigenous Lands'. Retrieved 16 March 2023 from https://www.crcna.com.au/file-download/download/public/534.

———. 2020a. 'Business on Country Diversification Strategy: For Enterprise, Economic Development and Health and Productive Lands and Seas: Growing Benefits from Land Ownership, Use and Management'. Cooperative Research Centre for Developing Northern Australia. Retrieved 16 March 2023 from https://www.crcna.com.au/sites/default/files/2020-11/BOC%20Strategy.pdf.

———. 2020b. 'Western Yalanji Land Use and Economic Diversification Plan. Cooperative Research Centre for Developing Northern Australia'. Retrieved 16 March 2023 from https://www.crcna.com.au/resources/publications/western-yalanji-land-use-plan.

———. 2020c. 'Cooperative Research Centre for Developing Northern Australia. Normanby Land Use and Economic Diversification Plan'. Retrieved 16 March 2023 from https://www.crcna.com.au/resources/publications/normanby-land-use-plan.

———. 2020d. 'Waanyi and Garawa Land Use and Economic Diversification Plan. Cooperative Research Centre for Developing Northern Australia', https://www.crcna.com.au/resources/publications/waanyi-and-garawa-land-use-plan

Northern Land Council (NLC) 2022. 'Project Sea Dragon Setback "Disappointing" But Native Title Holders Will Still Benefit'. Retrieved 16 March 2023 from https://www.nlc.org.au/media-publications/project-sea-dragon-setback-disappointing-but-native-title-holders-will-still-benefit.

NT Government. 2019. 'Project Sea Dragon'. Retrieved 16 March 2023 from https://theterritory.com.au/invest/investment-opportunities/project-sea-dragon.

———. 2020. 'Why the Territory?' Retrieved 16 March 2023 from https://theterritory.com.au/invest/why-the-territory.

———. 2022. 'Northern Territory Economy: Agriculture, Forestry and Fishing'. Retrieved 16 March 2023 from https://nteconomy.nt.gov.au/industry-analysis/agriculture,-foresty-and-fishing.

Nuthall, Peter, and Kevin Old. 2017. 'Will Future Land Based Food and Fibre Production Be in Family or Corporate Hands? An Analysis of Farm Land Ownership and Governance Considering Farmer Characteristics as Choice Drivers: The New Zealand Case'. *Land Use Policy* 63: 98–110, https://doi.org/10.1016/j.landusepol.2017.01.018

O'Callaghan, Cian, Cesare Di Feliciantonio and Michael Byrne. 2018. 'Governing Urban Vacancy in Post-crash Dublin: Contested Property and Alternative Social Projects'. *Urban Geography* 39(6): 868–91, https://doi.org/10.1080/02723638.2017.1405688.

O'Neill, Lily, Lee Godden, Elizabeth Macpherson, and Erin O'Donnell. 2016. 'Australia, Wet or Dry, North or South: Addressing Environmental Impacts and the Exclusion of Aboriginal Peoples in Northern Water Development'. *Environmental and Planning Law Journal* 33(4): 402–17.

O'Neill, Phillip. 2019. 'The Financialisation of Urban Infrastructure: A Framework of Analysis'. *Urban Studies* 56(7): 1304–25, https://doi.org/10.1177/0042098017751983.

Oosterveer, Peter. 2007. *Global Governance of Food Production and Consumption: Issues and Challenges.* Cheltenham: Edward Elgar.

Ord, Duncan, and Tim Mazzarol. 2007. 'Unlocking the Economic Potential of an Australian Indigenous Community', in *International Handbook of Research on Indigenous Entrepreneurship.* Cheltenham: Edward Elgar, pp. 508–25

Orhangazi, Özgür. 2008. *Finanzialization and the US Economy.* Cheltenham: Edward Elgar.

Ortiz, Horacio. 2014. 'The Limits of Financial Imagination: Free Investors, Efficient Markets, and Crisis'. *American Anthropologist* 116(1), 38–50.

Ostrander, Susan. 1995. '"Surely You're Not in This Just to Be Helpful": Access, Rapport, and Interviews in Three Studies of Elites', in Rosanna Herz and Jonathan Imber (eds), *Studying Elites Using Qualitative Methods.* London: Sage, pp. 133–50.

Ouma, Stefan. 2014. 'Situating Global Finance in the Land Rush Debate: A Critical Review'. *Geoforum* 57: 162–66.

———. 2015a. 'Getting in between "M and M" or: How Farmland Further Debunks Financialisation'. *Dialogues in Human Geography* 5(2): 225–28.

———. 2015b. *Assembling Export Markets: The Making and Unmaking of Global Food Connections in West Africa.* Chichester: John Wiley & Sons.

———. 2016. 'From Financialisation to Operations of Capital: Historicizing and Disentangling the Finance-Farmland-Nexus'. *Geoforum* 72: 82–93.

———. 2018a. 'This Can't Be an Asset Class: The World of Money Management, "Society", and the Contested Morality of Farmland Investments'. *Environment and Planning A: Economy and Space* 52(1): 66–87, https://doi.org/10.1177/0308518X18790051.

———. 2018b. 'Opening the Black Boxes of Finance-Gone-Farming: A Global Analysis of Assetization', in Hilde Bjørkhaug, Andre Magnan and Geoffrey Lawrence (eds), *The Financialization of Agri-food Systems.* London: Routledge, pp. 85–107

———. 2020. *Farming as a Financial Asset: Global Finance and the Making of Institutional Landscapes.* Newcastle: Agenda Publishing.

Ouma, Stefan, Leigh Johnson and Patrick Bigger. 2018. 'Rethinking the Financialization of "Nature"'. *Environment and Planning A* 50(3): 500–11, https://doi.org/10.1177/030851 8X18755748.

Overbeek, Henk. 2012. 'Sovereign Debt Crisis in Euroland: Root Causes and Implications for European Integration'. *International Spectator: Italian Journal of International Affairs* 47: 30–48.

Owen, Michael. 2016. 'Anna Creek Cattle Station Sale Settles'. *The Australian*, 16 December. Retrieved 16 March 2023 from https://www.theaustralian.com.au/business/news/anna-cre ek-cattle-station-sale-settles/news-story/335dca0085be0d68bbd17b88fddf4ac2.

Palomera, Jaime, and Theodora Vetta. 2016. 'Moral Economy: Rethinking a Radical Concept'. *Anthropological Theory* 16(4): 413–32, https://doi.org/10.1177/1463499616678097.

Pardoo, Wagyu 2022. 'Transforming the Pilbara Pastoral Industry'. Retrieved 16 March 2023 from https://www.pardoo.com.

Pascoe, Bruce. 2014. *Dark Emu: Aboriginal Australia and the Birth of Agriculture*. Broome: Magabala Books.

Peakcocke, Frank. 2017. 'Submission No. 12A – Herron Todd White (Northern Territory) Pty Ltd. Submission to the Pastoral Land Legislation Amendment Bill'. Retrieved 16 March 2023 from https://parliament.nt.gov.au/__data/assets/pdf_file/0009/462717/Sub mission-No.-12A-Herron-Todd-White-Northern-Territory-Pty-Ltd.pdf.

Pearson, Michael, and Jane Lennon. 2010. *Pastoral Australia: Fortunes, Failures and Hard Yakka: A Historical Overview 1788–1967*. Collingwood: CSIRO Publishing.

Pearson, Cecil A.L., and Klaus Helms. 2010. 'Releasing Indigenous Entrepreneurial Capacity: A Case Study of the Yolngu Clan in a Remote Region of Northern Australia'. *Global Business & Economics Review* 12(1–2): 72–84, https://doi.org/10.1504/GBER.2010.03 2318.

Pearson, Cecil Arthur Leonard and Yi Liu. 2016. 'A Chronicle of Indigenous Entrepreneurship, Human Development and Capacity Building in East Arnhem Land of Australia', in Maria Fay Rola-Rubzen and John Burgess (eds), *Human Development and Capacity Building: Asia Pacific Trends, Challenges and Prospects for the Future*. London and New York: Routledge, pp. 161–84.

Pearson, Cecil, and A Rota. 2010. 'Business and Employment for Indigenous Australians: The Case of the Bunuwal Industrial Venture at Yirrkala'. *SDM IMD Journal of Management* 1(2): 4–15.

Peck, Jamie, and Adam Tickell. 2002. 'Neoliberalizing Space'. *Antipode* 34(3): 380–404.

Pedersen, Howard, and Stuart Phillpot. 2019. 'North Australian History: Dispossession, Colonisation, and the Assertion of Indigenous Rights', in Glenn James Russell-Smith, Howard Pedersen and Kamaljt K. Sangha (eds), *Sustainable Land Sector Development in Northern Australia: Indigenous Rights, Aspirations and Cultural Responsibilities*. Baton Rouge: CRC Press, pp. 35–52.

Pierce, J. 1995. 'Reflections on Fieldwork in a Complex Organization: Lawyers, Ethnographic Authority, and Lethal Weapons', in R. Hertz and J. Imber (eds), *Studying Elites Using Qualitative Methods*. Newbury Park, CA: Sage Publications, pp. 94–110.

Pike, Andy, and Jane Pollard. 2010. 'Economic Geographies of Financialization'. *Economic Geography* 86(1): 29–51, https://doi.org/10.1111/j.1944-8287.2009.01057.x.

Poljak, Vesna. 2018. 'Quintis: Inside the Year That Broke the Sandalwood Grower'. *Australian Financial Review*, 24 January. Retrieved 16 March 2023 from https://www.afr.com/compa nies/quintis-inside-the-year-that-broke-the-sandalwood-grower-20180123-h0n4pz.

Poovey, Mary. 2015. 'On "the Limits to Financialization"'. *Dialogues in Human Geography* 5(2): 220–24, https://doi.org/10.1177/2043820615588159.

Powell, Alan. 2009 [1982]. *Far Country: A Short History of the Northern Territory*. 5th edn. Darwin: Charles Darwin University Press.

Preda, Alex. 2005. 'The Investor as a Cultural Figure of Global Capitalism', in Karin Knorr Cetina and Alex Preda (eds), *The Sociology of Financial Markets*. Oxford: Oxford University Press, pp. 141–62.

Preunkert, Jenny. 2017. 'Financialization of Government Debt? European Government Debt Management Approaches 1980–2007'. *Competition & Change* 21(1): 27–44, https://doi .org/10.1177/1024529416678072.

Prince, Russell, Matthew Henry, Aisling Gallagher, Carolyn Morris and Stephen FitzHerbert. 2021. *Markets in Their Place: Context, Culture, Finance*. Abingdon: Routledge.

Pritchard, Bill. 2009. 'The Long Hangover from the Second Food Regime: A World-Historical Interpretation of the Collapse of the WTO Doha Round'. *Agriculture and Human Values* 26(4): 297–307.

208 • References

Pritchard, Bill, David Burch and Geoffrey Lawrence. 2007'. Neither "Family" nor "Corporate" Farming: Australian Tomato Growers as Farm Family Entrepreneurs'. *Journal of Rural Studies* 23: 75–87.

Pritchard, Bill, Jane Dixon, Elizabeth Hull and Chetan Choithani. 2016. '"Stepping Back and Moving in": The Role of the State in the Contemporary Food Regime'. *Journal of Peasant Studies* 43(3): 693–710.

Pritchard, Bill, and Matthew Tonts. 2011. 'Market Efficiency, Agriculture and Prosperity in Australia', in Matthew Tonts and Muhammed Abu B. Siddique (eds), *Globalisation, Agriculture and Development: Perspectives from the Asia-Pacific*. Cheltenham: Edward Elgar, pp. 29–53.

Qi, Hanying. 2019. 'A New Literature Review on Financialization'. *Journal of Accounting, Business and Finance Research* 7(2): 40–50.

Quattrone, Paolo. 2015. 'Value in the Age of Doubt', in Martin Kornberger, Lise Justesen, Jan Mouritsen, and Anders Koed Madsen (eds), *Making Things Valuable*. Oxford: Oxford University Press, pp. 38–61.

Rabobank. 2023. 'Why Rabobank'. Retrieved 26 April 2023 from www.rabobank.com.au/banking/.

Riemer, Frances J. 2011. 'Ethnographic Research', in Stephen Lapan, MaryLynn T Quartaroli, and Frances J. Riemer (eds), *Qualitative Research: An Introduction to Methods and Designs*. New York, NY: Jossey-Bass.

Rose, Nikolas, and Peter Miller. 1992. 'Political Power beyond the State: Problematics of Government'. *British Journal of Sociology* 43(2): 173–205, https://doi.org/10.2307/591464.

Rosin, Christopher J., Katharine A. Legun, Hugh Campbell and Marion Sautier. 2017. 'From Compliance to Co-production: Emergent Forms of Agency in Sustainable Wine Production in New Zealand'. *Environment and Planning A* 49(12): 2780–99, https://doi.org/10.1177/0308518X1773374.

Rowley, Linda. 2019. 'Movement at the Station: Recent Property Listings'. *Beef Central*, 14 August. . Retrieved 16 March 2023 from https://www.beefcentral.com/property/weekly-property-review-movement-at-the-station-12.

Ruddy, Melville. 2018. 'Royal Commission into the Misconduct in the Banking, Superannuation and Financial Services Industry: Submission of Melville Ruddy'. Retrieved 4 May 2023 from https://financialservices.royalcommission.gov.au/public-hearings/Documents/Round-4-written-submissions/mel-ruddy-written-submission.pdf.

Rural Bank. 2021. 'Australian Farmland Values 2021'. Retrieved 16 March 2023 from https://www.ruralbank.com.au/siteassets/knowledgeandinsights/publications/farmlandvalues/national/afv-national-2021.pdf.

———. 2022. 'Australian Farmland Values 2022'. Retrieved 16 March 2023 from https://www.ruralbank.com.au/siteassets/_documents/publications/flv/afv-national-2022.pdf.

Russi, Luigi. 2013. *Hungry Capital: The Financialization of Food*. Alresford: Zero Books.

Rylko-Bauer, Barbara, Merrill Singer and John van Willigen. 2006. 'Reclaiming Applied Anthropology: Its Past, Present, and Future'. *American Anthropologist* 108(1): 178–90, https://doi.org/10.1525/aa.2006.108.1.178.

Salerno, Tania. 2014. 'Capitalising on the Financialization of Agriculture: Cargill's Land Investment Techniques in the Philippines'. *Third World Quarterly* 35(9): 1709–27.

Sayer, Andrew. 2015. 'Time for Moral Economy?' *Geoforum* 65: 291–93.

Schmidt, Ted. 2016. *The Political Economy of Food and Finance*. New York: Routledge.

Schwartz, Dominique. 2017. 'Gina Rinehart Ushers in a New Kidman Cattle Era with Big Plans for Australia's Most Famed Pastoral Estate'. *ABC News*, 4 June, Retrieved 16 March

2023 from https://www.abc.net.au/news/2017-06-04/gina-rinehart-ushers-in-a-new-kidm an-cattle-era/8586540.

Scoones, Ian, Ruth Hall, Saturnino M. Borras, Ben White and Wendy Wolford. 2013. 'Politics of Evidence: Methodologies for Understanding the Global Land Rush'. *Journal of Peasant Studies* 40(3): 469–83, https://doi.org/10.1080/03066150.2013.801341.

Seafarms. 2022a. 'Project Sea Dragon Review – Investor Briefing Presentation'. Retrieved 16 March 2023 from http://seafarms.com.au/wp-content/uploads/2022/04/Project-Sea-Drag on-Review-Investor-Briefing-Presentation-March-31-2022-1.pdf.

———. 2022b. 'Project Sea Dragon Update: ASX Announcement 21 June 2022'. Retrieved 16 March 2023 from http://seafarms.com.au/wp-content/uploads/2022/06/2022_06_21-Ma rket-Update-732.pdf.

———. 2022c. 'Project Sea Dragon Is Implementation Ready, with the Following Key Milestones Complete'. Retrieved 16 March 2023 from https://seafarms.com.au/about-project-sea-dragon.

Seaver, Nick. 2017. 'Algorithms as Culture: Some Tactics for the Ethnography of Algorithmic Systems'. *Big Data & Society* 4(2), https://doi.org/10.1177/2053951717738104.

Sharma, Aarzoo. 2022. 'A Comparative Analysis of the Financialization of Commodities during COVID-19 and the Global Financial Crisis Using a Quantile Regression Approach'. *Resources Policy* 78: 102923–102923, https://doi.org/10.1016/j.resourpol.2022.102923.

Sinclair, Stephen. 2022. 'Seafarms Boss Mick Mcmahon Resigns after Deeming Giant Prawn Farm Plan "Unviable"'. *ABC News*, 6 May. Retrieved 16 March 2023 from https://www .abc.net.au/news/2022-05-06/seafarms-ceo-mick-mcmahon-quits-after-review-of-prawn -farm-plan/101044026.

Sippel, Sarah Ruth. 2015. 'Food Security or Commercial Business? Gulf State Investments in Australian Agriculture'. *Journal of Peasant Studies* 42(5): 981–1001.

———. 2018. 'Financialising Farming as a Moral Imperative? Renegotiating the Legitimacy of Land Investments in Australia'. *Environment and Planning A* 50(3): 549–68.

———. 2022. 'Agri-investment Cashing in on COVID-19', in Victoria Stead and Melinda Hinkson (eds), *Beyond Global Food Supply Chains*. Cham: Springer, pp. 23–36.

Sippel, Sarah Ruth, Nicolette Larder and Geoffrey Lawrence. 2017. 'Grounding the Financialization of Farmland: Perspectives on Financial Actors as New Land Owners in Rural Australia'. *Agriculture and Human Values* 34(2): 251–65, https://doi.org/10.1007/s1 0460-016-9707-2.

Sippel, Sarah Ruth, and Timothy Weldon. 2021. 'Redefining Land's Investability: Towards a Neo-nationalization of Resources in Australia?' *Territory, Politics, Governance* 9(2): 306–23, https://doi.org/10.1080/21622671.2019.1703797.

Sippel, Sarah Ruth, and Oane Visser. 2021. 'Introduction to Symposium "Reimagining Land: Materiality, Affect and the Uneven Trajectories of Land Transformation"'. *Agriculture and Human Values* 38(1): 271–82, https://doi.org/10.1007/s10460-020-10152-3.

Smith, Erin. 2015. 'Structuring for Serendipity: Family Wealth Creation, Farmer Autonomy and the Pursuit of Security in an Uncertain Australian Country Side'. Ph.D. thesis. Sydney: University of Sydney. Retrieved 16 March 2023 from http://research.usc.edu.au/vital/acce ss/manager/Repository/usc:16471?query=.

Smith, Erin, and Bill Pritchard. 2016. 'FactCheck: Is 30% of Northern Territory Farmland and 22% of Tasmanian Farmland Foreign-Owned?' *The Conversation*, 21 September. Retrieved 16 March 2023 from http://theconversation.com/factcheck-is-30-of-northern -territory-farmland-and-22-of-tasmanian-farmland-foreign-owned-65155.

Smith, Kiah. 2016. 'Food Systems Failure: Can We Avert Future Crises?', in Mark Shucksmith and David Brown (eds), *Routledge Handbook of Rural Studies*. Abingdon: Routledge, pp. 250–61.

Smith, Kiah, Alexandra Langford and Geoffrey Lawrence. 2023. 'Tracking Farmland Investment in Australia: Institutional Finance and the Politics of Data Mapping'. *Journal of Agrarian Change*, https://doi.org/10.1111/joac.12531.

Sokol, Martin. 2017. 'Financialisation, Financial Chains and Uneven Geographical Development: Towards a Research Agenda'. *Research in International Business and Finance* 39: 678–85. https://doi.org/10.1016/j.ribaf.2015.11.007.

Sommerville, Melanie, and André Magnan. 2015. '"Pinstripes on the Prairies": Examining the Financialization of Farming Systems in the Canadian Prairie Provinces'. *Journal of Peasant Studies* 42(1): 119–44, https://doi.org/10.1080/03066150.2014.990894.

Sommerville, Melanie. 2018. 'Old Roots, New Shoots: Thickening the Local Histories of Agri-food Financialisation', in Hilda Børkhaug, André Magnan, and Geoffrey Lawrence (eds), *The Financialization of Agri-food Systems: Contested Transformations*. New York: Routledge, pp. 223–43.

Sorensen, Hayley. 2017. 'Water Fight to Continue'. *NT News*, 13 February.

Sowden, William. 1882. *The Northern Territory as It Is: A Narrative of the South Australian Parliamentary Party's Trip, and Full Descriptions of the Northern Territory; Its Settlements and Industries*. Adelaide: W.K. Thomas.

Staritz, Cornelia, Susan Newman, Bernhard Tröster and Leonhard Plank. 2018. 'Financialization and Global Commodity Chains: Distributional Implications for Cotton in Sub-Saharan Africa'. *Development and Change* 49(3): 815–42, https://doi.org/10.1111/dech.12401.

Stephens, Phoebe. 2021. 'Social Finance for Sustainable Food Systems: Opportunities, Tensions and Ambiguities'. *Agriculture and Human Values* 38: 1123–37, https://doi.org/10.1007/s10460-021-10222-0.

Stein, Ginny. 2014. 'Indigenous Pastoral Stations Join Forces, Look to China to Revive Industry'. *ABC News*, 5 June. Retrieved 16 March 2023 from http://www.abc.net.au/news/2014-06-05/chinese-business-buying-into-pastoral-stations/5503086.

Stilwell, Frank. 2002. *Political Economy: The Contest of Economic Ideas*. Victoria: Oxford University Press.

Stockhammer, Engelbert. 2013. 'Financialization, Income Distribution and the Crisis'. *Investigación Económica* 71(279): 39–70, https://doi.org/10.22201/fe.01851667p.2012.279.37326.

———. 2015. 'Rising Inequality as a Cause of the Present Crisis'. *Cambridge Journal of Economics* 39(3): 935–58, https://doi.org/10.1093/cje/bet052.

Stoeckl, Natalie. 2010. 'Bridging the Asymmetric Divide: Background to, and Strategies for Bridging the Divide between Indigenous and Non-Indigenous Economies in Northern Australia', in Rolf Gerritson (ed.), *Northern Australia Political Economy: Issues and Agendas*. Darwin: Charles Darwin University, pp. 106–29.

Storm, Servias. 2018. 'Financialization and Economic Development: A Debate on the Social Efficiency of Modern Finance'. *Development and Change* 49(2): 302–29.

Suehrer, Juri. 2019. 'The Future of FDI: Achieving the Sustainable Development Goals 2030 through Impact Investment'. *Global Policy* 10(3): 413–15, https://doi.org/10.1111/1758-5899.12714.

Šunde, Charlotte, Jim Sinner, Marc Tadaki, Janet Stephenson, Bruce Glavovic, Shaun Awatere, Annabelle Giorgetti, Nick Lewis, Aneika Young and Kai Chan. 2018. 'Valuation as Destruction? The Social Effects of Valuation Processes in Contested Marine Spaces'. *Marine Policy* 97: 170–78, https://doi.org/10.1016/j.marpol.2018.05.024.

Sutton, Peter. 2021. *Farmers or Hunter-Gatherers? The Dark Emu Debate*. Melbourne: Melbourne University Press.

Szelényi, Katalin. 2013. 'The Meaning of Money in the Socialization of Science and Engineering Doctoral Students: Nurturing the Next Generation of Academic Capitalists?' *Journal of Higher Education* 84(2): 266–94, https://doi.org/10.1353/jhe.2013.0008.

Tarim, Emre. 2012. 'Storytelling and Structural Incoherence in Financial Matters'. *Journal of Interdisciplinary Economics* 24(2): 115–44.

Tellmann, Ute. 2021. 'The Politics of Assetization: From Devices of Calculation to Devices of Obligation'. *Distinktion: Journal of Social Theory* 33–54, https://doi.org/10.1080/160091 0X.2021.1991419.

Terrill, Leon. 2016. *Beyond Communal and Individual Ownership: Indigenous Land Reform in Australia*. Abingdon: Routledge.

Teubner, Gunther. 2011. 'A Constitutional Moment? The Logics of "Hitting the Bottom"', in Poul Kjaer, Gunther Teubner and Alberto Febbrajo (eds), *The Financial Crisis in Constitutional Perspective: The Dark Side of Functional Differentiation*. Oxford: Hart Publishing, pp. 3–42.

Thomas, Robert J. 1995. 'Interviewing Important People in Big Companies', in Rosanna Hertz and Jonathan Imber (eds), *Studying Elites Using Qualitative Methods*. London: Sage, pp. 3–17.

Thompson, Jesse. 2022. 'NT Government Insists $56 Million Spent on Project Sea Dragon Roads Will See a Return on Investment'. *ABC News*, 5 April. Retrieved 16 March 2023 from https://www.abc.net.au/news/2022-04-05/project-sea-dragon-seafarms-viability-nt -government-nlc/100967572#:~:text=Project%20Sea%20Dragon%20was%20set,questio ns%20over%20the%20project's%20future.

Tilzey, Mark, and Clive Potter. 2006. 'Neo-liberalism, Neo-mercantilism and Multi-functionality: Contested Political Discourses in European Post-Fordist Rural Governance', in Lynda Cheshire, Vaughan Higgins and Geoffrey Lawrence (eds), *Rural Governance: International Perspectives*. London: Routledge, pp. 115–29.

Treloar, Alexandra. 2022. 'School Leavers Opting or Gap Year of Outback Aussie Adventures Instead of Overseas Travel'. *ABC News*, 29 March. Retrieved 16 March 2023 from https:// www.abc.net.au/news/rural/2022-03-29/outback-life-appeals-to-school-leavers-to-spend -gap-year/100944998.

Tsing, Anna L. 2005. *Friction: An Ethnography of Global Connection*. Princeton: Princeton University Press.

Tung, Irene. 2014. 'Financializing Urban Governance', Ph.D. thesis. New Brunswick: State University of New Jersey.

Undurraga, Tomas. 2013. 'An Interview with Philip Mirowski'. *Estudios de la Economía*. Retrieved 16 March 2023 from https://estudiosdelaeconomia.wordpress.com/ 2013/07/22/facebook-teaches-you-how-to-be-a-neoliberal-agent-an-interview-with-philip-mirowski.

Vail, Michael. 2014. 'What Is the "True", Going Concern Value of a Pastoral Zone, Grazing Enterprise Investment in Australia and, Why Beast Area Valuation (BAV) Is Wrong?' Master's thesis. Rockhampton: Central Queensland University. Retrieved 16 March 2023 from https://www.beefcentral.com/wp-content/uploads/2014/12/Michael-J-VAIL-s02341 80-Property-Valuation-Research-Project-B-PROP29002_25-09-2014-v0.3.pdf.

Van der Zwan, Natasha. 2014. 'Making Sense of Financialization'. *Socio-economic Review* 12(1): 99–129, https://doi.org/10.1093/ser/mwt020.

Vatin, François. 2013. 'Valuation as Evaluating and Valorizing'. *Valuation Studies* 1(1): 51–81, https://doi.org/10.3384/vs.2001-5992.131131.

Visser, Oane. 2017. 'Running out of Farmland? Investment Discourses, Unstable Land Values and the Sluggishness of Asset Making'. *Agriculture and Human Values* 34: 185–98.

———. 2021. 'Persistent Farmland Imaginaries: Celebration of Fertile Soil and the Recurrent Ignorance of Climate'. *Agriculture and Human Values* 38: 313–26, https://doi.org/10.1007/s10460-020-10154-1.

Visser, Oane, Jennifer Clapp and S. Ryan Isakson. 2015. 'Introduction to a Symposium on Global Finance and the Agri-food Sector: Risk and Regulation'. *Journal of Agrarian Change* 15(4): 541–48.

Wagstaff, James, and Ted Miles. 2022. 'The 50 Biggest Aussie Farm Sales of the Past Five Years'. *Weekly Times*, 3 August.

Ward, Callum, and Erik Swyngedouw. 2018. 'Neoliberalisation from the Ground up: Insurgent Capital, Regional Struggle, and the Assetisation of Land'. *Antipode* 50(4): 1077–97, https://doi.org/10.1111/anti.12387.

Warakirri Asset Management. 2020. 'Is It Time to Consider an Investment in Australian Agriculture?' Retrieved 16 March 2023 from https://warakirri.com.au/wp-content/uploads/2020/10/Agri-Topic-Paper_Sept-2020.pdf.

Warren, Carol. 2001. 'Qualitative Interviewing', in Jaber F. Gubrium and James A. Holstein (eds), *A Handbook of Interview Research*. London: Sage, pp. 83–102.

Watson, Ian, Andrew Ash, Tony Grice, Andrew Higgins, Leigh Hunt, Cuan Petheram and Peter Stone. 2013. 'Is There a Place for Intensification of Northern Beef Production Systems?' *Northern Beef Research Update Conference Proceedings 2013*. Retrieved 16 March 2023 from https://publications.csiro.au/rpr/download?pid=csiro:EP136333&dsid=DS3.

Webb, Janette. 2019. 'New Lamps for Old: Financialised Governance of Cities and Clean Energy'. *Journal of Cultural Economy* 12(4): 286–98, https://doi.org/10.1080/17530350.2019.1613253.

Weber, David. 2005. 'Landowners Approve Biggest Australian Irrigation Scheme'. *ABC News*, 6 October. Retrieved 16 March 2023 from https://www.abc.net.au/radio/programs/am/landowners-approve-biggest-australian-irrigation/2118986.

Weller, Sally, Erin F. Smith and Bill Pritchard. 2013. 'Family or Enterprise? What Shapes the Business Structures of Australian Farming?' *Australian Geographer* 44(2): 129–42, https://doi.org/10.1080/00049182.2013.789592.

Weller, Sally, and Neil Argent. 2018. 'Royal Commission Shows Bank Lenders Don't "Get" Farming, and Rural Economies Pay the Price.' *The Conversation* 2 July. Retrieved 25 April 2023 from https://theconversation.com/royal-commission-shows-bank-lenders-dont-get-farming-and-rural-economies-pay-the-price-99086.

White, Ray. 2019. 'Wollogorang and Wentworth Station'. Retrieved 16 March 2023 from https://raywhiteruralqld.com.au/properties/rural/nt/tennant-creek-0860/livestock/2158954.

Williams, James W. 2014. 'Feeding Finance: A Critical Account of the Shifting Relationships Between Finance, Food and Farming'. *Economy and Society* 43(3): 401–31, https://doi.org/10.1080/03085147.2014.892797.

Williams, Karel. 2000. 'From Shareholder Value to Present-Day Capitalism'. *Economy and Society* 29(1): 1–12, https://doi.org/10.1080/030851400360532.

Williams, S. 1981. 'Interview with Max Sargent, 23 June 1981'. NT Archives.

Wilson, Malcolm. 1982. 'A Tax-Deductible Mango for Everyone'. *Sydney Morning Herald*, 9 January.

Wolford, Wendy. 2005. 'Agrarian Moral Economies and Neoliberalism in Brazil: Competing Worldviews and the State in the Struggle for Land'. *Environment and Planning A* 37(2): 241–61, https://doi.org/10.1068/a3745.

Woods, Michael. 2007. 'Engaging the Global Countryside: Globalization, Hybridity and the Reconstitution of Rural Place'. *Progress in Human Geography* 31(4): 485–507.

Woods, Michael. 2014. 'Family Farming in the Global Countryside'. *Anthropological Notebooks* 20(3): 31–48.

Wright, Alexis. 1997. *Grog War*. Broome: Magabala Books.

Zander, Kerstin K., Beau J. Austin and Stephen T. Garnett. 2014. 'Indigenous Peoples' Interest in Wildlife-Based Enterprises in the Northern Territory, Australia'. *Human Ecology* 42(1): 115–26, https://doi.org/10.1007/s10745-013-9627-3.

INDEX

absentee owners, 43–44, 52
agency
  in assemblage, 25–28, 30–32, 159,
    173–178
  farmer, 116, 118–121
  human, 18–21, 34, 96, 103, 105,
    163–167
  nonhuman, 5, 21–23, 86, 167–170
Alberta Investment Management
  Corporation, 148, 150
Alice Springs, 46
anthropology of finance, 20–21
Asia, 38, 41, 44, 46, 127–128, 130, 152,
  169
assemblage thinking
  'cuts' to the assemblage, 33, 56, 160, 179
  exteriority of relations, 28–30, 174–175,
    178
  nonlinear causation, 26, 30–31, 175–176,
    178–179
  process of assembling heterogeneous
    parts, 26–29, 32–33, 174, 176, 178
  structure and dynamism, 31–32,
    176–178
assetisation, 5, 21, 22, 24, 27, 75, 76, 77,
  85, 114, 123, 126, 139, 164, 192
aquaculture, 62, 64, 133, 138, 143, 172
Arnhem Land, 57, 70–71, 124, 145
Auston Corporation, 148, 150
Australian Agricultural Company, 61
Australian Land and Cattle Company, 50

bank
  incentives, 102–103
  lending to agriculture, 93–95
  lending oversight, 104

  lending ratios, 93–94
  sustainability, 102, 161
bankers, 4, 8, 19–20, 34, 74, 84, 85, 88, 90,
  91–106, 116, 152, 160
Beast Area Value, 75–82, 85–90, 164,
  166–168, 170, 175–177
biosecurity, 126, 129–130, 132
black-box, 2, 18, 116
BlackRock Advisors LLC, 63, 143
Brett Blundy, 61, 150, 154
Brisbane, 48, 99
buffalo, 41, 123, 133, 140

Canada, 15, 59, 60, 148, 150
Cape York, 51, 168
Cape York Partnership, 168
capital gap, 161–162
capitalised farm family entrepreneurs,
  116–188
carrying capacity, 77, 79–80, 86, 88, 167
cattle
  breeds, 154
  breeding, 90, 99, 154
  grazing, 39–40, 44, 47, 50, 77, 79, 132,
    167
Central Land Council, 70, 135, 137
China, 20, 42, 59, 60, 67–68, 128, 147,
  150, 151, 165
clean and green, 127, 129, 130, 169
commensuration, 8, 75, 77, 134
commodification, 24–25, 75
concessional finance, 55, 60, 139, 145–147
Consolidated Pastoral Company, 61, 152
control, 4, 7, 8, 13, 38, 100, 109110,
  114–115, 118–119, 123–124, 128,
  136–137, 163–167

COVID-19, 8–9, 20, 142–147
crocodile eggs, 123, 140
Crown Point Pastoral Company, 62, 147
CSIRO, 51–52

Darwin, 41–42, 45–47, 51, 57, 64, 68, 128, 166, 169
Davidson, 38, 47
debt, 13, 16, 18, 45, 84, 90–107, 109–111, 123, 141
default, 92, 104
Department of Primary Industries, 165–166
Developing Northern Australia, 4, 7, 54–73, 89, 127, 142–157, 160, 169, 174, 177
drought, 39, 43, 91, 94–95, 99–100, 103–104, 107, 155

Earnings Before Interest, Tax, Depreciation and Amortisation, 85
Elders Rural Services, 3, 5, 97
equity partnerships, 108–120, 161, 163, 166, 171, 175
ethics, 7, 34–35
ethnography of finance, 18–20
Europe, 15, 69, 60
exit strategy, 114, 115, 136, 163, 164, 165

farm family entrepreneurs, 108
Fiera Comox, 148, 150
finance-led development, 65, 70, 140–141, 155–157
financialisation
    agrifood, 1–2, 9, 12, 15–17
    for development, 121–141
    of development, 121–141
    global, 11–13
    industry, 15–17
    as an organising principle, 13–15
    as a regime of accumulation, 11–13,
Foreign Investment Review Board, 59, 60, 147–149, 153
foreign ownership
    of land, 59, 147–149
    of water, 60, 148
Free Prior Informed Consent, 135
'free' water, 62, 127–130, 169

Gateway to Asia, 41, 127–128, 169
Gina Rhinehart, vii

government officials, 67–70, 128, 165, 169, 172
grassroots, 71, 139
greenfield agriculture, 3, 8, 56, 62, 65, 68, 69, 71–72, 127, 129, 132–133, 145, 154, 157, 171, 172
Gulf Country of Queensland, 61, 83
Gunn Rural Management, 51–52

Hancock Agricultural Investment Group, 149–150, 152
Hewitt Cattle Company, 62, 154
Heytesbury Cattle Company, 61
Hughes Pastoral Company, 61
Humpty Doo Barramundi, 129,
Holmes, 38, 44, 47,
Hong Kong, 59, 60, 151

impact investment, 23, 126, 138–140
Indigenous Australian
    Aboriginal Land Economic Development Agency, 124, 137, 155
    agribusiness, 57–58, 121–141
    asset-making, 123–141,
    branding, 123, 130–131
    bush foods, 130, 141
    Business on Country program, 124, 131–132
    entrepreneurship, 121–141
    food security, 122–123, 155–157
    Free, Prior and Informed Consent, 135
    economic development, 56–58, 121–141
    history, 40–41
    Indigenous Procurement Policy, 122
    Inquiry into food pricing and food security in remote Indigenous communities, 156
    investment prospectuses, 32, 67, 71, 111, 129, 131, 139, 155, 168–170, 176
    land, 127–128, 132, 134
    land rights, 40, 55, 61, 121–122, 127–128, 132, 134–136
    Native Title Representative Bodies and Service Providers, 40, 124, 137
    North Australian Indigenous Land and Sea Management Alliance, 124, 131
    Traditional Owners, 57, 125, 135, 137–138, 168
    wildlife enterprises, 41, 123, 130

216 • Index

infrastructure development, 9, 24, 38, 55–56, 60–62, 65, 67, 71, 75, 78, 85–89, 93, 96, 114, 117, 122, 127, 139, 145–147, 153, 157, 159, 162, 165, 170–171, 176
interest rates, 47–48, 93, 98–99, 104, 107
intermediaries, 3–7, 26–27, 34–36, 67–74, 104, 115, 133–134, 137–138, 159, 161–162, 164–179
interviewing professionals, 36–37
investment ready, 108, 11–111
investors
  farmer perceptions, 109
  meeting, 113
  negotiating with, 114

Kakadu plum, 123
Katherine mangoes, 50–52
Kimberley Agricultural Investment Company, 62, 150
Kimberley Agriculture and Pastoral Company, 61, 156

Land Development Corporation, 70–71, 124, 129, 133, 162, 168–169, 172
land
  Indigenous, 8, 32, 40, 55, 57–58, 71, 121–141, 140, 147, 162, 164, 165, 168, 171–179
  market volatility, 88, 93–95, 160–161, 166, 168, 175
  pastoral, 3, 7, 44, 62, 74–90, 147, 155, 161, 167–168, 172
  speculation, 41, 42–43, 52, 75–76, 89, 110, 161, 163, 165–166, 175, 178
  valuers, vii, 4, 74–90, 125, 134, 160–161, 166, 172, 179
lawyers, 34, 115–116, 136
leaseholds, 40, 43, 46, 76, 128
legitimacy, 137–138
Legune Station, 64
liquidity, 135–137
loyalty, 98–99

Macquarie Bank, 61, 149
managed funds, 124–125, 137, 155, 164, 172
Managed Investment Schemes, 50, 62

mangoes, 49–51, 144–145, 165–166
moral economy, 91–106, 161
Mt Isa, 46
Murray Darling Basin, 149

national interest (Australian), vii, 58
nationalism, 165
Netherlands, 59, 60, 151
North Australian Pastoral Company, 61
Northern Agricultural Development Corporation, 50
Northern Australia
  environment, 78–79
  history, 38–53
Northern Australia Infrastructure Facility, 56, 60–61, 145–147
Northern Land Council, 70, 124, 135, 137, 140, 144
Northern Territory, 3, 38–51, 56–58, 62–73, 121, 124, 129, 135–137, 143–145, 155, 160, 165–166, 169

Ord River Irrigation Area, 47, 49, 62–64, 143, 155

Paraway Pastoral, 61
patient capital, 68
pension fund, 59, 108, 114–116, 148, 150–151, 176
political economy, 11, 25
Ponzi scheme, 63, 143
Potential for Profit, 126–133
postructuralism, 2
power, 34–37
procyclical lending, 93, 95, 101, 105
professional networks, 5, 17, 19, 20, 96, 97, 112–113, 116
PSP investments, 59, 148–150, 154

qualification, 74, 77
qualculation, 169
Queensland, 38, 43–44, 47, 61–62, 83, 121, 124, 131, 145, 150, 155
Queensland-British Food Corporation, 47–48
Quintis, vii, 62, 63, 143

Rabobank, 97
railways, 45–46

ranking, 78, 80, 81, 90, 134
'real'
    assets, 153
    economy, 11–12
    financial process, 18
    growth, 12
relationship lending, 95–100, 104–105
remoteness, ix, 3, 7, 23, 25, 27, 52, 56–58,
    60, 65–67, 71–73, 76, 78, 82, 84, 89,
    96–100, 104–106, 107, 122–123,
    125–130, 132, 134, 136, 139–142,
    146–147, 155–157, 160, 162,
    171–172, 175, 180–181
Return on Investment, 84–90, 166–168
    from capital appreciation, 82–84
    from income, 82–83
risk, 101–102
risk-taking, 20
roads, 55, 60–61, 65, 71, 127, 144, 146
role of the state, 7, 20, 70, 72, 93, 108,
    160–161
Royal Commission into Misconduct in the
    Banking, Superannuation and Financial
    Services Industry, 91–92, 92, 100–101,
    104, 106, 161
Ruddy (Melville), 99–100

S. Kidman & Co., vii, 58–59, 147, 150
sandalwood, vii, 62, 63, 143
scarcity, 77, 132–133
Seafarms, vii, 64–65, 138, 143, 144
Shanghai, 20, 67–68
Shanghai CRED, vii, 58, 147
shareholder value, 11, 13–17, 21
social enterprise, 139
speculation, 41, 42–43, 52, 75–76, 89, 110,
    161, 163, 165–166, 175, 178
speculative development, 85–87

standardisation, 133–134
Stanbroke Pastoral, 62

Territory Rice Ltd, 48
TIAA-CREF, 149, 152
Tipperary Land Corporation, 49–50
Tiwi Islands, 70–71, 129, 133, 143, 155,
    168, 172
tick fever, 44
trust, 24, 96, 98–101

underutilization of land, 127–128
underdevelopment, ix, 38, 66, 170
United Kingdom, 59, 60
United States, 15, 59, 60, 152

valuation
    using the Beast Area Value, 75–82,
        85–90, 164, 166–168, 170, 175–177
    -qua-capitalisation, 75, 86
    -qua-marketisation, 75, 86
value proposition, 4, 55, 66, 127, 129
Vesteys, 45–46

water
    ground, 40, 129
    surface, 39, 129
war
    Indonesian Confrontation, 47
    Korean War, 47
    Second World War, 46–47, 29
Western Australia, 38, 43, 49–50, 62, 65,
    121, 124, 143, 145, 155
White Paper, 4, 8, 54–57, 60, 62, 66, 69,
    72–73, 128–129, 142, 145, 157, 160,
    169, 177

xenophobia, 166